Hitler's Stormtroopers
and the Attack on the
German Republic,
1919–1933

HITLER'S STORMTROOPERS AND THE ATTACK ON THE GERMAN REPUBLIC, 1919–1933

Otis C. Mitchell

McFarland & Company, Inc., Publishers
Jefferson, North Carolina, and London

The present work is a reprint of the illustrated case bound edition of Hitler's Stormtroopers and the Attack on the German Republic, 1919–1933, *first published in 2008 by McFarland.*

LIBRARY OF CONGRESS CATALOGUING-IN-PUBLICATION DATA

Mitchell, Otis C.
Hitler's stormtroopers and the attack on the
German Republic, 1919–1933 / Otis C. Mitchell.
p. cm.
Includes bibliographical references and index.

ISBN 978-0-7864-7729-6
softcover : acid free paper ∞

1. Germany — History — 1918–1933.
2. Nationalsozialistische Deutsche Arbeiter-Partei.   I. Title.
DD240.M52   2013   324.243'023809042 — dc22   2008034160

BRITISH LIBRARY CATALOGUING DATA ARE AVAILABLE

© 2008 Otis C. Mitchell. All rights reserved

No part of this book may be reproduced or transmitted in any form or by any means, electronic or mechanical, including photocopying or recording, or by any information storage and retrieval system, without permission in writing from the publisher.

On the cover: An SA "march-out" from 1930

Manufactured in the United States of America

*McFarland & Company, Inc., Publishers
Box 611, Jefferson, North Carolina 28640
www.mcfarlandpub.com*

For Darlene and Lindsay, again

Contents

Preface 1

ONE. Origins and Inspirations: Prewar Imperial Germany 3
TWO. The Weimar Republic Rises Among the Ruins 12
THREE. The Appearance of Hitler 29
INTERPOLATION I. The Munich Matrix of Right Radicalism 38
FOUR. The Infancy of Nazism (1919–1923) 46
INTERPOLATION II. The Bavarian Paramilitary Scene (1919–1923) 57
FIVE. The Failed Putsch 72
SIX. The Years of Preparation (1924–1930) 83
SEVEN. The Reichstag Elections of 1930 and the SA 96
INTERPOLATION III. Battleground Berlin (1925–1933) 106
EIGHT. The Shape and Meaning of the Depression SA 117
NINE. Nazism into Power 139

Epilogue (1933–1934) 154
Chapter Notes 171
Bibliography 181
Index 189

Preface

"Hitler was Nazi Germany and Nazi Germany was Hitler." Thus it is often presented. In essence, the personality, leadership style, and ideological convictions of Hitler, according to this view, shaped the nature of government and life during the Third Reich. This perspective often led writers from the end of World War II until the eighties to concentrate on Hitler to the exclusion of most other aspects of Nazism. This meant that the best-known studies of Hitler and Nazism for that period were almost always biographies, although various groundbreaking studies appeared here and there along with those books about the *Führer*. Then, with the 1980s, more works began to appear concerning specific organizations like the SA and SS. I myself have contributed articles and books on the SA. There have also been studies examining closely the voting patterns of the late Weimar Republic. In most of these studies of organizations and voting, as well as in specific examinations of class origins for party members such as Michael Kater, the early assumption that the Nazi Party was exclusively of lower-middle-class origin is confronted. This work remains cognizant of all these newer trends in scholarship.

Hitler is featured here more in the early chapters when his career was beginning, and there is a brief digression into psychoanalytic theories about him, most of which I find do not tell us much that is dependable. And what I find most lacking in them is that they do little to inform us about what he shared with considerable portions of a generation returning from the trenches; a number of these men emerged from four long years of seeing men mowed down in windrows to display aberrant mental characteristics. One can best discover the impact of this group of men, who were what novelist John Hersey called "war lovers," by examining the paramilitary scene existing in Germany nationwide and Bavaria particularly in immediate postwar Germany. For this reason, in addition to looking at Hitler and the beginnings of the Weimar Republic, the explosion of paramilitary groups on which Weimar initially depended and then had to try to resist is given considerable space. After the failure of the Beer Hall Putsch in 1923, this special attention to things paramilitary is focused on the Nazi SA — the *Sturmabteilung* (stormtroopers).

The initial thrust of this work is aimed at deciding why and how Hitler was able to create a political party which came to rival the German Social Democratic Party as a second mass party in Germany. That the Social Democrats formed a mass workers' party in the nineteenth century comes as not much of a surprise in that its growth was a natural by-product of, and grew apace with, rapid industrialization. As this party entered the postwar period, its constituency, as one might expect, was industrial workers. Rather naturally, it became the one mass party, as it had been just before World War I, which stood alone. What were the circumstances allowing the Nazis with a companion organization of massed paramilitary segments to appear so suddenly on the scene to rival Social Democracy? What allowed Hitler to establish the first "umbrella party" in German history, drawing from across social lines so that white-collar workers, non-union workers, and others could fill the Nazi ranks? This book attempts to answer such questions. And it provides a more elaborate examination of the Nazi Party as it expanded and surged toward power from 1930 to 1933 and the *Machtergreifung* ("Seizure of Power").

The paramilitary tradition in the Prussian, then Germanic, world is the subject most examined in this book. And beyond the early chapters most of that concentration falls upon the Nazi SA. This organization, by the depression years, was full of young stormtroopers, often self-styled revolutionaries, who helped the politically novel Nazis ascend to power over state and society. Given the eventual terrible fate of the Nazi "Storm Detachment," to have its leadership eliminated in a bloody purge on the night of 30 June 1934, the decisive role that the SA played in the ascendency to power is perhaps ironic. That purge will be covered in a more succinct form here in the epilogue than if this book's chronological limitations reached out to the period beyond January of 1933.

This book developed from a series of questions I asked myself after a years-long concentration on the uses and abuses of power. Most particularly this interest has centered on the Weimar period in Germany. Within that context, I looked primarily at two decisive periods. The first of these is 1923–24 when Hitler became a central figure in the racist-nationalist movement. During this time, despite the earlier-mentioned works that concentrate upon Hitler's career, it is apparent that the Nazis were only one of the more important pieces in an intricate mosaic. And significant aspects of this pattern, inside Nazism and beyond it, were paramilitary in nature.

The second decisive period studied in greater detail is 1930–33. It was during this time that the Nazi SA assumed the nature and proportion of a mass organization which helped march Hitler through the gates of power. It was at this historical juncture that the mass formation of brown-shirts began to proceed more fully into the world of the "propaganda soldier" and further from the old combat-seeking dwellers in the world of the putsch.

In the preparation of this work, a number of people have aided me. First, there is Charles F. Sidman who, as my major professor for a doctoral degree, first guided me into the world of the Nazi stormtroopers. Conversations in more recent years with my friends in the field, Jay Baird of Miami of Ohio, and the late George Mosse, generally seen during his day as one of the most prominent of German historians, have given me considerable stimulation. The personnel at the National Archives helped me initially during the sixties, and many times since. During the eighties, I received assistance from the archival staff at the Bayerische Staatsarchiv. During the same time, I was aided by Anton Hoch and Thilo Vogelsang of the Institut für Zeitgeschichte in Munich. None of these people are responsible for any of the shortcomings of this work. These are my responsibility alone.

Otis C. Mitchell
Professor Emeritus of History
University of Cincinnati

Chapter One

Origins and Inspirations: Prewar Imperial Germany

General Background

Over the long course of German history, perhaps the most prominent displayed theme is that of political fragmentation. The Germans have been unlike most other Europeans in following their path of historical development, unable as they were to form a viable nation-state at the beginning of modern times. When they did finally form such a nation-state in 1871, it was not the result of a broad consensus of the people, but rather the outcome of military victories accomplished by the Prussian army. The new Prussianized Germany had many notable positive qualities. It displayed an institutionalized respect for authority, a dedication to hard work, and a sense of good order. Unfortunately, unification had established a split Prussian personality. One part was capable of producing high culture. The other was hostile to it. The newly established, Prussianized Germany was militaristic. It quickly institutionalized militaristic values anachronistic in the Europe of that day. To come close to an approximation of the military indoctrination imposed upon Germans one had to look beyond Europe to the cultural model of Japan. Both the German and the Japanese models presented the concept of the idealized warrior.[1]

In imperial Germany, the military establishment stood aloof from other institutions. The military caste possessed its own code of honor and its own code of law. But the military was not subject to civil law. It was like a Roman praetorian guard for the emperor.[2] The emperor in 1914 was the very epitome of the Prussian love for all things military. William II was contemptuous of civilians. He turned away from the Reichstag and the constitution. His public statements tended toward the belligerent. Typically, while addressing a German contingent of troops designated to help suppress the antiforeigner Boxer rebellion in China, he ordered them to take no prisoners and act like "Huns." This bit of bombast allowed Allied propagandists in two wars to refer to Germans as "Huns."

An old-style militaristic monarchy was anachronistic in the Europe of 1850–1900. For most western societies, the late nineteenth century was a time of rapid industrial growth and the German monarchy seemingly remained unaware of that fact. There were thus anomalies present in a German society rapidly transforming along the path to modernity. Unfortunately, the shape given to the new empire at the point of unification in 1871 provided powers for the government more appropriate to the era of absolute monarchy. The state tradition in Germany was paternalistic, going back to patterns established by Prussian monarchs like Frederick the Great.

Paternalism also shaped the nineteenth-century form of government. There was a bicameral parliament (Bundesrat and Reichstag), but Otto von Bismarck and his successors in the chancellorship excluded the parliament from decision making. The country was directed by a conservative elite. Demands for democratic participation were blunted or made to serve the purposes of the monarchy. Despite this seemingly anachronistic style, political life in imperial Germany was relatively free and social democracy made steady progress. In 1903, the Social Democratic Party (SPD) became the second largest party in the Reichstag. And yet participation in the political process was one of form rather than substance. Effective power remained in the hands of the old dynastic order. There were no fundamental civil rights. All of this was supported by what has been dubbed the "industrial-feudal state." Within that order there existed a linkage between large private cartels and state-managed enterprises.

It was not a cruel society. The more odious consequences of industrialization — unemployment, pestilence sweeping through the slums of cities, accidents in factories producing beggars on street corners, poor working conditions leading directly to illnesses and bodily harm, conditions so troubling in European societies industrializing earlier — were avoided. These were handled more effectively from the top down than they were in many democratic societies where the negative impact of unbridled capitalism had been more widely injurious. Prussian paternalism evolved in the united Germany into a progressive social-welfare state, physically industrial but socially feudal, socialistic and capitalistic simultaneously.[3] The state paternalism conditioned the German populace to obedience and dependency. It fostered the illusion that nothing great or even just positive could be accomplished without state intervention. But to the objective observer, no amount of paternalism could hide the disparities in the social order. Class conflicts abounded.

Instead of trying to work with the laboring classes, as those classes grew larger, the imperial elite increasingly walled itself off against the masses and often assaulted them with strident rhetoric.[4] Beyond rhetoric, which had potentially negative by-products, there appeared a need to integrate the disenfranchised masses behind the conservative order. The idea was to make the people at large enthusiastically loyal, essentially comfortable, and caught up in a participatory myth. This was done, not as part of genuine reforms, but by a series of stop-gap measures aimed at blunting or co-opting Social Democratic issues.

Bismarck was able to manipulate the state and society because he avoided foreign entanglements while Germany industrialized. His assumption was that the new Reich had not been sufficiently stabilized since its establishment in 1871 to allow foreign adventures. When Bismarck was gone, prudence slipped away. The German people were then exposed to deliberately stimulated enthusiasm for imperialism, taking the form of a naval race with Great Britain and the development of strident patriotic associations. What came from the proponents of this new "world politics" (*Weltpolitik*) was mobilization inside Germany and expansion outside. These tactics prefigured later Nazi crusades in a milder form.

The Kaiser saw himself as freed from Bismarck's policy of restraint. He wanted to transform his country into a world power surpassing even the British Empire. The Kaiser, in turn, inspired others to become imperialistic. One example of this removal of restraints imposed by the retired chancellor was to be seen in the person of Alfred von Tirpitz, secretary of the navy, and his activities. He was instrumental in building the second most powerful naval force in the world. He was also the orchestrator of a brilliant public-relations campaign urging the adoption of imperialistic policy. These arguments urging an imperialistic course issued from popular associations like the Pan-German League, the Naval League, and the Colonial Society. These were organizations that popularized war, especially wars of expansion, as noble causes.[5]

The imperialistic policies of the Second Reich thus, to an important extent, furnished the background for the foreign policy of the Third Reich.[6] There is a continuity between the policies of ruling prewar elites and the Nazis leaders of the thirties. This does not mean that there are many direct causal links between the Second and Third Reichs. There were remote linkage areas. The first was the attachment of Germans to paternalistic authority. The second was the concept, vaguely drawn before the war, of National Socialism. These two factors were not dangerous in a society restrained by religious conscience and scientific intellect. But, by 1933, a new generation had reached maturity, scarred by war and economic ruin. Then it became possible to subordinate intellect to emotion and surrender Germanic destiny to a deviant strain of ideologically driven elements.

Ethnic and religious hatreds were as intense in Germany as elsewhere in Europe. And the most virulent form of racism was anti–Semitism. For centuries, the Jews had been seen as "Christ-killers." They were pariahs who had to be excluded from society. It was a supreme irony that there were affinities between Germans and Jews. A close linguistic relationship between Germans and Jews evolved into Yiddish, a dialect developed as an offspring of medieval high German. This dialect also had words derived from Hebrew and various Slavic tongues. Moreover, it was spoken across much of Eastern Europe among lower-class Jews. Most Germans had little difficulty in understanding Yiddish.

Jews had been treated as religious outcasts since the Middle Ages. But the key word here is "religious." They had been excluded from Christian communities by all possible means. While excluded, the Jews of Germany themselves felt exclusive, and they usually refused to participate in the general cultural pattern of societies in which they resided. This characteristic of German life has been called by scholars of medieval Germany "otherness." It helped make the Jews a target for discrimination.

It is only with the advent of the eighteenth century Enlightenment that the Jews began to participate in the cultural and social life of Germany. The Germans and German Jews developed a closer relationship, albeit often antagonistic, than Jews and gentiles elsewhere.[7] A scholar described Germans and Jews as the two people who were admired and hated, "both equally unable to make themselves liked."[8] Germans and Jews of the eighteenth and nineteenth centuries shared thought patterns and expressed themselves in the same language. Most Jewish writers, including Zionists, assimilated German culture and wrote in German. When tensions between the two groups intensified, the Yiddish dialect was regarded by Germans as a stigma.

Whatever real or perceived cultural differences existed between German Jews and German Christians, the awareness of them was intensified by the influx of eastern Jews (*Ostjuden*) into Germany. These immigrants increased in number in the early twentieth century. And they were more removed from the mainstream than the original German Jews. They spoke Yiddish, wore ghetto attire, and formed clans. Even many a native German Jew saw these "intruders" as totally alien. They presented an "unpleasant" sight as they searched German cities for economic opportunity. A government minister during World War I, Walther

Rathenau, an assimilated Jew himself, said that the Jews from the East were a "foreign organism in the German People's body."[9]

If Rathenau, a Jew, was offended by *Ostjuden*, then how much greater must have been the feelings of a young Adolf Hitler. What Rathenau saw as a foreign organism became for the racists, often speaking in pseudobiological terms, a "bacillus." This was a deadly organism or virus requiring total expulsion from the host. Some Jews, particularly *Ostjuden*, did stand out in terms of physical appearance. But assimilated Jews stood out in their intellectual endeavors. The evidence is persuasive that Jews had displayed equal, if not superior, intelligence whenever competing with other Germans. This displayed ability was not "racial," but rather the product of a culture in which scholarship was valued. Jews, therefore, constituted a much higher percentage than that of the general population in professions like law, medicine, and higher education. Such a disproportionate representation of Jews among intellectuals has fostered much speculation as to causes of the phenomenon. Some have explained it, as explained here, by focusing on the long-term tendency to form an intellectual community. Others, unscientifically, have seen clear genetic factors.

The Jews were an ancient, cultured people who, during the Middle Ages, found themselves among primitive natives who were suspect of their intellectuality and business abilities. The two peoples lived side by side, but were at different stages of cultural evolution. The genetic argument, as is the case with other "racial questions," has been accepted by only a few. To embrace it would amount to a kind of racism arguing that there is something in the Jewish "race," not culture, that is marked by higher intelligence. Whichever view was held, Jews were forced to bear the brunt of ethnic prejudices.

From the Middle Ages, Jews had been the focus for prejudicial assaults. By the late nineteenth century, such anti-Jewish prejudice was greatly enhanced by their participation in radical causes as they joined liberal and leftist movements. Some of the leaders of radical movements were Jewish. Despite the fact that during the nineteenth century all the elements of what is now called "anti–Semitism" were present, it did not become politically organized until its last two decades.

One of the first spokesmen of organized anti–Semitism in Germany was Court Chaplain Adolf Stöcker. Stöcker founded the "Christian Social Party" in 1878 to rescue the lower classes from Marxian-Socialism. He presented himself as the representative of a troubled lower-middle class. He used the Jews as a scapegoat for widespread financial and economic problems resulting from intense industrialization. There had been a great depression in 1873 and widespread scandals in high finance during the same decade. Stöcker insinuated that "Jewish capital" was somehow responsible. He identified himself with the complaints of small business owners who claimed to have been ruined by corporations and banks. Since these institutions were often owned by Jews, the Jews were thus the source of misfortune.[10]

Stöcker failed in founding a mass movement, but his anti–Semitic rhetoric was well received by some conservatives. One rightist newspaper, the *Kreuzzeitung*, singled out a close financial confidant of Otto von Bismarck's for attack because he was Jewish. In this way, Gerson Bleichschroder was seen by some as the author of German financial difficulties during the 1870s.[11] This pattern of anti–Semitism was similar to that displayed elsewhere in Europe. At its core, it was the resentful expression of displaced social groups damaged by late nineteenth-century industrialization.[12]

In the shorter term, unsuccessful anti–Semitic political vehicles developed. The League of Anti–Semites was founded in 1879. In 1880, the Social Reich Party and the German Reform Party were launched, with anti–Semitism providing most of their platforms. Moreover, Germany was saturated in the 1880s by a proliferation of minor anti–Semitic parties, books, magazines, and pamphlets. Theodor Fritsch, later to become a Nazi, founded his own anti–Semitic publishing house in Leipzig, the Hammer Publishing Company. Hammer issued a steady stream of anti–Semitic books. The themes presented in all these books were similar: the Jews were in secret league with Freemasons, Catholics, and Jehovah's Witnesses to control the world. This was linked with the illogical assumption that these disparate groups would actually have anything to do with each other.

Admittedly, all this in Germany did not represent the thinking of a significant portion of society. The theme of "national interests" of an anti–Semitic kind was more pronounced in Austria. Ethnic conflicts were intense within the multiethnic empire. The Germanic population, although it contained the ruling class (the Habsburgs), felt threatened. The result was a recurrent xenophobic Germanism with stridently anti–Semitic overtones.[13] Vienna was governed by an anti–Semitic mayor, Karl Lueger, in 1907. This was the case when Hitler appeared there. Lueger was a Christian Socialist supported by the middle class. He found targets in the financial community, in his view the "natural home" of society's "scoundrels" and "scandals." Unrealistically, Lueger held that all the financial problems of a modernizing society could be solved by a return to a more "organic" racial community. Lueger and his ilk held that one could be rid of all the vices spawned by modern finance capitalism by removing all Jews from banking.

Lueger's chief political rival in Vienna was Georg Ritter von Schönerer, a landowner, who sat in the Austrian House of Delegates. In addition to the anti–Semitism that was so much a part of the time's political currency, Schönerer commonly issued calls to end the influence of the Catholic Church. Central to his thought was the need to merge Germanic Austria with Germany.

Such anti–Semitic politicians and parties were ineffective in imperial Germany. On the social level, there were few serious anti–Semitic disturbances before World War I. Some of the racial groups and parties mentioned here did incite latent prejudice. But their public influence was negligible. In sum, before 1914, blatant and political anti–Semitism was rarer in Germany than in the ethnically fractioned Austrian Empire. And yet, cultural anti–Semitism was often just beneath the surface.

There were obscure pamphleteers here and there who provided a "literature" which could be bought in newsstands in both Germany and Austria. One author whose name appeared on many booklets was Georg Lanz von Liebenfels (whose real name was Adolf Lang). It was his cheap pamphlets which provided Hitler with many of his ideas. Liebenfels had founded the "Order of the Temple" in 1901, whose members had to be fair-haired, blue-eyed men who were urged to mate only with "pure Aryan women." His racist ideas were spread through *Ostara*, a magazine usually adorned with a swastika. Hitler went to him on one occasion in Vienna to ask for back issues of *Ostara* and discover the swastika's origins. He also wished to examine Lang's racist theories of history, and the idea that "ape-like" humans should be exterminated.[14]

Actually, there was considerable cross-fertilization of racialist ideas in the Germanic world, with personal contacts between academics and racist popularizers. In 1900, for example, industrialist Alfred Krupp announced an essay competition on the subject: "What can we learn from the principles of Darwinism and its application to the inner political development and the laws of the state?" The majority of the contestants were believers in Aryan superiority. First prize went to a Munich physician who recommended stringent eugenic efforts to keep the Aryan race pure. Another contestant in Krupp's competition was Ludwig Woltman, who later published a racist journal. This publication was one of many to be found in Germany and Germanic Austria, almost every one of which had bibliographic and citational paraphernalia that imitated scholarship.

When Hitler read a popularizer, he was absorbing ideas to be found both in a pseudointellectual fringe of academic circles and the popular arena. The message was always basically the same: any organism of any biological kind is constantly engaged in a ceaseless struggle for existence and is doomed to extinction if it does not fight. Moreover, nations were "very much like individuals"; they too were involved in an unending fight to survive. The fighting quality of a nation depended on its racial purity. It was proclaimed by racist ideologue Eugen Fischer that the Bismarckian empire and the *Realpolitik* that established it was too tolerant of minorities and their "impurities." What was needed, held Fischer, was a way to rid the entire Germanic world of "defilers." Fischer offered that his ends could be accomplished by appropriate state measures, for only government intervention could prevent further "infection" by inferior races. Thus, governments, especially the one in Germany, should develop and implement a coherent racial policy.[15] Nazism would one day put into effect such a policy.

Paramilitary Antecedents

We return at this juncture to the Prussian military tradition. The power of the military in German life and particularly the Prussian officers corps derived from a long historical tradition. In the seventeenth and eighteenth centuries, the Prussian state had gradually expanded. This expansion was based on a polity organized along military lines. It was dominated by a neo-feudal system of landowners, the Junker class. This class had intermeshed with the military recruiting system.[16] This system was dismantled with the end of serfdom. The prestige of the Prussian army was then damaged considerably by its defeat in fighting against Napoleon. It has often been maintained that the Prussians fought the French in the humiliating battles of the first decade of the nineteenth century with the army that had been used by Frederick the Great a generation earlier. In some instances this was precisely the case, as it was reported that at Jena one old Prussian general had to be lifted into the saddle on his horse so as to ride into battle.

In 1848 and again in 1862, Prussian reformers came close to bringing the old Prussian officers corps under civilian control. Then Otto von Bismarck was appointed chancellor to save the army from interference by reformers. He quickly used a revived Prussian army in three wars to unify Germany. And reformist zeal was turned aside permanently in 1871.

After unification, the army was greatly influential in Germany society. Its continuing prestige, secured through the wars of unification, was enormous. Noncommissioned officers, who had stayed in the army for some years after initial tours of compulsory military service, were given an automatic right to a position in state employment when they finally were discharged. In time, the majority of police, postal workers, and various other state functionaries were veterans who carried out their jobs in a militaristic style.

As years passed, a popular militarism spread. There was by the early twentieth century a "Navy League" and a considerable variety of veterans' organizations.[17] By the beginning of World War I, military professionalization made the army increasingly less open to reform. This pervasive professionalism made the army even less potentially democratic. Also, military arrogance became increasingly prominent in German life. This phenomenon was enhanced by Germany's entry into *Weltpolitik*, the competitive pursuit of colonies in what would later be called the "third world." The German army in South-West Africa (now Nambia) slaughtered thousands of a people called the "Herero." They then drove the rest of the natives into the desert where a great many more of them died because of starvation.[18] Even in Alsace-Lorraine, within Europe itself, German troops behaved like conquerors, causing a hostile response and a lasting hatred among French natives.

The political life of prewar Germany developed in a way that made the society easily paramilitarized after the end of the war. It was greatly factionalized into coalitions which were normally hostile to each other. These coalitions spanned the political spectrum from conservative to liberals. Unlike Great Britain, Germany had a prominent element of politicized Catholicism. But Catholicism in politics displayed some characteristics of a class-based party even while displaying a strongly unifying religious theme. There was something of a paranoid style at work in political life. Particularly the Marxists saw themselves as "just" defenders of their beliefs, eternally watchful against attacks from all sides. In a system like this, lasting coalitions were impossible so that the goals of any one or few groups could not be achieved.[19]

Of all the political formations, the only one that had any chance of success was the Social Democratic Party (SPD), which came closest to developing a program with a significant attraction for the masses in Germany. But no political party appeared that came close to the umbrella parties that had developed in England or the United States, sheltering diverse factions as they did. The process of oppositional block building then carried over into postwar Germany. And during the postwar period, blocs were reinforced by paramilitary associations. Without World War I, the tensions between and among blocs would likely have spawned little actual physical confrontation. But the war acted as a catalyst for change in terms of rigidifying the opposition, and sometimes confrontations, between these disparate groups.

In this way the initial cause for the emergence of political associations in the immediate postwar period was obviously that conflict itself, followed as it was by humiliating defeat. But to observe the war by itself as a primary causational factor is to oversimplify. Certain aspects of German society had become highly militarized before the "Great War."[20] It is necessary to return to the fact that Wilhelmine society greatly honored the military which had been its unifier. Therefore, as early as 1900, in addition to the veterans' organizations mentioned earlier, there had appeared the first ancestors of the postwar Free Corps. As early as 1900, there existed the Kyffhäuser *Bund* counting some 3 million members over time. This formation was established to oppose socialism and did so with government assistance.[21]

That the appearance and growth of such formations was sparked in opposition to the spread of Social Democracy was demonstrated in individual cases. For example, in 1903 the SPD emerged from Reichstag elections as the second largest party in Germany, taking some one-third of the votes cast. This success on the left caused widespread panic on the right. The first fruit of this rightist apprehension was the formation of the National Association against Social Democracy. When the SPD put together youth organizations, the imperial government backed the founding of the Young German League. This league was a sort of Boy-Scout-like formation, in some ways resembling the later Hitler Youth. It also provided military training in its time. It eventually numbered some three-quarter million young men.[22] In this way, before the common linking between the military and the political Right was seen throughout the world, it was seen in prewar Germany.

A picture is provided of an imperial Germany politicized to some extent and militarized to a greater extent. This situation pertained because the German army had gained and maintained enormous prestige as the instrument of unification. A concept appeared which had it that the army should and would act as the "school of the nation," conforming civilian life to military standards. Any military service gave the veteran returned to ordinary life prestige and enhanced social standing in a fairly highly stratified society. It became true that a middle-class individual obtaining even a reserve commission would gain social advancement. And this military cast returned to the civilian order to enter the anti–SPD lists through auxiliary organizations.[23]

When the war came in 1914, it built on the tendencies toward militarization well entrenched in German life. Its impact was built on two chronological segments of the war. Before 1916, societal chasms were bridged and the Germans unified in an unprecedented manner. After 1916, the year which saw two catastrophic tragedies at Verdun and at the Somme, the strain of a large conflict of attrition diminished that earlier spirit of unified resolve. Germany to a considerable extent was generationally divided along a fault line separating an older generation, which more easily put aside war fervor in the form of a desire to return to the peaceful prewar time, and the younger people represented by the mass of young manhood at the front. Many of this second group came to romanticize the war and the "front experience." Increasingly, the usual generational conflict was intensified by these two differing perceptions. The residual postwar impact of this divide was seen in older brothers who returned to civilian life unable to accept the defeat emotionally. These young men were quick to convey to younger siblings the idea that class divisions should be replaced by a new order in which societal stratification was meaningless.

The old social chasms were said by those who made the calls for a front-oriented society to be overridden by a nationalistic-militaristic orientation. The returning veterans became the national leaders of those too young to have served in the war. Among postwar university students, "it was interesting [in 1919] to observe closely the transformation of [their] political spirit. Representatives of liberal and democratic ideals were in the minority [obscured] by blustering soldiers of fortune, growing rapidly in number.... Just as later, before Hitler's rise, anti–Semitism emerged as the means for supporting such viewpoints."[24]

A basic aspect of this situation was that these returned soldiers in 1918 and 1919 seemed oblivious to the fact that they had been no more than civilians serving as soldiers for the duration of the war. In civilian life, they too had been among the faceless masses working at boring jobs for inadequate wages. The war had lifted them above all that and made them intolerant of returning to take up residence among those who were as they once had been. Hence, a more militarized and simultaneously participation-inclined German society, split between gradualism and radicalism emerged by the end of the fighting.

Particularly drawn to the new world of the militarized society for the common man were the younger siblings who could not serve because of age limitations in the war itself. Many of these had participated in a pre-service paramilitary program. One of these was later Nazi leader Heinrich Himmler who commenced his pre-service training in a militarized youth formation in 1917. This made him ready to join his veteran older sibling who was part of a group of would-be soldiers run out of the service by a restriction imposed by the Treaty of Versailles limiting the total army to 100,000 men.[25]

The war had involved the population of Germany in the affairs of the nation and made it a much more participatory society. The first wave of a participation revolution had swept over Germany during the war. A second wave was realized after the war, having both Left and Right spearheads.[26] Over time, the Nazi stormtrooper would become an integral part of the second wave. The German revolution at war's end and the simultaneous abdication of the Kaiser played double causational roles in shaping the postwar participation explosion. These were a double link between the Empire and the emerging Republic. They were also a stimulative cause for the emergence of the many paramilitary groups appearing in the immediate postwar era. The feature of the German revolution most commonly seen throughout Germany and most abhorrent to the Right generally was the appearance of the soldiers' and workers' councils with their own fighting forces. A negative image of such councils was spread throughout the "patriotic literature." The street fighters associated with the councils were commonly offered up in this literature as exclusively involved in atrocities and ruthless acts launched against the civilian population.

As the councils and their paramilitary "guards" became active on 9 November 1919, it appeared likely that the only sort of government to develop would grow out of the revolution. There was a vacuum of civil authority after the abdication of the Kaiser and it was quickly filled by the councils. This process will be covered more completely in the next chapter. It is sufficient to state at this point that this swirl of events drew together the various strands of militaristic tendencies proceeding from the nineteenth century and placed them completely at the service of the political Right.

Chapter Two

The Weimar Republic Rises Among the Ruins

It should not be understood that only anti–Semitism dominated the political and social thought of imperial Germany. Of great significance too were strains of traditionalist monarchist thinking, emerging socialism, some vague stirrings toward English-style parliamentarianism and, most important, nationalism. Of these, the only one to blend with anti–Semitism in any meaningful fashion was nationalism. German political development suffered from the absence of conservatives and liberals developed on the Western model. Before 1918, in fact, liberals had little influence. This was also true of the conservatives after 1918 who lost themselves in dreams of a vanished monarchy. German liberals failed to think in modern ways. Most of them never doubted the principles on which the Reich had been established in 1871. Western ideals of liberalism, meaning, in the nineteenth century, parliamentary limitation on the power of the executive, were not accepted.

Before 1914, the nationalistic forces in Germany were growing in numbers, but were not yet of overwhelming influence. The rise of German nationalism in the nineteenth century was based in part upon the idea of the Germanic *Volk* (literally "the people" with overtones of racial connectiveness and exclusivity). In this view the *Volk* was an entity held together by historical symbols and traditions. The rise of nationalism, even before Germany was a nation, stimulated the worship of "the people" and the nation as a secular religion. The idea was greatly enhanced after 1871.

The very beginning of the nineteenth century witnessed a feeling of disappointment with the disunity of German lands. After 1815, the Congress of Vienna's legacy was the Germanic Federation, a loose union of some thirty-nine states, large and small. This situation led to a glorification of the "wars of liberation" against Napoleon just ended. After it, Germans from each of the thirty-nine states formed into a loose union. They began, because of this, to think of themselves as a nation. The governments of the confederation were suspicious of this nationalism first developing against Napoleon. They worked to suppress it wherever it reappeared.

When the Second Reich came in 1871, it was the fulfillment of long-held hopes for unity. But this new Germany stressed the state's power rather than "spiritual" linking. The government moved to integrate the masses into the conservative social order, by using a common set of Germanic values. The ruling classes envisioned a strong central Europe under Germanic hegemony. Their vision embraced an expansionist policy aimed at the open space that lay eastward (the *Drang nach Osten* or "drive to the east") and the acquisition of colonies abroad. Bismarck had not acted in accordance with this expansionist dream. But his successors commenced to invoke both hyper-nationalism and imperialism to gain the support of the working classes, ever burgeoning in numbers because of rapid industrialization. Once Bismarck was gone and Wilhelm II was in power, the German people were exposed to deliberately stimulated enthusiasm for imperialism. Many saw war as a noble cause and demanded *Lebensraum* ("living room") for the German people. All of this prefigured the eventual Nazi crusades.

This does not mean that prewar Germany was rife with storm warnings of the Nazism to come. Wilhelmine society broadly was committed to law and order. Its laws protected property and persons. Political violence when it transpired, was generally condemned and prosecuted under law. This was the case regardless of who the victims were. The protective umbrella of Wilhelmine law covered Socialists and Jews despite the fact that both were unpopular. Anti-Semitic and antisocialist writings and actions were handled harshly in many cases, even though many judges were also antisocialist and anti–Semitic. This happened because the defendants, as they took action against "societal enemies," often violated rights of privacy and property. Hence, like many societies, the Second Empire had within it anomalies. But without an extraordinary set of circumstances these could not assume a central position in national life. It was the Great War of 1914 that provided the circumstances that disrupted stability.

The German people were enthralled when war was declared in August of 1914. Many of the initial participants in the first fighting shared a displayed euphoria about impending combat. In Germany, the intense nationalism of the prewar period caused those on the Left to join those on the Right in pledging themselves to suspend civil dissent until victory was achieved. The Emperor proudly announced a *Burgfrieden* (a moratorium on political confrontation).[1] Influenced by the Kaiser's promises that the war would be short, most Germans saw it as a brief respite from making a living wage, from boring assembly lines. Nothing was at all foreboding for, as the Kaiser and others had said, the war would be "over by Christmas."

By Christmas of 1914, however, there was no end in sight. Instead, particularly on the Western front, there was a war of attrition. The losses were staggering. And the home front was anything but united. Great societal fissures appeared. The Left voted funds along with the rest of the *Reichstag* at the outset of the war and expected in return to be granted significant political concessions. But none appeared. Even after it became clear that there were to be no concessions, support for the war continued. This can be attributed, in part, to a delight in conflict based on prewar nationalism. Important also was the constant war propaganda indicating that the nation's leaders would present Germany with the fruits of victory. This was unrealistic. Geopolitical and military situations signaled defeat over the longer term. Perhaps this should have been apparent to the German High Command from the outset. Germany was fighting on two fronts against enemies owning more extensive means of production and greater numbers of people.

Deadly threats from more than one quarter required careful coordination of strategic policy, especially with Germany's war-alliance partners. It required understandings between civilian and military authorities. But these did not exist.[2] Instead of developing a plan for coordinating the war, Germany's High Command began to subvert the power of the civilian government. This was very much the case when Paul von Hindenburg and Erich Ludendorff assumed supreme command of the German army and war effort in August of 1916. Having crippled the Russians at Tannenburg and the Masurian Lakes in 1914, Hindenburg and Ludendorff assumed the status of exalted heroes. Their reputations dwarfed the Emperor's and those of civilian leaders. This allowed them to establish the so-called "Hindenburg-Ludendorff dictatorship" for the last two years of the war. From late 1916 on, the Kaiser was politically impotent. This was also true in the cases of the chancellor, the cabinet, the *Reichstag*, the industrialists, and the trade unions.

In actuality, this German military, so exalted in myth, was little more than a pale reflection of earlier Prussian or German forces. Particularly was this the case at the strategic level. In 1914, the Germans quickly bogged down on the Western front. In 1915 and 1916, German strategists sacrificed a million men in futile battles. In 1916, the admirals made a failed effort to challenge the British navy off Jutland and break a war-long blockade. In 1917, the Hindenburg-Ludendorf command team guaranteed defeat by throwing away whatever chances they had for a moderate peace by bringing America into the war with unrestricted submarine warfare, transporting the Bolshevik leader V. I. Lenin from Switzerland into Russia to mount a Communist revolution, and committing Germany's last reserves to a final assault.

The army appointed civilians to arrange a cessation of hostilities and later created a myth blaming them for "stabbing the Germany Army, never defeated" at the front, "in the back." This, they said, had happened through "inadequate support" on the home front. This was the stab-in-the-back legend (*Dolchstosslegende*).[3] The German people thus believed until the final months of the war that victory was close at hand. Four years of positive propaganda followed by one piece of profoundly negative news made the shock from the loss much greater. If the Germans had allowed more accurate information to issue during wartime as had the English, the populace might have been more realistic. It took the nation a few years and a humiliating treaty to accept defeat. And some never accepted it. The generals acted in this manner because they wanted to maintain the position of the military in German life. It was axiomatic for them to blame everything on home-front defeatism.

Just before the end of the war, the High Command and the entrenched elites decided that the Allies did not want to settle peace with the monarchy. As the generals saw it, the old ruling order had become a liability. United States president Woodrow Wilson, inspired by lofty democratic sentiments, held that there could be no bargain with the emperor or the military. This provided Germans who wanted to replace the monarchy with an excuse; they would devise a parliamentary state.

Diplomatic pressure alone could not have brought about the abandonment of the monarchy. By the middle of 1918, the Allied blockade was creating starvation. There were food riots in major cities and strikes. The Kaiser's credibility was at its nadir. The Emperor had appointed Max of Baden, his liberal cousin, as chancellor. But that act improved his public image little. Meanwhile, Max of Baden indicated to the Allies that Germany was now under civilian control and ready to sign an armistice. On 11 November the armistice was signed by a civilian, Matthias Erzberger, who had sponsored earlier peace resolutions in the Reichstag.

The armistice terms were not lenient. The document was designed to let the Germans know that they had lost the war and to make them experience the humiliation of defeat. While the German delegation agonized over terms in a railroad car in the forest of Compiègne, on 9 November the Kaiser abdicated and went into Dutch exile. Quickly, a political vacuum came into being. Several factions, including the Communists, tried to fill the void.

Two. The Weimar Republic Rises Among the Ruins

In Moscow, Lenin saw the German situation as being much like that of St. Petersburg in 1917. Lenin's belief appeared confirmed by the appearance of councils of workers and soldiers. They also seemed confirmed by mutinous sailors in Kiel (28 October 1918) who had refused an order to take out the fleet for a final decisive battle with the British in the North Sea. Instead, they sang revolutionary songs and hoisted red flags over their ships. As news of the sailors' mutiny spread across Germany, a rash of revolts were inspired. The government, with few troops back from the front, could not suppress them.

These German rebels of 1919, however, were not followers of Lenin as that leader in far-away Russia believed. They were not interested in a Bolshevik-style revolution. They were merely war-weary and hoped that rebellious actions would bring a quick end to conflict. On 8 November the independent socialist Kurt Eisner, supported by councils of workers, soldiers, and peasants, overthrew the royal Bavarian government. Eisner and his followers then proclaimed a "Socialist Republic."

It thus appeared, superficially, that the first two weeks of November during 1918 constituted a reenactment of the Russian revolution. The fears of a Communist revolution were exaggerated. The German situation did not resemble Russia during 1917. In Russia, the urban working classes were proportionately much smaller. They were also less disciplined along formal political lines and lacked traditions of skilled craftsmanship. Those kind of traditions made the German workers much more moderate than the Bolsheviks. In Russia, under impact of a disastrous war, an elite cadre of revolutionaries skillfully manipulated deep-seated resentments. The eventual result was a one-party dictatorship.

In contrast to the Russian situation, the Germans produced a "revolution" that left the social structure of Wilhelmine Germany essentially the same.[4] The decisive political shift in Germany had actually transpired before the revolution when the ruling elites were temporarily displaced by Social Democracy, and some middle-class elements.[5] The largest of the political parties supporting change at the top of the governmental pyramid was the Social Democratic Party (SPD). In 1914, the SPD had reluctantly supported the war effort. But this had caused a basic split in its ranks. The dissidents walked out of the party and formed a new entity in 1917 called the "Independent Socialist Party." The aim of the new radicals was to establish genuine socialism in Germany. The new group first called for a quick halt to the war. These independent socialists were supported by even more radical Communists, admirers of the Bolsheviks in Russia.

German Communists were led by two notorious and highly effective revolutionaries—Rosa Luxemburg and Karl Liebknecht. Supported by angry workers, the "Spartacists" (instead of "Communists") were named after the ill-fated, insurrectionary Roman slave leader Spartacus. They called at war's end for a Bolshevik-style order. Out of this event, they expected an expropriation of industries, and the limitation of inherited estates. This all was to be enacted by "Soviets" (as in Russia). Spartacist leader Karl Liebknecht was the son of Wilhelm Liebknecht, a close friend of Karl Marx. Karl Liebknecht had broken with the rump majority of Social Democrats as early as 1914 over the voting of war credits. The younger Liebknecht was a person of unshakable determination and revolutionary zeal.

By May of 1918, Liebknecht was organizing a demonstration against the war to denounce government "warmongers." And he moved quickly to call for the violent overthrow of the government. This was called sedition by the government. He was seized by authorities, quickly tried, and given a four-year jail sentence. However, in October of 1918, as part of a general amnesty for political prisoners, he was released. He quickly returned to center stage in Berlin.[6] Soon thereafter a sizeable part of the German Left gathered around Liebknecht and his second-in-command, Rosa Luxemburg. Luxemburg was a brilliant ideologue, a combative agitator in her mid-forties. Born in Poland, she had come to Germany to study. She emerged as an intellectual at the forefront of the Left. She was one of the few in Germany who opposed the war from the beginning.

The majority socialists also claimed to be Marxists. In actuality, their rank-and-file showed little interest in ideology. They had the lifestyles of the petit bourgeois and wanted no revolution. Rather, the SPD desired to raise the general standard of living for working people in the context of a moderate democratic order. Typical of this new nonrevolutionary Left in Germany was their leader, Friedrich Ebert. Born in 1871, Ebert was the son of a tailor, who had apprenticed as a saddlemaker. He had became the chairman of the saddler's union in Bremen and was a member of the city council before he was thirty. In 1904, he rose to the cochairmanship of the SPD convention. A year later he was appointed secretary of the Central Committee. The majority socialists liked the fact that Ebert was not a rigid ideologue. He was a revisionist, who believed in parliamentary democracy. Parliamentary government, in his view, would best transpire in a republican form. But he was not averse to it developing as a constitutional monarchy.

The last thing in the world that a man like Ebert would support was a Bolshevik-like rising of the masses against the state.[7] In October of 1918, he feared such a revolution in Germany. For that reason, he threw his authority behind Max of Baden. Those close to Ebert thought much as he did, notably his chief lieutenant, Philip Scheidemann. By 9 November 1918, Berliners were in a state of tension. The radical Left had called for a general strike of all workers. There was an expectation of violence but little transpired. Most people expected to see the abdication of the Emperor. Suddenly Max of Baden forced the situation to change. On his own authority, he announced the Kaiser's abdication and issued a call for new elections. Unwillingly, the Kaiser departed. That same day, Philip Scheidemann was confronted, while at lunch in the Reichstag dining room, with the news that Liebknecht was speaking from the balcony of the imperial palace to proclaim a new Red republic.

Scheidemann later described the situation as follows: "Now I saw clearly what was afoot. I knew his Liebknecht's] slogan — supreme authority for the workers' councils. Germany to be therefore a Russian province, a branch of the Soviet. No, no, a thousand times no!"[8] Scheidemann then rushed to one of the large windows of the Reichstag and proclaimed the republic to a crowd below. This spur-of-the-moment announcement had been made even before the abdication. Ebert believed, because there had as yet been no abdication, that Scheidemann actually had no right to do as he did. Germany thus more or less stumbled into the republican form by accident. It was argued at the time, and has been argued since, that a more gradual move to a constitutional monarchy would have brought the new government a larger group of supporters and increased its survival chances.[9] However, pressure from the streets and the urgings of Woodrow Wilson suggested that the Germans did not have the time to move in a gradual manner away from the empire.

During the last days of 1918 and the early days of 1919, conservative forces were in disarray. The situation looked bleak. Conservatives, at least momentarily, were without resolve and energy and appeared incapable of opposing a Red takeover. Many people turned to the majority socialists as the best hope of preventing a revolution. Conservatives noted with alarm that the situation was reminiscent of the Bolshevik Revolution in Russia. The formation of councils by workers, soldiers, and left-wing intellectuals established a force competing directly with established, traditional Reichstag political parties. The party leaders were hostile to the councils.

One historian, although his is not the majority view, has argued that the councils could have played a positive role in Germany's future, helping to "restructure society."[10] But such an assumption is counterfactual. The reluctance of the majority socialists to use the councils was expressed in their public utterances and a program. This encouraged the political Right. The Right came to believe that, since it did not have to fear the councils, the needed concessions would be minimal.

The SPD leadership was in a quandary. It hoped to establish a state based on cooperation with moderate forces, and there was no wish to alienate such forces. They were much concerned that, should any reforms look radical, they might appear to be Bolshevistic. They were apprehensive not only that the broad sweep of the middle class might believe this, but that the English and French would as well. Their plight worsened through the surge of radicalism that appeared to dominate the period of November 1918 to April 1919. During this time span, revolution seemed to be in the air. But uprisings lacked the extent of organization present in the Bolshevik Revolution. There appeared to be no disciplined cadre of the kind seen acting earlier with Lenin to bring down the state's edifice.

In Munich, power was seized in a spontaneous rush by a collection of idealists led by journalist Kurt Eisner. Eisner and his associates were able to prevail for a time because there was a nearly absolute vacuum in Bavaria at war's end when King Ludwig fled his domain. But Eisner was no Lenin. No proletarian dictatorship was set in place. Instead, Eisner sponsored elections which took place in April and quickly threw him out of office. He was then assassinated. The killing of Eisner (an event described later in this book) inspired his followers to try to retain power by force. This meant establishing the Soviet-style government they failed to create initially. The eventual "Red Republics" which grew out of this circumstance lasted only a brief period and were soon crushed by German army and Freikorps elements.

Freikorps units were recent paramilitary arrivals on the scene. They formed at the end of the war when armistice and treaty negotiations were forcing men out of the military. They were assigned the task of defending German territory in the east against Poland.[11] These fierce fighters, most of whom would have liked to see World War I continue, believed that the more territory they controlled militarily the more Germany would receive in a peace settlement. The new German government believed the same thing, but the authorities in Berlin could not rely on regular army units to carry out the tasks necessary to achieve such a goal.

Many of the soldiers still in uniform had seen their units fall apart at the end of the war through desertions, casualties, and epidemics. For these reasons, special units were formed by drawing on volunteers. Not all the volunteer groups were formed of frontline veterans. Some members had been too young to enlist during the war, although they very much wanted to fight. Others had not been able to pass intelligence tests or had criminal records, keeping them out of the army.

Free Corps were usually led by men who had been wartime junior officers or noncommissioned officers. These Freikorps never employed regular army restraint. They were brutal fighters with brutal instincts. One indication of just how badly the times were out of joint was seen in the socialist government in Berlin being forced, as in Munich, to call in regular army troops reinforced by Freikorps to suppress rebellions. This practice led to a split on the Left between moderate and more radical socialists. This fracture was not healed for the duration of the Weimar Republic.

Revolutionary activity in Berlin was of the greatest importance, because it was the seat of government. Immediately after the war, Berlin had become a center of radical agitation. In January of 1919, a series of major disturbances erupted comprising the so-called Spartacist Revolt. The Spartacists had agitated against the war with intensity during its final stages and now called for a socialist revolution. However, the Spartacist leaders, Liebknecht and Luxemburg, were not planning revolution in January because the time was not ripe. The revolt that broke out in the capital was without design or meaningful leadership.

Some of the demonstrations had been called by revolutionary shop stewards Others seemed more spontaneous, boiling up on the spot.[12] Planned and spontaneous actions resulted in an uprising which presented Liebknecht and Luxemburg with a quandary. The two leaders did not believe that Germany was ready to embrace far-reaching change. However, the people were in the streets and they had been presented with a premature action. They had to provide direction and a sense of purpose. Their decision to act turned out to be an unwise one. The duo's assumption of leadership led to their murders by troops charged with restoring order. Perhaps a *New York Times* editorial had the most perceptive observation on the events when it questioned the choice of the revolutionists' name: "[I]n choosing the name [Spartacist] the German leader [Liebknecht] forgot to take into consideration" that the Spartacus of Roman times had attached to his name both the glory of early victories and "the stigma of ultimate defeat."[13]

Without much of a plan and little hope of success, the uprising appeared preordained to fail. Ebert as spokesman for the government, called upon the military to restore order. He had established connections with members of the general staff during the war. His emissary to the army in the postwar period was Gustav Noske, an SPD moderate. Noske was a pariah in Leftist circles where he was called the "bulldog of the counterrevolution."[14]

General Wilhelm Groener was the representative of the general staff in negotiations with the majority socialists. The outcome was a deal struck between the generals and SPD leaders. The generals would dispatch troops to Berlin to deal with the revolutionaries. In return for this service, the Social Democratic government promised to leave the General Staff intact within the new state. An unintended outcome of this bargain was the creation of an essentially unreformed, unrepublican army. In the short term, army troops came to Berlin to put down the rising and hard upon the heels of the army came the far less disciplined and more violent Free Corps. This caused a number of anti-insurgent atrocities, including the killing of the Spartacist leaders. This fact led to a lasting enmity between the majority socialists and the radical Left faction of prewar Social Democracy. The majority socialists quickly moved to arrange the election of a National Assembly. This assembly was sent from the capital to congregate in Weimar away from Berlin's strife. After negotiations, the workers' councils went along with the idea.

In this manner, on 19 January 1919, Germany had its first important election. It produced a National Assembly charged with writing a new constitution. On 9 February the Assembly had its first meeting and selected Ebert president and Scheidemann his chancellor. Fear of

Two. The Weimar Republic Rises Among the Ruins

Shown are street scenes from Berlin demonstrating street fighting during the suppression of the Spartacist Revolt of 1918/1919. (From photographic montages in J. Goebbels, *Das erwachende Berlin*, Munich: Zentralverlag der NSDAP, 1934.

Two images of Rosa Luxemburg and one of Karl Liebknecht. Both were murdered during the suppression of the Spartacist rising.

radical socialist revolution had established a basis for temporary cooperation between conservatives and moderate socialists.

The Versailles Treaty now confronted Germany. It has been handled variously by historians. One view is that it had an initial negative impact for the Weimar Republic from which it was impossible to recover. It has also been offered that it "fell between two stools." In this view, it was neither harsh enough to make certain a lasting parliamentary state was established nor, on the other hand, lenient enough to obtain that same end. Instead of providing sufficient Allied control to prevent the emergence of effective anti–Republican forces, the Allies forced Germany to move forward with difficulty. Moreover, not only was Allied control not forthcoming, but the infant parliamentary order was not provided with the instruments to restrain foes.

Regardless of which position one takes on the Versailles Treaty, it is evident that the Republic did not recover from its economic impact until the mid–1920s. Moreover, the irritant quality of the treaty in German society remained. Over time, many anti–Republican nationalists called Versailles a "dictated peace." There was a widely held belief in Germany that the treaty was unfairly imposed upon Germans, that the people had no voice in it when the representatives of the new Republic had been forced to agree to its provisions. All of that was supposedly done by the Allies, particularly the bullying French. There was some truth in the notion. The German legation that went to Paris in 1919 was given little chance to modify the treaty. Perhaps the Germans should have had no reason to be surprised by this; they had been defeated in a long and costly war.

In sum, the treaty played a very large part in the history of the Republic. Its provisions need to be weighed against the almost unanimous German claim that it was unfairly punitive. This view was held by some notable non–Germans as well. Widely known English economist John Maynard Keynes called it a "Carthaginian peace, aimed at reducing Germany to a second rate power and leading to the impoverishment of the German people."[15]

Some of the key terms were: (1) Alsace-Lorraine was returned to France; (2) West Prussia and Pomerania were given to Poland; (3) Memel went to Lithuania; (4) Danzig was declared a free city under the League of Nations; (5) German colonies were parceled out to the Allies; (6) the Saar Basin was placed under administration of the League of Nations for fifteen years; (7) newly established European states made out of old empires had to be recognized; (8) the *Anschluss* with Austria was forbidden; (9) Germany was limited to a 100,000-man army; and (10) Germany was to pay restitution for all wartime damages. On a more positive note, the Allies did not try to separate the Rhineland from the rest of the German nation, although the French might have liked that. The treaty in final draft ignored separatist sentiment in both Bavaria and the Rhineland. Important for postwar chaos was the limitation of the army to 100,000 men, making it impossible for those who wished to remain warriors to stay in the regular military. Versailles had left the truncated Germany a large and highly populated nation with, perhaps most importantly, its industrial power still intact. But the treaty also caused a number of problems.

The reparations demands of the treaty were too high to make good sense economically. The plan to pay them out over an excessively long period of time was problematic. But the economic crisis of 1923, and the worldwide one in 1929, were by no means the sole product of the treaty. A relatively recent study of the negotiations at Versailles has argued persuasively that the terms of the treaty represented a compromise. It was, in this view, a bargain between those who wanted Germany to pay all war costs and those who wanted the new government to pay only damages suffered by civilians.[16] Unfortunately, to satisfy those who wanted a more punitive war settlement but had failed to achieve it, Article 231 was included. Article 231 was the infamous and intensely disliked "war guilt" clause. By it, Germany accepted "the responsibility" for initiating the war. Many German politicians seized upon this symbolic article to make of it an act of national humiliation unjustly imposed by the Allies.[17] And the Allies were not the only villains in this scenario. This infamous treaty had been signed, it was often held, by "treacherous" republicans practicing a "policy of fulfillment."

Some statesmen were aware of the difficulties involved in a treaty perceived as too harsh. David Lloyd George, the British prime minister, was one of these. Lloyd George believed that stationing troops of the victorious Allies in Germany would create lasting bitterness in a "proud people."[18] Lloyd George was aware of the warning left behind by one of the nineteenth century's most effective diplomats, Clemens von Metternich, Prince of Austria. Metternich had testified after the Congress of Vienna had ended the Napoleonic Wars that, when any party left the negotiating table totally bitter, the treaty just signed could not last long. Lloyd George was concerned about how successful the new German republic could be as it labored under a harsh treaty. Yet he could not argue his doubts in negotiations. Lloyd George wished to maintain his party in power in England. And he had promised voters during 1918 that Germany would be pressured mercilessly after the war and forced to compensate for the enormous losses that Britain had endured. To some extent the prime minister's hands were tied.

The U.S. president, Woodrow Wilson, had come to Europe in 1919 with a vision for a new and peaceful world. During the war, he had offered his "Fourteen Points." These promised a just peace. The Germans based far too much hope on the Wilsonian pronouncements. Wilson did not actually have sufficient support from his own Congress to exercise the freedom of action necessary to impose his vision at Paris.[19] Once the negotiations had ended, Wilson appeared to many Germans to have been a hypocritical liar. Germans came to fear Wilson when he spoke in idealistic terms. During the Weimar republican years, antidemocratic diatribes began by singling out Wilson as an example of how little the statements of the former Allies could be taken at face value. One such was writer Arthur Moeller van den Bruck who provided the title "the Third Reich" for the future Germany he hoped to see.[20]

Wilson's lack of realism and Lloyd George's political opportunism were noted by George Clemenceau, the prime minister of France. Clemenceau commented that sitting between the two was like "sitting between Napoleon and Jesus Christ." In hindsight, the Versailles Treaty was perhaps not grossly unfair in the moral sense, given the damage Germany had inflicted and the precedent of the Empire's highly punitive Treaty of Brest-Litovsk imposed upon Russia in 1917. However, even if the treaty was not completely unfair, it was unwise.

The Weimar leaders charged with the responsibility of signing the armistice had not wanted to do so, but the military leadership made it clear that Germany simply could not continue the fighting. Philip Scheidemann resigned as chancellor rather than sign the treaty. But finally, given little choice in that the Allies were clearly in a position to occupy Germany as far east as the borders with the new state of Czechoslovakia, the government signed. Many of those same generals who told the Republican government that they had to sign the treaty were later to call its members a group of "traitors" for having done so. Those who supported the national leaders in signing Versailles did not come close in their emotional support to matching the vehemence of rightist opposition.

Enemies of the Republic attacked it early and often in the period from 1920 to 1923. Coup attempts, political murders and popular risings threatened the state. The immediate impact of the Versailles Treaty on Germany was twofold. It led to the cabinet crisis resulting in Scheidemann's resignation. More ominously, over time, it led to a soldiers' revolt against the Republic. For a time, leaders of the German military thought seriously of armed resistance to the

Allies. But even the most diehard generals recognized that a revolt against the victors by a diminished army had no hope of success. Frustrated, it was not long before military figures shifted their rage to the Republic. The republican government, in the meantime, was under intense pressure from the Allies to reduce the army to a peacetime force of 100,000 men and disband all paramilitary forces. This only served to intensify military resentments. What resulted was a series of mutinous acts. The most serious of these was in March of 1920 when army officers conspired to overthrow the Republic. This episode known as the Kapp *Putsch* is named after an undistinguished Prussian civil servant, Wolfgang Kapp.

The plan for the Kapp rebellion was actually the work of General Walther von Lüttwitz, commander of the Berlin army district. The scheme was simple. A paramilitary group named after the Second Marine Brigade's former commander, Captain Hermann Ehrhardt (the "Ehrhardt Brigade"), was to march on Berlin and topple the government.[21] As the Kapp *Putsch* began, republican leaders discovered that the generals would not order their men to fire on Ehrhardt. The army leadership said that the paramilitary unit acting as the spearhead of the Putsch was "one of its own." The army saw most such units as groups which wished to be under its command and ought to be. Thus abandoned by its own army and under assault by a paramilitary force, the republican government fled the capital. It went first to Dresden and then fled to Stuttgart. Before leaving Berlin, it issued an appeal to all German workers to support a general strike. The general strike took place and the Ehrhardt men in their swastika-adorned helmets left Berlin as Kapp and Lüttwitz found they could not run the government when public workers would not provide basic services. On 20 March it was all over. Ebert returned to Berlin to resume control.

The retrospective significance of this failed coup was not just that it revealed the unreliability of the military if an assault came from the Right. The differing approach the army took was soon demonstrated by what happened when an assault from the radical Left transpired in the Ruhr. A Red army of some 80,000 moved in and took over that industrial region. The Ebert regime quickly called out an army that had proven unreliable a week before. This time, however, the German army showed few qualms in quelling the revolt. Ebert's hopes of dismantling an officers' corps full of anti–Republican rightists to replace it with a truly republican force were in this way disappointed permanently.[22]

The Kapp *Putsch* had other significant results. It forced the government to call its first national election, perhaps prematurely. It brought rightists into control of the Bavarian state regime. In Bavaria, the majority socialist government was forced to resign. On 16 March 1920 Gustav von Kahr was elected prime minister by the Bavarian diet. Kahr harbored separatist notions. Bavaria now became the domain of the far Right (often called the "Orderly Compartment of Bavaria"). Munich then, under Kahr, spearheaded opposition against the Republic in Berlin.[23]

In the spring of 1921, the final reparations bill (left blank in the Versailles Treaty), came due. It was thirty-five billion dollars in gold marks. The Germans were given a six-day ultimatum to accept the reparations bill. Not to do so would have resulted in an invasion of the Ruhr. The government accepted the ultimatum. As with the treaty itself earlier, there was no alternative. The nationalists, cloaking themselves in hyperpatriotism, screamed about "treason." The Right complained about the fact that the man assigned to the task of complying with reparations was Walther Rathenau, a Jew. From the Right there emerged a popular and reprehensible couplet: "Shoot down that Walter Rathenau, that cursed, god-damned Jewish sow."[24]

The Kapp Putsch is depicted here. Every photograph shows members of the supporting Ehrhardt Brigade which, when leaving the city, shot people indiscriminately who jeered at them.

Under Rathenau's leadership, Weimar Germany scored its initial success in foreign policy. Rathenau attempted to thwart France's desire to isolate Germany through encircling alliances by turning to the Soviets. The U.S.S.R. was also isolated in foreign affairs. The two international outcasts concluded a treaty of friendship at Rapallo near Genoa. The bilateral document contained an agreement to establish relations on a permanent footing and a pledge not to ask reparations of each other. They also initiated close economic relations and, in a secret clause, established military connections. Rapallo caused consternation abroad, particularly in France. Inside Germany, the treaty did not provide public-relations dividends for the government. Instead, rightist hysteria continued and resulted in Rathenau's murder. The same clandestine group that killed Rathenau, the "Organization Consul," had also assassinated Matthias Erzberger. Erzberger's "sin" had been that he signed the armistice. There was a continuing economic crisis in Germany as all this happened because of runaway inflation. This phenomenon was caused by a series of unwise policies adopted by the government originating in World War I.[25] The war had hidden the problems, but the pressures imposed by defeat brought them to the surface. The immediate cause of economic collapse was the invasion of the Ruhr by a French force on 11 January 1923. The Germans had requested a moratorium on war debt payments. But the French had refused. French leadership had tried to persuade the British and Americans to believe that an Allied invasion of the Ruhr was justified. But they could not. Not dissuaded, Paris waited on a pretext to act on its own.

The pretext desired in France came when the Reparations Commission declared Germany in default on the delivery of some 140,000 telegraph poles to replace lines destroyed during the war. On 11 January a French-Belgian force marched into the Ruhr. Thus was the nearly nonexistent unity of the Reich further weakened.[26] French occupiers acted harshly and often brutally. The German government's answer to all this was "passive resistance." All economic activity came to a halt in the Ruhr. In an effort to subsidize the workers there who were out on strike, more paper money was printed. Inflation reached fantastic heights in consequence and unemployment soared. The German government could not meet its obligations. The majority of middle-class citizens were ruined by the inflation.

In hope of bringing a quick end to the inflationary crisis, Ebert appointed Gustav Stresemann, leader of the German Peoples' Party, as chancellor. The new chancellor faced staggering problems. The Ruhr was still occupied. Moreover, Communist and socialist regimes hostile to the Republic had been established in Thuringia and Saxony. And there were Communist insurrections in industrial centers like Hamburg. As all this transpired, the mark became so devalued that it stood at 4.6 million to one U.S. dollar. It was in this poisoned atmosphere existing from 1919 through 1923 that an obscure veteran of the Great War became leader of a right-wing party in Bavaria that was little more than a political club at the time. This leader decided, somewhat unrealistically, that he would soon lead an insurrection to overthrow the Weimar Republic. His name was Adolf Hitler.

At least one more immediate postwar phenomenon is to be examined here before turning to Hitler's rise, and that is the "military desperado." The word "desperado" used in this manner was first employed in a 1967 article by historian Wolfgang Sauer.[27] This idea holds that a distinct interest group was formed by a coalescence of men emerging from the war to find they could not become civilians again. Neither could they remain in the armed forces, which most would have liked to do, because of the restrictions imposed by Versailles.

These men had become primitive warriors in four years of battles. Most of them were individuals who had simply come to desire the adventure of mortal combat. They sought not only to return to the army life, but also to transform the civilian world into a facsimile of the front. Immediately after the war there was for a time a near vacuum of political and military power which was filled to some extent by a pluralistic system of militaristic activity. Initially, the postwar Free Corps provided the backbone of this system. But not too much later the context expanded to include all sorts of paramilitaristic activity and formations. There were leagues and a large number of organizations with "*Bund*" somewhere in their names. Among the elaborate mix of such groups was the fledgling Nazi SA. Typical of this group in Germany was Ernst Röhm, later to lead the Nazi SA, who wrote: "I discover that I no longer belong to the people. All I remember is that I once belonged to the German Army."[28]

All the German desperadoes shared a mythical belief in the life of the trenches. This was a vision that consecrated the total war experience. Such a myth may well have had its origins as early as the Napoleonic Wars, but it reached its fullest development immediately after World War I. This notion of a shared unique experience kept the desperado seeking its replication. This was difficult in the gray, drab world of peacetime. They also remembered their fallen comrades as heroes in Valhalla. If the desperado followed his vision into the paramilitary world, he could then believe, and many did, that their special shared meaning of life was continuing in the civilian sphere with like-minded comrades.

It would be a mistake to think that the desperado was a typology to be found in Germany alone. The Treaty of Trianon had come close to dismembering historic Hungary. The Hungarians had in fact been stripped of some two-thirds of their prewar territory. This loss exacerbated an intense Hungarian nationalism. Equally stimulative of this nationalism was a threat from the Left much like that of the Sparticist rising in Germany. Communist Bela Kun was successful in establishing a short-lived regime only to have it dislodged by a counterrevolution under Admiral Nicholas Horthy. The desperado played a pivotal role in this counterrevolutionary action. In Hungary, desperadoes returning from the front threw their violent support to one cause or another as it suited them. Oscar Jazi, an early postwar government official, described them as "those bands of political soldiers" who hastened, once having fought, to present their accounts to the government, demanding this role and that in the future Hungarian state. The eventual role played by the Nazis in Germany as a magnet drawing in the desperado was fulfilled in Hungary by the "Magyar Defense League." The League fought against leftist attempts to control the state. But the League was not alone; desperadoes played a role at one time or another in some 200 groups labeled by historians of Hungary as "fascistic."[29]

Many Hungarian veterans found postwar paramilitary life extraordinarily attractive as it, like Free Corps activity in Germany, was free from the regular-army discipline enforced upon them in the past. Some of this broad group, despite a general antipathy to Marxism, commonly shared, participated for a time in Bela Kun's Red Army because, apparently, they saw it as the most readily available way for the moment to follow a violent course of action. Of course, with this mindset they found it easy to shift sides later. Clearly the desperado, here and elsewhere, lacked a clear ideological profile. Of course, given a choice between Left and Right they normally preferred the Right. Because the treaty had dismembered historic Hungary, most of them were violently irredentist. It is just that some were casual about what part of the political spectrum could produce a "reunited" Hungary. In Hungary, however, strongman Nicholas Horthy as leader appeared capable of keeping under control what might well have become the core of a fascist party and, in that fashion, the example differs markedly from the German situation.

Similarly, in Italy, the peace settlement of 1919 gave Rome small pieces of territory. Larger ambitions were left unsatisfied. Many in nationalist circles believed that Italy, having been on the "winning" side, would receive an extended colonial empire. They did not. Then the

Italian government accepted a peace not including the desired territorial acquisitions. The things desired but not granted were an African colonial empire and the Dalmatian area of what became at war's end Yugoslavia. Most Italians came to believe that they had fought the war, emerging on the victorious side only to "lose the peace." But the further toward the Right the individual, the greater was the fury. The best known desperado elements associated with this angered Right were the Arditi.

The Arditi were a fabled group of Italian veterans. Like their counterparts called "stormtroopers" in the German Army, they were elite units maintained in the rear to be brought to the front to participate in suicidal assaults. The idea was, as it came to be with the German "Storm Detachments," to create a breakthrough for regular infantry through holes in the barbed-wire fences and sandbagged protections. Men such as these possessed no clear ideological profile, as was the case with Hungarian and German desperadoes. But they, like their counterparts in other countries, found it difficult to return to peaceful life at home. As one of them put it at the end of 1918, he felt that "every one of us" is obliged "to exclude the possibility" of putting our lives back together for "the war has become our second nature." But like these others, soon enough, they were drawn to the radical Right in Italy to follow Benito Mussolini.[30]

The phenomenon of the desperado is yet another case where the extraordinary importance for postwar life of World War I can be observed. This war was a major turning point in the history of the modern world and appears today, nearly a century after its beginning, as a juncture in time (1914) on a level of importance with the French Revolution of 1789. To the postwar generation, the perspective one saw was influenced by the triumph of Bolshevism in Russia, domestic chaos in many places, often appearing to originate on the left, and the chaotic economic situation of the early twenties. As for the desperado, he appeared as part of postwar chaos not only in countries which had been losers in the war, but even in Great Britain. Note the case of the infamous "Black and Tans" in Ireland.

Although only a small proportion of British forces were sent to suppress the Irish Republican Army's attempts to secure independence, the Black and Tans were by far the most ruthless of these. They were much feared. Their official title was the "Royal Irish Constabulary." Most of them had fought the "war to end all wars" and returned to find no jobs in the contracting economy of postwar Britain. By the time they entered the Black and Tans they had become severely demoralized. Author George Bernard Shaw wrote about the sort of men drawn to the Black and Tans: "Hardly a week passes without some soldier who risked death in the field" being involved in one petty criminal act or another. The call to arms in Ireland was a lifesaver for such men. But the government that hired them did not know how the war had brutalized them. They were given the authority to arrest and imprison. And there were documented instances of outright murder. Their uniforms were a mix of dark green tunics, khaki trousers, black belts, and odd headgear. The Irish gave them the nickname previously applied to a famous pack of wild dogs in County Limerick, the "Black and Tans." By 1921, they had outlived their usefulness. They were then disbanded.[31]

For the most elaborate and important development of the desperado, however, one must return to postwar Germany. In Germany, there came together after the war men disgusted with peacetime society. They had no capacity for civilian life. Instead, their taste was for adventurism and criminality. No matter how heinous their acts, the desperadoes saw them as simply exercising a proper spirit of nationalism. They were a group never at rest. One might well call the desperado in Germany an agent of permanent revolution. But they were unlike past European revolutionaries. Those former revolutionaries had a vision of a better future. The desperado was without a meaningful vision. He was instead driven by a constant restlessness. As far as there was any goal for him it was to eternalize the values of the trenches. But to achieve this aim in Germany they had to become political. It was this fact that would eventually drive many of them into Hitler's party.

The most typical German desperado was *Hauptman* (Captain) Ernst Röhm. Conditions immediately after the war were especially favorable for Captain Ernst Röhm of Reichswehr Group Headquarters 4 in Munich. In Bavaria, more than elsewhere in Germany, men like Röhm were free to develop counterrevolutionary and counter-societal activity. One of a large group of ambitious captains, this scarred veteran of trench battles rose to become important in Bavaria and the master of a secret weapons cache. He was often called the "machine-gun king" of Bavaria. Guided by his belief in the soldier's basic right to leadership in civilian or military realms, Röhm organized a special intelligence unit of the General Staff to watch the various political groups springing up like wild seedlings in postwar Munich. These groups that interested the captain were of both the Left and Right. He wished to know which might be useful to the army. It was in this connection that he first came into contact with a young soldier named Adolf Hitler. Hitler soon served as an agent sent out to evaluate various Right-leaning political groups.[32]

The war, the postwar period of upheaval, and the consequences of each played an important part in the lives of the men who made up this generation moving out of the trenches. This "Front Generation" had members who were eventually, to use one of Hitler's favorite phrases, "like iron filings drawn to a magnet," pulled toward Nazism. The initial appeal of Nazism for the desperado was not its anti–Semitism. Discriminating against Jews was more popular with lower-middle-class people looking for economic scapegoats to provide emotional cover for their own failures. For the desperado, the movement held out the chance for participation in irresponsible violence. Röhm and his colleagues sought to spread terror for its own sake. And the Hitlerian vehicle awaited them to achieve that end.

Chapter Three

The Appearance of Hitler

In 1837, a forty-one-year-old maid named Maria Anna Schickelgruber returned to her native village of Strones. She was pregnant, but unmarried. Her family cast her out and a tenant farmer took her in. Soon after, she gave birth to a baby boy. He was baptized as Alois Schickelgruber. On the birth records the space for the father's name was left blank. This was a common practice in an area where inbreeding and illegitimacy were the rule rather than the exception. The high rate of illegitimacy in rural Austria probably resulted from the lack of economic opportunity. As a result, couples often simply could not afford to marry when they owned no land or property.

Who the father of Alois might have been is uncertain. One possibility suggested was that a wealthy Graz Jew named Frankenberger impregnated Hitler's grandmother while she was in domestic service. While awaiting execution in Nuremberg during 1946, Hans Frank made a sensational statement about Hitler's possible roots. He revealed that a highly agitated Hitler in 1930 had asked Frank to look into allegations that the Nazi leader might have had a Jewish ancestor. If true, this would have been more than embarrassing for a leader of an anti–Semitic movement. Frank claimed that he had discovered at least some circumstantial evidence that Hitler had Jewish ancestry. To this date, no shred of evidence has surfaced proving that Hitler was one-quarter Jewish as such theories have it.[1]

After half a century's research, Hitler's biographers have not been able to identify Alois Hitler's real father. The most authoritative account has it that Johann Nepomuk Heidler, Anna's later husband's brother, is the likely candidate. It was the Heidler name which was mistakenly written down as "Hitler" in the parish registry later when Alois was legitimized after the fact. This was not a matter of any importance in a society and an era where rural Austrians were casual about names. It was a partially literate society. At any rate, henceforth, the later dictator's father was legally Alois Hitler and not Alois Heidler. Johann Georg Heidler, an itinerant millworker, had been married to Maria only five years before she died. The stepfather then resumed wandering. Alois moved into the home of the brother, Johann Nepomuk. Johann Nepomuk's role as surrogate parent is cited by some as evidence he was the father.[2]

Of course, this is circumstantial evidence. The truth is that no real biological father for Alois can be identified and the actual circumstances of his birth will likely never emerge. The only possible historical importance of all of this might be, if various psycho-historians are correct, that Hitler had mental problems because he doubted the purity of his background. Since this question of background did not materially shape the history of the Weimar Republic and Third Reich, it may well be historically moot. For Hitler, a shadowy ancestral past turned out to be an asset. It enabled him to fabricate dramatic stories with legendary origins. In *Mein Kampf,* Hitler merely indicated that his father served as a customs official while his mother was idealized as a devoted housewife.³

What is certain is that Adolf Hitler entered life on 20 April 1889 in the Austro-German border town of Braunau on the river Inn. In this town, not far from Germany, Hitler grew up as the fourth child of his father's third marriage. Klara Pölzl, Alois's third wife, was a domestic servant. Hitler had siblings named Alois, Angela, and Paula. Hitler's half brother married an Irish woman, Bridget Dowling, who later fabricated a story about the dictator and a supposed visit he made to England in the period 1912–1914.

Dowling's son, Patrick Hitler, traveled to Germany during the 1930s in hope of obtaining money and favors from his famous uncle. He was, however, turned away with a few marks and stern advice about working for a living. Adolf's half-sister Angela married one Leo Raubal. She remained closer to the *Führer* than his other relatives. Angela's son Leo was often near Hitler and the future dictator was fond of him. Eventually, Leo became a German army officer and was captured at Stalingrad. Hitler's younger sister, Paula, was the only other surviving member of the family. There is evidence that Adolf was somewhat attached to her. From 1926 on she was in charge of his household, but did not use the name Paula Hitler. Instead she called herself Paula Wolf. The reasons for this are obscure. Adolf Hitler liked the pseudonym "Wolf," which he had used when skirting the borders of legality in postwar Munich.⁴

It is difficult to find the origins of Nazism, Hitler's later cruelty, his extreme racism, and other features of the Nazi movement inspired by him in his family life. Hitler's childhood was outwardly normal. He was doted upon and spoiled by his parents. Particularly this was the case after two of his brothers and one sister died within a span of only two years. This was common in an era when children, especially those who grew up in remote rural areas or city slums, fell prey to all sorts of childhood diseases. Hitler's father, who died as a retired Austrian Imperial Customs official, left his family in decent shape financially. Hitler later claimed to have been beaten by his father. But there is scant evidence to demonstrate that Alois went beyond what was common in the way of punishment and thus was any more abusive than other fathers of his time and class.⁵

That said, Alois was apparently hot-tempered and so was his son. According to Hitler, he resisted his father's wishes concerning career choices. If there was such an ongoing conflict between Adolf and his father, we will never really know. One must remember that this story is drawn from a political autobiography where Hitler liked to place himself in dramatic settings. The reported father-son conflict may thus well be the result of calculated invention. Alois died suddenly of a heart attack in 1903. By then, Hitler had received an excessive amount of smothering care from his mother. She made it known that she feared Adolf might expire, as had his siblings. It is Hitler's relationship with his mother that many have centered upon as the source for his later self-indulgences.⁶

There have been numerous attempts to reconstruct Hitler's childhood from psychological perspectives. They are speculative because it is impossible to obtain clinical evidence. Instead, many of the assumptions about Hitler's childhood and resultant psychological development are based on unverifiable evidence and are thus less than compelling. For example, we know nothing of Hitler's toilet training. It therefore cannot be maintained, as some have, that he needed to retain his feces in his body ("anal retentivism") and thus had a preoccupation with manure. Similarly, it can not be assumed that since Hitler had an undescended testicle that this caused a lasting distortion of his psychosexual maturation. This theory rests on a Russian autopsy describing a charred corpse assumed to have been Hitler's retrieved from near his Berlin bunker in 1945.[7]

The adult Adolf Hitler was obviously not normal. His abnormalities eventually came to shape aspects of public policy. And this can be assumed without retroactive psychoanalysis. It can be assumed as well that Hitler shared psychological problems with a large number of people thrown off the normal track of their lives by the war.

One thing that does appear to have emerged from examinations of Hitler's early life is that he could not have enjoyed a happy or tranquil existence. This can be ascertained from an examination of his adult emotional traits displayed before the public.[8] Some of these traits could have been rooted in simply too much moving about or the death of too many siblings. But even given the abnormal amount of moving, Braunau to Passau, Passau to Hofeld, and emerging from the initial grade at Fischlam on Traum to enter his second year in a Catholic school of the Bendedictine Order, he received high grades in his early education. He also was a choirboy and apparently admired the Catholic priesthood. One particular cleric caught his eye. The Abbot Hagen displayed a coat of arms, and a large ring. Featured on his devices was the swastika.[9]

Adolf Hitler's father spent much of his time in retirement keeping bees, visiting local taverns, and nagging some of his children to make something of themselves. An example of the elder Hitler's attempt to shape his children's' future can be seen with Adolf's half-brother Alois who fled his father's demands. Young Alois thereafter moved to England, back to Germany, then to England once more. As a result, Adolf then became the recipient of his father's well-meaning but often ill-founded judgments. This situation was not enduring, of course, as the elder Hitler died suddenly in 1903.

In 1897, the family had moved once more to a location near Linz on the Danube. Since his father had singled him out for a technical career, Adolf was sent to a state secondary school. There, young Adolf Hitler's interest in academic matters began to wane.[10] Once his father had died, Hitler was at home with four women — his mother, an aunt, a female lodger, and his sister Paula. In 1904, Hitler transferred to another school in Steyer. This institution was located fifteen miles from his residence. In this new school his grades slipped. There is nothing unusual in this circumstance. Many examinations of American school systems have noted the adverse impact on children uprooted from an educational situation they liked, to be placed in unfamiliar surroundings. Claiming an illness, Hitler left school in 1905.

In fact, it appears that the actual reason for Hitler's leaving school was his failing grades. Even in geography and history, which he later claimed as "favorite subjects," he received mediocre marks. He dropped out of school to spend the next two years in Linz, drifting, writing poetry, drawing, going to the theater, and daydreaming. Much about the life he lived in those days is revealed to us by August Kubizek. Kubizek was a friend and companion. Kubizek tells us that Hitler was a dreamer, a young man who always selected fantasy over reality. He envisioned in his realm of daydreams redesigning and reconstructing cities. He developed grandiose plans for completely rebuilding the city of Linz. Kubizek testified that Hitler actually came to believe that he had finished projects never even started.[11] He also became impatient, cranky, and irritable if contradicted.

His outbursts of temper rather naturally ensured he would have few friends beyond Kubizek. During his stay in Linz, he thus dreamed of becoming a great painter or architect. He also read a great deal. But his consumption of literary works revealed his lack of formal education. He read bits of this and that. He later claimed to have read Schopenhauer, Nietzsche, and Schiller. If he looked at these, he likely did not read them but only glanced through them. He appears not to have been capable of examining ideas objectively. Like many another uneducated person with pretensions, he left the work of serious authors to spend his time with fanciful and distorted pieces of writing. In fact, Hitler was developing an almost universal characteristic of the radical Right in any Western culture; he had a pigeon-hole mind, turning to the printed page to confirm a bias already held.

Since Hitler wanted to make his mark as a great artist in the world, he looked to Vienna instead of Linz. Not even his mother's operation for breast cancer in January of 1907 could deflect him from the notion that that he must pursue artistic greatness. In the summer of 1907, his mother gave him enough money from his father's estate to support him as an art student in Vienna. Hitler moved to Vienna only to face failure when he took the entrance examination. He was apparently crushed by this rejection. The rector of the academy told him that he had little aptitude for painting and that what talent he had was better suited to architecture.[12] Despite this setback, Hitler swore to retake the examination in the fall of 1908. As this transpired, he was forced to rush home, as his mother was dying. A radical mastectomy in January of 1907 had done nothing to arrest her cancer. Soon after his arrival, Hitler's remaining parent died and he was prostrate with grief. Now alone, young Hitler faced a world around him which might well pose dire threats.[13]

Initially, his share from his father's inheritance, added to an orphan's pension from the state, amounted to a respectable sum. It took him some time to squander it through his aimless and self-indulgent lifestyle. Only then did he come close to facing the fate he described in his vivid *Mein Kampf* account.[14] Over the short term, he returned to Vienna and shared an apartment with Kubizek who was studying at the Conservatory of Music. In the autumn of 1908, he sat for an examination and failed again to qualify for entrance to the art academy. At this juncture, Kubuzek left Vienna for a brief period of military training. He returned to discover that Hitler had moved out without leaving a forwarding address.

Between 1908 and 1913, Hitler's movements are obscure. Once he exhausted his legacy, he lived in men's hostels and cheap apartments. He managed to secure a marginal living. His only source of regular income was his orphan's pension. This he shared with his sister Paula, but it amounted to barely enough for food. He therefore rented beds in private homes or sought shelter in the mass quarters available to the homeless of Vienna. In the summer, he slept in the open, in parks or under archways. When the weather turned cold, he sought refuge in a hostel for the homeless, operated, ironically, by contributions from a Jewish family.[15]

In this kind of life, Hitler mingled with desperate men who regarded daily existence as a kind of jungle where survival of the fittest was the basic rule. In late 1909, Hitler teamed up with a vagabond named Reinhard Hanisch. Hanisch became Hitler's sales agent, hawking his "art." Adolf produced a steady stream of small pictures, most of them copies of postcards or prints. In the summer of 1910, the partnership halted abruptly as Hanisch urged Hitler to produce more pieces. Hitler complained to the police that Hanisch had defrauded him of the income from two pictures. This complaint resulted in Hanisch's arrest. Hanisch would later take his revenge by spreading false tales about Hitler once his former associate became prominent in politics. In turn, Hitler took his vengeance after the *Anschluss* with Austria. Hanisch was tracked down and killed on Hitler's orders.[16]

Hitler displayed at this point a worldview born of poverty and disappointments. This view had three major components: Social Darwinism, anticommunism, and extreme anti–Semitism. The first of these he displayed on the streets of Vienna and in *Mein Kampf*: "He who does not want to battle in this world of eternal struggle does not deserve to be alive."[17] In this prewar Vienna sojourn Hitler was a declassed outsider, but he maintained views drawn from his middle-class background. Hitler's reaction to proletarian ideology, Marxist or Social Democratic, was unbridled condemnation. Marxism he saw as a "pestilential whore covered with the mask of social virtue and brotherly love."[18]

His hatred of "the Jew" went beyond the usual prejudice of his time and became an irrational detestation. Although this was the case, evidence of why this was so is lacking. There was much ethnic discrimination in the prewar Austrian empire of some twenty separate nationalities. Germanic dislike for Slavs was nearly as great as that held for the Jews. Perhaps the intensification of this enmity resulted from a fear and resentment of Jews coming into Vienna escaping persecution in the East and competing with those native Austrians already there scratching out a marginal living. Young Hitler too, like many another racist in our own time, could associate personally with a Jew or other despised category of people without seeing the contradiction in such behavior. He was fairly close to one Jew on a personal level. This man's name was Josef Neuman, a companion also down on his luck and a frequenter of hostels.[19]

Hitler was much influenced by living in the central magnet of an empire with some twenty or more ethnic groups. Personal contacts with Jewish people much like himself did little to impede the development of his anti–Semitism. Hitler became a rabid and frequent reader of the various anti–Semitic tracts that appeared all over Vienna. He liked Lanz von Liebenfels' *Ostara,* on sale in tobacco shops. He also maintained a collection of tabloids which provided nauseating articles on Jews and their supposedly perverted sexual attitudes. He was a particular fan of pan–German nationalist Georg Ritter von Schönerer, a favorite author of Hitler's since having been introduced to his publications by an early teacher, Leopold Poetsch.[20]

In conjunction with the twisted ideas he absorbed, Hitler became aware of the growing presence of Jews on the streets of Vienna. In the years before World War I, those of the Jewish faith were nearly twenty-eight percent of the enrollment at the University of Vienna. These, however, were not the Jews arousing Hitler's disgust. The traditional Viennese Jews were well assimilated. They looked and sounded very much like non–Jewish Austrians. Fueling local anti–Semitism, a demographic movement transpired with large numbers of "Eastern Jews" moving into Vienna. Regardless of how down and out the inhabitants of the slum locations in Vienna were, they thought of themselves as German, Slavic, or even assimilated Jews and thus better than these new arrivals.

What Hitler had in common with others is that he saw "intruding" *Ostjuden* as alien competitors. Hitler was perhaps more disturbed than most by the "Eastern Jew" and he came to see them as the cause of most of his problems. To Hitler and others of his ilk, Jews could never be Germans because they were "racially" different. These aliens were so different that they needed to be removed from German society. Hitler's perception of the Jews as alien beings was intensified by his belief that they smelled bad. How a Viennese down-and-outer, sleeping outside and seldom bathing, could have smelled anyone else is difficult to understand. Of course, the answer lies in an emotional reaction. Apparently, Hitler's behavior was a common product of primitive ethnocentricity and he returned to it in *Mein Kampf*, claiming that the "smell of these caftan wearers often made me ill."[21]

Like many of the racists of his day, Hitler learned from his pamphlets to use pseudo-biological terms. He regarded Jews as "leeches." Like a leech, the Jews had grafted themselves onto a foreign body, in this case all human society. Hitler's analysis of this situation was developed over the years until it appeared full blown in *Mein Kampf*, where Hitler claimed that, in society, we always "find a little Jew, blinded by the sudden light, like a maggot in a rotten corpse."[22]

The tendencies described have caused some psycho-historians to see Hitler as a "borderline personality." In this view he was paranoid, with tendencies to fantasize about his supposed magical omnipotence. Such personality quirks, it has been held, would perhaps have made of him a man who behaved in selfish and narcissistic ways with phobias about filth.[23] This, of course, does not explain why so many of Hitler's generation appeared to have shared similar mental traits. There is little doubt that the young Hitler had the described characteristics. On the other hand, he and like-minded Germanophiles in Austria exhibited other traits which did not fit such a profile well. It is likely that Hitler did experience personality disorders which would, after having been exposed to the hard crucible of trench warfare, likely be categorized as some sort of sociopathic or antisocial behavior.[24] More than that one cannot state with certainty. What is fairly certain is that his anti–Semitism and antisocial behavior were pretty much fully developed during the flophouse years in Vienna.

In May of 1913, Hitler left Vienna and arrived in Munich to rent a small attic room from a tailor named Josef Popp. Despite the fact that he continued a solitary life, he saw Munich as far superior to Vienna. This was a city of ethnic solidarity, a city almost entirely made up of Germans. Despite being alone, Hitler clearly appears to have been euphoric about his new urban home. Munich also seemed the place to stimulate his artistic abilities. It was a city known for major developments in art and literature.[25] By fluke, a considerable number of important historical personalities lived in prewar Munich. Lenin had spent part of his exile there. And he had lived on the same street where the young Hitler eventually rented a room, Schleissheimerstrasse. Four streets over, Oswald Spengler had lived, as a still obscure writer collecting material for his seminal work, *The Decline of the West*. There were many others, including the famous novelist Thomas Mann.

Two famous *Kaffehandliteraten* (coffeehouse intellectuals) also lived in Munich before the war. One was Eric Muhsam, who loved to frighten the citizens of Munich with high-flown, vague rhetoric about liberating the downtrodden masses. The other was Kurt Eisner. Eisner was a small, unkempt man who told all who would listen that he was ready to help free people from the shackles of exploitive capitalism. His belligerent political style, impractical at the same time it was utopian, caused respectable citizens to desire nothing more than to see him jailed or killed. Eisner seemed to fit the stereotype of the unwashed radical, the sort of man a respectable German loved to hate. Some said he looked like a shaggy dog. The son of a Jewish Berlin shop owner, he had come to Munich, after study at Berlin University, to work as a journalist. He became theater critic for a prominent socialist newspaper, the *"Münchener Post."*[26]

Hitler, for his part, moved through the excitement and glitter of prewar Munich like a shadow. Few actually remember him from that era. It is unlikely that he was alone in this circumstance. The city drew young people with artistic and intellectual ambitions. Few of them made a mark either. His unimpressive paintings were produced in his attic room. He liked to paint pictures— the Hofbräuhaus, the Town Hall, and other local scenes— to sell them through Munich art dealers. His paintings from this period were almost always of buildings without people. This has drawn some to theorize that this was a result of his disdain for others. That is a theoretical leap. This pattern could just as easily have resulted from the fact that the human form is more difficult to render than straight-lined buildings.

Only one prewar experience transpired which appeared to interrupt what was for him a pleasing life. In January of 1914, the Austrian authorities tracked down Hitler and charged him with evading military service.[27] Hitler was persuasive in arguing that it was beyond his means to travel back to Linz and he was allowed a delay. Soon thereafter, he pled his poverty in a letter to authorities while maintaining he was anxious to serve in the Austrian army. He also asked if he could report in Salzburg, closer to Munich. He then went before Austrian authorities who rejected him as "too weak" for military duty, thus completing what was likely a hoax. The great irony here is that this is the same man, declared unfit for military service in February of 1914, who joyfully reported with other volunteers to join the German army when war was declared later the same year.[28] He was in time to claim in a self-serving manner that he fell to his knees and thanked heaven for the war and the good fortune to live in such times.[29]

By simple random fortune, Heinrich Hoffmann, who was one day to become Hitler's private photographer, snapped a picture of a large crowd in Munich's Odenplatz. Its members were listening to a reading of the war declaration. Following the announcement, they cheered wildly. Hitler told Hoffman years later that he had been near the front rank of that crowd. A microscopic search revealed the young Hitler, standing enraptured, displaying a broad smile. As Richard Hanser has written, this Hoffman picture "freezes forever the precise instant at which the career of Adolf Hitler becomes possible."[30]

Hitler was carried away by his excitement and rushed to enlist. Two weeks later he was in basic training. After only ten weeks, his regiment, the Sixteenth Bavarian Infantry Regiment ("the List"), was in combat. Hitler's regiment had been sent down the Rhine in mid-October, then to Belgium by way of Aachen. On 29 October it went into action, suffering heavy losses. On 1 November 1918 Hitler was made a Lance Corporal.[31] Although he was to serve with courage for the rest of the war, this was as high as he rose in the ranks. Perhaps this was because Hitler was a loner. Unlike his comrades, he received no mail from home. He appeared to many of his fellow soldiers to be overly zealous and too quick to curry favor with officers.[32] While other soldiers relaxed, he gratuitously cleaned his equipment. One of them recalled later that he acted "as if we would lose the war if he were not on the job every minute."[33]

War tends to form extraordinary bonds among men, but Hitler obviously did not build these bonds. Too much can be made of this. The description of his mind-set by his fellow soldiers probably did not differ much from those made of colleagues in other armies deciding to remain outside the world of comradely sentiments displayed by their brothers-in-arms. It was perhaps his desire to remain outside the bonds of soldierly comradeship that explains why he never received promotion to noncommissioned rank. The adjutant of his regiment,

Fritz Wiedemann, later testified in the docket at Nuremberg that Hitler was not promoted because his officers thought that he was a "Bohemian." Apparently, his superiors believed him to be a good soldier without leadership qualities.[34] Hitler's bearing, reported Wiedemann, was unmilitary. He often dressed in a slovenly fashion and slouched. Most of the time he spoke little except when, in the pattern of his prewar days, some remark caused him to launch into a tirade.[35] Moreover, Hitler apparently did not desire promotion.[36]

However limiting his quirks might have been, Hitler was more than willing to take on dangerous missions. He took part in over thirty battles and risked his life with sufficient frequency to be cited by officers. He earned the Iron Cross First Class near the end of the war. For Hitler, as for most young Germans, the war was the focal point around which the future would revolve. Many Germans lost their youthful idealism in the trenches. Others, like writer Ernst Jünger, glorified what was to some soldiers a terror-filled experience. Jünger wrote after the war that when one dies in combat "there is no lovelier death in the world."[37] Hitler and a number of others like him also displayed this attitude. He was to provide an opinion later that his time at the front was worth thirty years of university study.

In a war where so many died, Hitler was relatively fortunate. He had been temporarily disabled by combat twice, first in the autumn of 1916 when wounded in the left thigh. The second time was in 1918, less than a month before the armistice, when he became a victim of a heavier-than-air gas discharged into the trenches. This gassing caused temporary blindness and he was returned home. He was recuperating from his injury when he received the shattering news in his hospital bed that the war had ended in defeat.

It has been observed that the war redeemed Hitler from an aimless life to find a purpose. Of course, he was faced with the challenge after the war that bothered many of the desperadoes; he needed to eternalize the meaning of the trenches. In the war, he found a surrogate home in the List Regiment. His new surrogate home was to be a political party. For many of the early Nazis there developed this tendency to install the sprit of the trenches in any manner possible in German political and social life. This meant it was necessary to extinguish class differences. This did not mean that they were Marxists. This was a notion born during the war and in part the result of government propaganda. This propaganda campaign, issuing from the imperial government during the 1914–1918 period, had it that class differences could be submerged in a common nationalism.

Hitler was five months in fully recovering from his injuries. He was then sent to a reserve battalion in Munich. At this point, although momentous events appeared to be tearing apart the fabric of traditional Bavaria, Hitler was as yet politically uninvolved. In February of 1919, he volunteered for guard duty in a prisoner-of-war camp near the Austrian frontier. After only a month of this, he was returned to Munich when the camp closed. Munich was at that point in a state of upheaval. Bavaria had fallen under the disorganized leadership of Kurt Eisner. Eisner's assassination in February 1919 ushered in a time of even greater confusion. This brief flurry of abnormal events resulted in the establishment of a short-lived leftist regime followed by a short-lived Soviet Republic in April. In May, Free Corps elements sent by Berlin overthrew this second regime and killed its leaders. All of this will be covered in greater detail in the interpolation that follows. Suffice it to indicate at this juncture that, for those who already had developed a fervent anti–Marxism, the series of events just described hardened their attitudes and made them a permanent part of their beliefs.

As a fervent nationalist, Hitler, like many other returning veterans, temporarily found himself in a precarious position. But when the Red terror ended, he was eager to offer his services to a board of inquiry established to examine possible treachery within the army. His new work involved giving evidence on his fellow soldiers who perhaps had been "infected" with revolutionary fervor. He did his job of testifying so well that pleased military authorities assigned him to a course on proper civic thinking. In charge of the course was Captain Karl Mayr, head of the local army unit's Department of Press and Propaganda. It was Mayr, with some of Hitler's instructors, who discovered that the Austrian veteran owned compelling powers as a public speaker.[38] What happened was that Hitler's prewar tirades, and similar outbursts in the trenches, were now being channeled for political purposes. Hitler's talent so impressed his superiors that they made him an "instructional officer." He was charged with indoctrinating his fellow soldiers with correct nationalistic ideas.

For a time, Hitler's influence through oratory was limited. Then, with the help of the army, he was given the opportunity of addressing much larger groups. His reputation blossomed. One observer described his style thusly: "Hitler is a born demagogue; at a meeting his popular appeal compels his audience to listen to him."[39] In September of 1919, Hitler was assigned a new duty by Captain Mayr. He was to investigate an obscure new party (actually little more than a political discussion group) called the " the German Workers' Party."

This *Deutsche Arbeiterpartei Partei* (or DAP) held meetings and talked in the backrooms of small taverns about the usual combination of nationalistic, anti–Semitic, and anti-democratic ideas. The men in Munich's army headquarters viewed it positively. It was seen as yet another vehicle for use in spreading views held in the army's local command circles. Hitler went to a DAP meeting and liked what he heard. After reporting to superiors, he returned for subsequent meetings on his own. He then joined the fledgling group and became a popular speaker. In time, as part of a pattern of soldiers leaving the army because of treaty limitations, he left the military in order to devote his full energies to the DAP.

Hitler liked to call his "granite foundation" psychological quirks and ideas developed during his down-and-out prewar years in Vienna and then Munich. The postwar Bavarian capital provided the setting where Hitler managed to merge with others displaying similar ideas.

Interpolation I

The Munich Matrix of Right Radicalism

Between 1871 and 1914, the nature of European life was altered substantially. Industrial society promoted growing populations and the spreading of urban centers. Germany industrialized late, but rapidly. The organization of factory production in the *Reich*, as elsewhere, caused a concentration of people in cities. These cities also proliferated in number. Throughout Europe, with each passing year, proportionately fewer people remained in the countryside pursuing agricultural careers. Those who did stay in the agricultural sector were linked to cities more than before and were tied into national cultures by new transportation and communication networks. This all caused massive changes in political life. Mass movements made an appearance. Political parties developed as narrow interest groups. This forced the development of multi-party coalition-based systems. Demagogues appeared, shouting out messages in impromptu settings. Messages of a socialistic and Marxist bent attracted mass followings as did messages typified by antilabor, anti–Semitic and antiliberal themes.

Propaganda, the ability to control the spread of information, became the avenue to success. Anti-Semitism in politics became a challenge in Austria. Socialism became the foil to established norms in Germany. And political scandals stirred the masses in France.

As Munich grew after 1871, it gained a reputation as the most tolerant, democratic, and fun-loving city in Germany. In the popular mind, Munich meant baroque buildings, fine-art museums, and easygoing *Gemütlichkeit*. The atmosphere was such that it was easy to forget one was in Germany where urban centers were typified by authoritarianism and strutting militarists. Perhaps Munich was so amiable because life there was shaped by a beer-hall culture. To many outside observers, it appeared that great beer halls like the Hofbräuhaus had been established in an atmosphere where little distinction appeared to exist between the local social classes mixing in their celebration of leisure time. This was, however, a mere surface impression.

Munich had experienced the same rapid population growth as the rest of Germany. Between 1880 and 1910, the population doubled. It was by 1910 a city of around 600,000 people. Most of them came from parts of Germany beyond Bavaria or from Eastern Europe. Around 1900, nearly half of the city's population was not from Munich originally. And this was the capital of the most particularistic and xenophobic state in all Germany where resentment of all things "Prussian" was the order of the day. Moreover, rapid population growth brought the usual urban ills seen elsewhere. Typically, municipal authorities could not organize the services necessary to deal with exploding populations.

Munich's poor were forced to move about continually because of high-priced rentals. The upper levels of many buildings had in them small spaces transformed into rental units like the one Hitler lived in before the war. The expanding number of poor people caused a plague of begging and an increase in prostitution. There was a proliferation of open homosexuality, disturbing traditional and prudish Munich residents. There was organized pedophilia, resulting in a growing trade in young boys.

Prewar Munich's economy was in a state approaching upheaval. Small business, the traditional backbone of the local economy, was challenged by the growth of a manufacturing base demanding new labor forces. Small shops run by artisans were transformed into little factories. Munich became typified by labor unrest. There were repeated strikes against employers who hired cheaper foreign labor. In turn, threatened employers then banded together in protective associations which relied on cheap immigrant labor to fill the workplace. There were fewer strikes in the immediate postwar period, but primarily because employers became better organized. The animosities between classes remained and intensified.

Workers had not made significant progress in Munich as the war began. This was reflected in politics. In 1887, Social Democracy arrived in Munich. The party quickly began to grow and gained seats in the Bavarian state parliament. Along with the growth of Social Democracy, at the other end of the spectrum, there appeared political anti–Semitism. Cultural and political anti–Semitism thus developed, although there was much less of a Jewish population to react against than had been the case in Hitler's Vienna. Bavarian Social Democrats tended to be more moderate than the party nationally, so much so in fact that they were popularly called "his majesty's loyal SPD."

For quite some time, the phenomenon of anti–Semitism was not as intense in Munich as in prewar Vienna. But then few places in Europe before World War I were typified by the intense anti–Semitism of Vienna. The most significant cause of the upsurge of anti–Semitism in Munich in the immediate prewar period was Jewish population growth. As in Vienna, although tiny in comparison with Viennese numbers, an influx of Eastern Jews moved into Munich, fleeing persecution. The established Jewish community in Munich, although noticed because of their seeming overconcentration in the professions, was not readily distinguishable from the rest of the city's population. But the Eastern Jews were.

As Social Democracy entered organized politics, so did anti–Semitism. In December of 1891, a group calling itself "the German Social Union" registered with the police as an anti–Semitic party. As was common in Munich, a small newspaper appeared and was soon aligned with the movement. The emerging political anti–Semitism made common cause with Pan-Germanism. Munich had the largest group enrolled in the Pan-German League of any city by 1900. This transpired in a city also typified by strong sentiments for separatism. Munich was a city in flux and people imbibed of the various socio-political brews available there.

Men like Hitler, whose ideological constructs continued to develop in small attic rooms, dreamed radical dreams. These sorts of personalities were described by author Thomas Mann in his story "At the Prophets" (1904): "Strange regions there are, strange minds.... At the edge of large cities, where streetlamps are scarce ... are houses where you can mount no further, up into attics under the roof, where pale young geniuses, criminals of the dream, sit with folded arms and brood.... Here reign defiance ... the ego supreme ... here freedom, madness, and death hold sway."[1]

Despite the societal fault lines mentioned, Munich rejoiced in 1914 when the guns of August sounded. That Munich developed war fervor should provide no surprise. Since Bismarck's armies had unified Germany in 1871, military enthusiasm had become a part of Munich's atmosphere along with the frivolity of its beer barns. As one observer wrote in 1914: "They are glad to fight for king and fatherland."[2] However, once the war began, government spokesmen had continually demanded unqualified support for it. Then signs of disarray began to show across the Reich. Particularly was this true after 1916. A stalemated conflict appeared where thousands of men fought raging battles with massive losses of life and only a few miles of front would move one way or the other. Moreover, this protracted war had commenced to cause suffering at home.

While mounting disillusionment was almost universal in Germany from 1916, it became particularly intense in Munich. Those living there between 1914 and 1918 came to believe that their suffering was greater than in other parts of Germany. It seemed worse than in favored "Prussia" (a term sometimes used to refer to almost all of Germany north of Bavaria). It was true that, in Munich, the war had greatly accelerated social and economic change. Weapons factories had appeared there for the first time. A larger workforce was required to operate these and thousands of laborers came from the rest of Germany. Eventually, many of these outsiders became part of leftist insurrections after the war ended. Replacing men sent to the front, women began to be called to the factories unprecedentedly. Over 9,000 women were in Munich factory jobs by 1917.[3]

Such changes in the gender composition of the work force were unpleasant for many and seemed to mean an end to the old Munich. There were many bankruptcies and mounting unemployment. The war also dramatically exacerbated Munich's housing shortage. To add to the housing problem, food shortages were widespread. Munich city government began rationing food in May of 1915 and constantly added items to the scarcity list.[4] Food distribution nationally was coordinated by a large bureaucratic structure in Berlin called the "War Food Office." This caused constant complaints in Munich about food being produced in Bavaria only to be carried away to the north. With foodstuffs in short supply, the people in Munich, like other Germans, were forced to consume ersatz supplies. Most of these were less than appetizing. Most serious for many who frequented the great beer barns was the fact that their "beer" was dosed with water. According to one witness, after consuming some *ersatz* foodstuffs, "people [began to] collapse, feel sick, [and] grew desperate."[5]

In June of 1916, the first of a series of wartime food protests transpired. This featured people milling in the street and denouncing local authorities as "Prussian Lackeys."[6] It was rumored that King Ludwig of Bavaria had shipped milk from a model royal dairy northward to reap large profits. Bavarian hops were widely rumored to have been exported there as well, thus lessening the local supply. In the summer of 1917, it was rumored that Ludwig was so unpopular that he had fled to Saxony. All these rumors were untrue, but they led to the widely held impression that Ludwig was a stooge of Berlin's *Saupreussen* ("Prussian Pigs"). The costs of the war elevated. And it became common in Munich to blame the Bavarian government for dragging the local people into a conflict they had not wanted.

The people of Munich had obviously forgotten the wild celebration in the Odeonsplatz in August of 1914. Soon enough, in response to deprivations caused by the war, the first pacifist flyers appeared. These sheets were handed out in the streets and were pasted on walls or kiosks. They called the war a great "swindle." By 1917, the "Independent Social Democratic Party," or USPD, had made its appearance in Munich. And it came under the control of the suddenly and surprisingly politically prominent Kurt Eisner.[7]

The rise to prominence of Eisner coincided with the end of the war. Out of the volatile mix of emotions that was Munich at war's end came a revolution which preceded the rest of Germany by thirty-six hours. It began on the Thereisenwiese, the traditional site of the *Oktoberfest*. It commenced as an ordinary beer festival with a political slant. Those who appeared as speakers were pacifist intellectuals. Eisner was prominent among them. Most represented the USPD. The speeches given blamed the war on Germany and announced that independent socialists had broken with the mainstream Social Democrats led by Erhard Auer. The demonstration was about to become a silent protest march into the city when one of Eisner's followers, waving a red flag, jumped on stage and shouted: "Off to the barracks! Long live the Revolution!" Within a few hours, without a shot fired, Eisner's group had occupied barracks, ministries, and the parliament building. King Ludwig III fled Munich into exile.

Eisner's governing effort went badly. On 21 February 1919 he was on his way to the parliament to resign after an election defeat when a young army officer (Count Anton Arco–Valley) stepped from a doorway and shot him. Eisner died immediately. Within an hour, in retribution, an Eisner follower stormed into the parliament building firing shots. This opened the way to yet another revolution.[8] Eisner's funeral was held on 26 February 1919. The day before, the "Congress of Bavarian Councils" had met for a while in the parliament building.

During this period, elsewhere in Germany, workers and veterans from the front proclaimed conciliar republics. There were general strikes in Thuringia and Leipzig. In the Bavarian Diet a number of radical proposals were brought forward. The leader of the radical Left was Max Levien. The news of Eisner's willingness to resign and have his government step down, followed by his assassination, inspired hard-core Communists to leap into the breach. Local Reds formed a Munich chapter of the Spartacus League. The Spartacists transformed themselves nationally into the German Communist Party (KPD). The KPD's sudden prominence on Bavarian soil was the work of Levien. Levien was a Russian-born disciple of Lenin's who had escaped to Germany after the 1905 Russian revolution's failure. He became a German citizen and served in the army during World War I. After the war, he chaired the initially unimportant Munich Soldiers' Council.

During the week after Eisner's "revolution," a network of councils had appeared in Bavaria. There were peasants' councils in the countryside and a pyramid of workers' councils in urban settings. In all, during November, seven thousand conciliar organizations, some quite tiny and some larger, appeared in Bavaria. For a time, a workers-and-soldiers council had come into being in Augsburg and controlled that partially industrialized center located north of Munich. Max Levien moved to seize the leadership of this mix of organizations. Levien, despite his name, was not Jewish. He actually was descended from French Huguenot immigrants who came to Russia escaping the persecutions of Louis XIV. Despite this heritage, the Right made anti–Semitic charges against him. As early as Eisner's admission that he could no longer form a government, Levien had called for a permanent Soviet Republic.

As Eisner's funeral was announced, Levien was calling openly for a "second revolution." On the eve of the funeral, some five thousand of the Radical Left assembled in a Munich beer barn to cheer the reading of a five-point program demanding a permanent cessation of all functions of the Bavarian parliament, proclamation of a Bavarian Soviet Republic, diplomatic relations with the Soviet Union, arming of the workers, and formation of a Red Army. When the Bavarian Congress convened, a motion that Bavaria he transformed into a Socialist Soviet Republic was soundly defeated. Max Levien and another USPD representative immediately resigned from the council's deliberative body. A few hours later the radical Left issued calls for a protest rally. Early on 1 March 1919 several thousand demonstrators appeared on the Thereisenstrasse. Violence ensued, followed by days of moderate-radical negotiation. Eventually, an unstable government under moderate socialist leader Johannes Hoffman appeared.

While the Hoffman government struggled with the economic situation, tremors of activity from elsewhere in Europe reached Munich. Vienna sent out feelers signaling a desire to discuss a possible *Anschluss* with Germany, then withdrew them. In early March, Lenin had begun the Communist International (Comintern) in Moscow. Moscow soon sent word to Munich that it was not in the best interests of international Communism for the radical Left in Munich to cooperate with the mainstream Social Democrats. In Budapest on 22 March 1919, Communists under Bela Kun overthrew a parliamentary government and set up a Soviet regime. The revolutionary tide in Europe, beginning with the Bolsheviks in Russia during 1917 and coming to states like Hungary, seemed to be rushing westward. Elsewhere in Germany, the government in Berlin had found it necessary to use troops to smash a general strike in the Ruhr. Prompted in part by all these events, and by intense Bavarian internal pressures resulting from a nearly Arctic winter, beer-hall meetings promoted radicalism nightly.[9]

The situation caused moderate Social Democratic leader Johannes Hoffmann to recall the parliament. Before much could be done to reconstitute that body, various of the councils merged in Augsburg to discuss courses of action for the radical Left. The councils endorsed enthusiastically a Bavarian conciliar republic, an alliance for the nation with Communist Russia, and another with Bela Kun's Hungary. There were various other radical measures issued, among them, a call for a Bavarian general strike.

A delegation was then sent from Augsburg to Munich to negotiate with the Hoffmann regime. But Hoffmann had taken the train for Berlin to consult with the central government. Remaining officials in Munich would not negotiate with the councils. A power vacuum developed into which the radical Left moved. Another meeting produced a demand to eliminate all political parties and the proclamation of a Soviet Republic. On 6–7 March 1919, arrangements were finalized for the First Soviet Republic in Bavaria.[10]

This new left-wing government was never fully in control of Bavaria, but only ruled over Munich and an area immediately around it, including Augsburg. The vast majority of people in Munich remained in stunned silence as this group of "foreigners" took over. The Hoffman government simply moved to Bamberg. It claimed still to be "the single possessor of power in Bavaria." Ernst Toller, at twenty-five probably the youngest head of state in German history, was proclaimed the new chief executive of Bavaria. Toller was a businessman's son from East Prussia who had been invalided out of the army in 1916. He became active in a student peace movement at Heidelberg University and wrote antiwar poems. He joined the Bavarian Left at war's end.[11]

This was a regime which faced major obstacles from the outset. On 9 April 1919 leaflets were dropped by planes flying over Munich. These came from the Hoffmann regime in Bamberg. The leaflets had it that the farmers in north Bavaria had suspended food deliveries to the capital. Meanwhile the short-lived first Soviet Republic was increasingly opposed by hard-line Communists. Militants poured out of the factories denouncing the new government's lack of purpose and calling for the Communists to take control. By 11 April 1919, Munich was a scene of confusion. Newly printed paper money was held to be worthless and, by 13 April, there was gunfire in the streets between workers and soldiers of the First Infantry Regiment. Of course, veterans from World War I were present on both sides and the weapons they used were ones brought home with them. Moreover, Munich had many stockpiles of weapons stored in the basements of various buildings, even monasteries. Some of these stockpiles were still available as late as the Beer Hall Putsch of 1923. The putative heads of the Second Bavarian Soviet Republic met at the Hofbräuhaus and proclaimed the new regime. A new administration was installed under Eugen Leviné.[12]

Leviné was born in St. Petersburg into a family of emancipated Russian Jews. After his father's death, Leviné had moved to Germany with his mother. As part of his university courses, he had been involved in Russian studies and had returned there to participate in the 1905 rising. After the collapse of the revolutionary movement in that year, he was sentenced to imprisonment. He was released in 1908 and returned to Germany. He later joined the Spartacus League in Berlin. He was sent to Bavaria to take of the Communist Party there.

Once the second Soviet Republic had been established, a Red Army (consisting of armed factory workers) replaced a disbanded police force. It became common at this juncture to refer to the regime in control as "Reds" and to those who opposed it as "Whites." On 16 April there was a Red-White firefight in Dachau. Counterrevolutionary forces began to organize outside Munich and there were further clashes. There were atrocities committed by both sides.

The White force assembled at Dachau had in it hardened desperadoes and they shot down without cause some twenty medical orderlies and eight surrendered Red soldiers. Most infamously, the Reds executed ten people by firing squad, including the Countess Westarp. This killing was the direct result of the White atrocities at Dachau which had caused Red soldiers to ask superiors if they could take revenge. Permission was granted and the victims were rounded up and brought to courtyard of the Luitpold gymnasium. In pairs, they were placed against a wall and shot. The news of this horrific event spread quickly and, by midday of 1 May, the killings had become public knowledge. There were protest meetings all over the city, and firefights erupted.

The Luitpold event moved up a White timetable to move on Munich and dislodge the Second Soviet regime. The Whites had decided to move on 2 May. They now advanced the attack to May Day. It was held to be just and proper that they were moving into the capital on the traditional workers' holiday. As the Whites took Munich, atrocities appeared seemingly everywhere. All White killings were said to be justified by the Luitpold executions. The Luitpold killings had also had a demoralizing impact on Red troops not involved but who had heard of them. They began throwing down their arms, as the Whites entered the city to encounter scant opposition.[13]

The Munich political scene, immediately after the demise of the Red Republics, was profoundly altered. The disappearance of the two republics resulted in an atmosphere changed lastingly. It is to be noted that the two Soviet republics were shaped, as would be Hitler's movement, largely in the beer halls of Munich. This beer-hall phenomenon was based on prewar tendencies from the nineteenth century. During this earlier time, to the outside observer, the beer-hall scene was classless and democratic.[14] However, beneath this boisterous surface, was another aspect of beer-hall life. There were frequent brawls and riots. Beer steins were thrown and swung. Made of heavy earthenware, they were formidable weapons. These conflicts were often sparked by ideological disagreements. The great halls saw orators of all political stripes. And commonly their remarks would lead to open conflict. This was the heritage which carried over into the scene after the war.

As the White Terror began to subside, Munich returned to a superficial normality. But the atmosphere in Munich was not the same. The period of revolutionary chaos had led to community life featuring a kind of electric tension. There was bitterness, apprehension, and a widespread expectation of more upheaval. The population was in full reaction to the Soviet regimes and appeared ready to listen to reactionary views from nearly any source on the Right. Munich appeared now ready to interpret the turmoil of the immediate past as the unavoidable product of "aliens" come from outside Bavaria to arrive in Munich and disturb its tranquility.[15]

The darker dimensions of Munich's prewar society now came to the fore (racism, calls for Bavarian separation from the rest of Germany, and the enshrining of extreme voices). There emerged a mix of rightist groups nearly as confusing as the mix of conciliar organizations. Generally these groups are called *völkisch*. This is a nearly untranslatable term with overtones of hyper-nationalism of a definitely anti–Semitic type mixed with the idea of "rootedness" (the notion that only those of pure blood are truly rooted in Germanic soil). Nazism was to be one of these movements. One major difference between Nazism and these other groups was that most had originated outside Bavaria and what became National Socialism was a native movement of that state.[16]

Conditioning the Munich welter of discontent was the fact that, on 9 May 1919, the victorious Allies announced the terms of the Versailles Treaty. Its perceived harsh nature raised an outcry in Munich beyond that heard elsewhere. The most important, but certainly not the only, grievance in Munich with the treaty was that the Allies demanded some reparations in grain and hops. This seemed but yet another drain on Bavaria's resources. Moreover, Bavarian particularism with this set of stimuli reappeared in full force. The Social Democratic Hoffmann government had been reinstalled. Particularists now charged Hoffmann with being an anti–Bavarian culprit for his association with those who had penned a much-disliked Weimar constitution that had not protected Bavarian rights.[17]

Munich continued to be a city in ferment and an armed camp. The army could not maintain order because it was in flux. Men were urged out of its ranks as the Republic adjusted to the limitations on military strength imposed at Versailles. The Hoffmann government gave its blessing to "Civil Guards," composed of ex-soldiers. But the Guards felt accountable only to their own leaders. Munich was still littered with stockpiles of weapons, some of which probably came directly from the German army, now called the Reichswehr. Arms reported to the Allies as destroyed had been spirited away to various rightist groups including the Guards. The Guards' commander, Georg Escherich, presided over an organization which came to have in it some 300,000 members. Thirty thousand of them were within the city limits of Munich. Despite claims of nonpoliticization, the Civil Guards reached out to similarly inclined groups. Escherich directed an umbrella organization which eventually came to be called "Orka." This group worked its way into Western Austria and as far away as the Ukraine.[18]

It is apparent that the upsurge of the masses building in all Germany was especially intense in Munich. In Munich there had been a surge from the Left and now there was a surge from the Right. But the total socio-political picture there was still composed of various differing parts floating about seeking a channel to the future. What was needed was an inaugurator of reform, a figure or a movement to coalesce disparate elements. It was a time calling out for a movement into which all things flow and from which all things emerge. A metaphor to describe this need might be a bundle of varicolored threads drawn through a ring, twisted in passing through, so that every thread emerges on the other side with the pattern changed lastingly. Given the tendencies to list toward the right in Munich, the movement could have been produced by any one of various shades of rightist opinion. But the ring through which the threads of history were drawn in this south German state was to be formed by the Nazis.

Chapter Four

The Infancy Of Nazism (1919–1923)

Between November 1918 and May 1919, a political breakdown produced in Bavaria a power vacuum that established an opening to the left followed quickly by opposition on the right. The extreme Left had occupied a momentary opening vowing, "The Revolution will not allow itself to be voted down."[1] The Left made good on its threat, but the counterrevolutionary Right had the last say. The major focal point of White activities in Bavaria had been the army headquarters in Munich. In that headquarters, Colonel Ritter von Epp commanded the remnants of a Bavarian "Life Guard," a local militia called to active duty during the war. Before the war, he had been in Southwest Africa participating in the earlier described genocidal assault on a native people called the Hereros, punished for disobedience to their German masters. The Hereros were practically wiped out by 1911.[2]

During World War I, Epp was appointed to command the Bavarian Life Guard. This was an elite commando unit. Because of his Life Guard activities, he received the highest Bavarian decoration, the Max-Josef *Ritterorden* (which also made him a nobleman). During the rising of the Left, Munich became too unstable for the orderly operation of Epp's counter-revolutionary paramilitary activity. Epp transferred his theater of operations outside Bavaria and established a Free Corps in Thuringia. It was placed under the command of the Ministry of Defense as were other desperado units springing up to form a loose coalition of fighters without political affiliation.

With Epp in Thuringia was Captain Ernst Röhm, a battle-scarred man who had proven a daredevil at the front. Röhm, like Epp, belonged to the military caste. This specialized order felt threatened with extinction in Bavaria by the rise of the Soviets. Both Röhm and Epp believed that there was only one way to deal with the revolutionary Left and that was to annihilate it. Both men also considered the possibility that the German middle-class might have become "infected" by parliamentary liberal ideals. They were ready to wage war on both leftists and moderates.

Röhm was the scion of a family of Bavarian civil servants. But he distanced himself from that background to become a risk-taking soldier, rising to the rank of captain. In the course of four year's fighting he was wounded several times. He had a deep bullet scar on one cheek. He was short and sturdy, with a ruddy complexion, a swashbuckling manner, and an obvious fondness for good-looking young men. He, like others, felt betrayed by the government's surrender at war's end and came to blame the "November Criminals" in Berlin for Germany's defeat. Another major focus of the counterrevolutionary movement was the Thule Society. (Countess Westarp's membership in the Thule Society put her against that wall in Munich). This was a conspiratorial and racist organization. The society grew out of the "Germanic Order" which had been founded in prewar Munich. It took the name "Thule" in 1918, after a legendary, pure Germanic order which supposedly had vanished into the dim mists of time.[3]

The headquarters of the society was in the fashionable *Hotel Vierjahrzeiten*, where the group rented meeting rooms. Membership depended upon proving "Aryan descent." Just how one did that with accuracy was not well defined. Perhaps this was because the *völkisch* ideological community was awash in differing definitions of what it mean to be Aryan.[4] The Thule society spawned many of the pioneers of the Nazi movement. Among them were Dietrich Eckardt, editor of an anti–Semitic journal and mentor of Hitler; Alfred Rosenberg, destined to become Nazism's official "philosopher"; Gottfried Feder, a somewhat economically confused "financial expert"; Hans Frank, Hitler's future lawyer; Rudolf Hess, eventually Deputy *Führer*; and Father Bernhard Stemple, who helped Hitler write *Mein Kampf*.

In the winter of 1918, Rudolf von Sebattendorf (Adam Glauer), another Thule member, became interested in a new political club calling itself the "Free Workers Committee for a Good Peace." This informal group of workers had been founded in Munich during March 1918 by Anton Drexler, a toolmaker in the Munich railroad works. Sebattendorf saw an opportunity to use this small circle as a means to convert other German workers to the cause of the *völkisch* movement. Sebattendorf suspected that many German workers would not defect to Communism because their loyalty to the nation was stronger than their allegiance to class.[5] In October 1918, Sebattendorf instructed Karl Harrer, a sports journalist and Thule Society member, to combine forces with Drexler in a "political worker's circle."[6] Shortly thereafter, this small club became the Deutsche Arbeiter Partei (DAP).

The initial program for this "German Workers' Party" was promoted by the slow-witted Drexler. Anton Drexler meant to save the workers of Germany from international Communism. He imagined a pure Germanic state, purged of all "alien" forces. In truth this club was simply another beer-hall debating society with a vague program and an ill-defined agenda. Like other rightist associations with grandiose names, it had difficulty maintaining even a small membership. While the two Red republics held sway, Drexler had a hard time of it, barely escaping a firing squad of Red guards.[7] The defeat of the Communists allowed the DAP to operate in public and to recruit. At this point, in spite of its small size, the "party" had important contacts like Ludendorff, through a friend of the general's. Ludendorff had left Germany briefly after the defeat of 1918. He returned, memoirs in hand, to reside in a villa near Munich.[8]

What was required at this point was to make the DAP something more than a debating society. Every political group noticed in Munich possessed a fiery beer-hall orator to draw in crowds. The DAP considered Hermann Esser, a talented rabble rouser, to fill this role. Esser, some held, might just provide the spark to ignite the proper fires. After the war, Esser had become involved in beer-hall politics. He was cunning and quite unscrupulous. Konrad Heiden, perhaps the first serious historian of Nazism, described him as the prototypical Nazi — crude, brutal, without morality, and callous.[9] Esser, like Hitler and Joseph Goebbels to come later, had a gift for making vivid phrases. But Esser was disqualified as the potential firebrand the DAP needed. He seemed far too selfish. He was not likely to attract members in the numbers required.

What this party waited upon was what Bruce Mazlish has termed the "revolutionary ascetic." Such zealots, once they have seen the "light," are galvanized into a kind of continuous action typified by intense charisma. The masses are soon converted to the ideology professed. In everyday life the revolutionary ascetic appears to be immune to the usual human problems. Leaders of this kind are sometimes perceived as somewhat godlike within their movements.[10] It happened that Adolf Hitler, not Esser, possessed enough of these qualities to fill the role.

When Hitler joined the party in September of 1919, he was shocked by the beer-hall slovenliness that characterized business procedures. He was also disturbed by the lack of proper authority as the organization seemed to be so casually democratic in nature. This was because the DAP was still a club. After Hitler came, he set to work with feverish energy, sending out invitations to meetings, building lists of potential members, and personally seeking support. All of this disenchanted some of the older members, content as they were with membership in an obscure political club. Because it was required that they move into the big beer barns where the SPD and Bavarian separatists operated, some accused Hitler of delusions of grandeur.[11]

People move into mass movements when times are bad. Times were very bad in Munich even after martial law had been removed and the state government was brought back. Insecurity for the local populace was heightened as economic distress became the order of the day. A close handmaiden of this distress was social dislocation. Prices continued to soar because of the scarcity factor. Inflation was rampant. But it seemed especially difficult in Munich. The city had within it a high percentage of vulnerable groups such as small businessmen, civil servants, white-collar workers, and retired people on fixed incomes.

One product of this situation which opened the way for the DAP was a wave of anti–Semitic agitation produced by socio-economic distress. There were attacks on Jews who were said by the attackers to be responsible for increases in profiteering. Moreover, the trials of Reds accused of participating in the Luitpold gymnasium took place in the fall of 1919. The six defendants were found guilty and executed immediately. This very public trial and sentence helped heighten animosity toward the Left with a linking of these views, illogically, with anti–Semitism. There were calls for the immediate deportation of all Eastern Jews.

While this transpired, Hitler argued with the old guard at the DAP that now was the time to move into the beer barns. This argument continued until finally Hitler won a victory. A party meeting was held with an audience of nearly 2,000 attending. Hitler was not billed as the main speaker, but in the *Hofbräuhaus* on 24 February 1920 he got his chance. When he rose to speak he was confronted by loud opposition and fighting on the floor of the hall resulted. This was represented in *Mein Kampf* as a unique situation. It was hardly that. Hitler claimed as he wrote about it that he alone mastered the uproar. He then secured agreement from the floor to change the name of the party to the National Socialist German Workers Party (or NSDAP). It was abbreviated soon enough to "Nazi" from the sound of the title in German and perhaps in response to the Socialists' long-term use of "Sozi" as shorthand for "member of the SPD."

As the writ of Nazism continues, Hitler announced the twenty-five points of the party's "unchangeable" program through an up-or-down vote.[12] According to later Nazi hagiography, this mass meeting was the equivalent of Luther's presentation of his ninety-five theses for debate at Worms. Whatever happened at the meeting, Hitler painted a great success for himself. Contemporary press accounts based on police reports do not bear out the significance of this event. But within the narrow universe of the NSDAP as it existed at that time, it does appear to have been a decisive moment.

Shortly after this speech Hitler was discharged from the army, but he did maintain links with his old comrades. After this, Hitler became a full-time agitator, finding such support as he could while living, like the proper revolutionary ascetic, in a single poorly furnished room. It is clear, from what he said to many around him, that Hitler wanted to mobilize the masses in the service of the radical Right. He had only scorn for conservative nationalists who remained separated from the broad ranges of the German social order by class barriers. He also disliked the small racist societies because they only spoke to each other in tiny groups. Hitler had looked long and hard at the Social Democratic Party during his Vienna days and its use of mass followings. He wanted to establish the rightist equivalent.

A week after the *Hofbräuhaus* "triumph," Hitler's wish to make the name change invoked in the mass meeting permanent was agreed upon in a party leadership conference. The term "National Socialist" was hardly new in that it was used by groups in Germany and Austria before the war. Hitler's insistence on the name may have been a simple attempt to confuse workers, who might normally have opted for socialism. The party's next step was to use Hitler as their main attraction to bring in the crowds and enroll them in Nazi ranks. The Party also commenced to create "locals" outside of Munich.[13]

In December of 1920, a newspaper was obtained in the manner of many small Rightist groups which had preceded the fledgling Nazis. It became in time the *Völkischer Beobachter* (loosely translated, the "Racist Observer"). By this juncture, Hitler had become the propaganda chief of the party. It fell to him to determine the editorial policy of its newspaper. Despite the earlier mentioned demand from some quarters that the "Eastern Jew" be deported, there were additional persecutions in Eastern Europe and refugees continued to flow into Munich. Along with them came East European Christians. These immigrants were lumped together in the popular mind despite their religious differences. Such refugees automatically sunk to the lowest social levels.[14]

As a result of popular attitudes, there were attacks on the Easterners in the press. Often these were anti–Semitic in character. To some extent, the more respectable press criticized the bizarre stories appearing in the racist media. A mainstream German newspaper denounced a story appearing in one racist sheet. The story had it that some 200 children were missing from the city. It was offered that these children had likely been butchered by Jews and the flesh used to make wurst.[15] This story was actually a variation of an old folk tale, likely dating back to the Middle Ages. Like similar fables collected by the Brothers Grimm, this story was an old cannibalistic folk story.

All of this was not lost on the various racist-nationalist groups in Germany. The early Nazis quickly became aware that such gutter-level messages satisfied some. The tendency to ape such material appeared in Hitler's speeches during 1920. Hitler, like other rabble-rousers of the Right, used them to stir paranoia. He presented lists of those plotting to sabotage the German nation. Among these were capitalists, Bolsheviks, black marketeers, profiteers, and unspecified anti–German conspirators. Hitler's displayed racism was extended beyond Jews to include Africans. One way of demonstrating how vengeful the French were was for him to hold that they had put African troops from their colonial empire into the Rhineland. They did this, he said, so that these "sub-humans" could rape white women. When the war ended, the French had moved back to Alsace-Lorraine, lost to them in 1871. Hitler talked of the shame involved for Strasbourg where church bells had tolled for two hours to celebrate French victory. It was promised that they would one day ring for three hours when the French were thrown out.[16]

What Hitler offered in 1920 meetings differed little from what he believed while still in Austria. Germany, he said, was surrounded by malevolent powers set on destroying the Fatherland. His proof was the Allied appropriation of livestock, ships, and coal through reparations. He accused Clemenceau of saying malevolently that there were "twenty million Germans too many." This was the justification for the "stealing" of "German food" by the Allies.[17]

Hitler was like many of the orators on the Right in that he kept his diatribes uncomplicated. England, Hitler said, controlled world commerce. While London exported merchandise, Germany had to export people who were wage slaves for other countries.[18] He talked generally about politics, calling it only a means to an end. That end was the flourishing of Germany's people. The form of government that accomplished this was not important. The only question was what was best for the *Volk*. Hitler continually compared and contrasted prewar Germany with its order, cleanliness, and precision with the disorderly Germany of the 1920s.

Hitler's speeches from his early days as an orator were racist "wisdom" interlaced with attacks on Versailles. Hitlerian principles had also been included in the party program. The treaties of Versailles and St. Germaine had to be abrogated as soon as possible. Only real Germans should be allowed citizenship in the Reich. These were defined as people of "pure blood." The Jew could not be a German even if he or his ancestors had converted to Christianity. Only those who worked deserved incomes. War profits should be confiscated by the Reich. A "people's army" should be built nationally. Hitler was gathering a following with all this. He did not suggest answers for problems, but his strength was in the keen discernment of the biased views and grievances shaping the views of those who listened to him. The result of his approach was that increased numbers came into the party.

On 22 January 1921, the party assembled for its initial national congress in Munich. Hitler appears to have been carried away by his apparent successes. But, of course, the Nazi Party was still only one of many similar organizations. Many rival groups in Bavaria had equal or greater strength. The party was about 3,000 strong. It had become respectable on the Right. Julius Streicher led a branch of the similarly racist German Socialist Party in Nuremberg. Otto Dickel directed a branch of the same party in Augsburg. This "socialism" had nothing to do with the SPD but rather was yet another part of the broad *völkisch* movement.

Hitler hoped eventually to establish a homogeneous party organized along military lines. As his confidence in his own leadership abilities grew, he tried increasingly to shape Nazism in terms of his ambitions. As he moved to do this, he became quite heavy-handed and the old guard resented it. Charges were made that Hitler wanted to make himself dictator of National Socialism. Those who held this view were likely correct. In time, there was an open breach between Hitler and his detractors over a plan to bring into the party the whole German Socialist Party from Nuremberg and Augsburg. This seemed practical enough on the surface. Both organizations were much alike. A merger could mean a beneficial pooling of financial resources and talents. The proponents of this plan argued that the Nazi Party would be strengthened by such a step. It could become part of a broader movement with its headquarters in Berlin. Hitler felt threatened by ideas of this sort. He saw the move by the old guard as an attempt to dilute his growing support by swelling the ranks with recruits of uncertain loyalties. Moreover, Hitler saw the idea of moving the headquarters to Berlin as an attempt to isolate his followers in Bavaria.

The emerging Nazi Party, in many ways, already belonged to Hitler. He had gradually built an elaborate ritual around the mass meeting. It reflected a distorted vision of Catholic ceremony. Regardless, an approach of this sort was appealing and enjoying some success in Catholic Bavaria. This was not part of some brilliant master plan. The young Nazi Party did not possess experienced strategists. It was instead a fortunate stumbling onto something that worked.

Among the devices now produced to attract new members were posters and banners. Hitler deliberately picked red for these to provoke the Left and added the swastika. He developed the "Heil Hitler!" salute. He also employed mass parades and the dedication of party standards. He spent many hours hunting through magazines to find an eagle for the party emblem. Members were then ordered to wear the emblem at all times.[19] At a typical party meeting, tension was built up in advance with martial music and patriotic songs. Such meetings were announced (time and place) by a special section of the party newspaper entitled "From the Campaign."

Hitler's successes caused more rumbling among the founding members of the DAP. Many of them seemed prepared to limit the Hitlerian role. For a party he had shaped so personally to slip from his control was more than Hitler could bear. His response was daring. Hitler resigned from the Nazi Party suddenly on 12 July 1921. The Executive Committee was caught off guard. They maligned Hitler, accusing him of dictatorial ambitions. An absurd charge was made that he was in the pay of Jews.[20] Hitler then said that he might rejoin the Party, but only on condition that he be given dictatorial powers. Drexler played a central role at this point in the inner-party struggle.

Drexler was also suspicious of Hitler's intentions. But he saw that, if Hitler left, the DAP might become a club again. He knew that its recent growth was due in large part to Hitler's talents. Drexler persuaded his colleagues to accede to Hitler's demands. The Party Congress, held 29 July 1921, was a triumph for Hitler. He proclaimed at it that he would structure the party as he saw fit. Mixing politics with stagecraft, he put on a series of gaudy events. It became common for some on the Right to refer to him after this as the "King of Munich."

Hitler's political style now became belligerent. His speeches were especially provocative. His meetings were commonly violent. Meetings of opponents were invaded to cause disruptions. Sometimes people were seriously injured. The police monitored Nazi gatherings and related meetings on a regular basis. The authorities repeatedly warned Hitler to keep his followers in check. Leaflets, pamphlets, and posters were often censored because of venomous content.

On 12 January 1922 Hitler was sentenced to three months in prison for disrupting a meeting at the Lowenbräu beer hall where the speaker was severely injured.[21] To serve time in jail was a badge of honor. Hitler emerged from his cell to be welcomed by the Nazis as a hero. But the confrontational style often caused the Nazis problems. Speakers at Nazi meetings, particularly Hitler, created extreme sentiments in audiences. On 31 August 1920, for example, Hitler told an audience: "One should hate the Jew simply because of his race."[22] Earlier, he said the "eternal Jews" were responsible for providing "ninety percent of all racketeers and usurers."[23] It was natural that such assertions as these would produce extreme responses. His Nazi listeners responded with shouts of: "Hang them! Kill them!"[24] As early as September 1920, it became necessary to throw people out of the meetings who responded negatively and physically to such vitriolic statements.[25] These people were ejected by so-called "monitor troops."

The Pre-Putsch SA

One of the often made and inaccurate generalizations about this early Nazi Party was that what was to become the stormtroopers was built out of men drawn from war veterans like those found in many of the Free Corps.[26] In fact, the Nazis would have preferred men from the trenches, but most of these became involved in earlier developing paramilitary groups. Instead, the initial defense formations of the Nazi Party appear to have been constructed of "loud young students" and elements drawn from other radicalized youth.[27] It was out of material like this that Emil Maurice, former member of the paramilitary Bund Oberland, built the initial small groups of monitor troops.[28] In November of 1920, a "Sport Section" or SA was built out of hall guards. It is difficult to tell when the term "*Sturmabteilung*" ("Storm Detachment") was first used to describe the organization formed in late 1920. "Stormtrooper" was clearly in common use by mid-1921. The Nazi SA was at some point renamed (from "Sport Detachment" to "Storm Detachment") after the party leaders had become assured that the authorities would not respond negatively to a more aggressive sounding name. Perhaps it was because the initials "SA" for "Security Section" were already in common use on the Left. The SPD had established SAs in Munich and Coburg by 1921.[29]

The name Sturmabteilung had come directly from the trenches. Storm Detachments were specialized units used in the World War I German Army, charging the opposing lines to create breakthroughs for infantry.[30] There thus was a kind of romantic aura about the name, contributing to the attraction for the brawlers recruited for the early SA. World War I stormtroopers had been highly mobile, nearly suicidal, and much-honored units.[31]

The basic notion in forming the SA was to transform the party's meeting guards over time into a mass organization. In the short term, it was believed that its "heroic" actions would attract many to Nazism.[32] On 11 August 1921, an appeal appeared in the party media addressed to all German youth.[33] This emphasis on youth demonstrates the difference between the SA and other paramilitary formations. Most of the rest desired to make only desperadoes the bulk of their rank and file. The SA sought desperadoes primarily to act as leaders. The party was fairly consistent in seeking recruits between seventeen and twenty-one years of age.[34]

One can argue, and scholars do, that not all postwar radical–Right organizations should be dubbed "fascist," since only two ever bore that name in their title. Of course, intense nationalism was at the core of each movement, so that each country had its unique variety of the radical Right. It might also be argued that there is no "fascism," but only "fascisms." Nevertheless, the fervently nationalistic kind of ideology called fascism was very much a "revolt of the younger generation" in all the states where such movements appeared.[35]

Similar calls for violence in service of a cause to those made by the Nazis emerged in France. Rightist George Valois argued in 1924 that the old order had to be destroyed. It was time for the youth of his country to rise up en masse and destroy decadent, old structures. It was useful for young people to be ready to employ violence to establish the new order. His well-known injunction was as follows: "Two plus three makes naught, the barbarian replies, smashing his head in."[36]

Hitler was very much of the same mind, indicating, "If you do not wish to be German, I will bash in your skull."[37] The Nazi emphasis on youth during this period may have been simple practicality. If the SA was to be made into a propaganda organization rather than a standard paramilitary formation, it suited that purpose better to have malleable young men. Membership roles dating from 1921 demonstrate the emphasis on youth. One list has on it 25 members. Most of these were not veterans (only eight were). Half the men listed were eighteen or younger.[38] These original SA men were soon brought under the influence, arranged by Ernst Röhm, of desperadoes from the Ehrhardt Brigade.

Once Ehrhardt became established in Bavaria after the forced dissolution of his Brigade for involvement in the Kapp Putsch, he and his men moved in several directions. One of these was clandestine in nature. The Ehrhardt cohort in this shadow world was the Organization Consul (OC), the secretive band of assassins that murdered Rathenau in 1922. After the Rathenau killing, the OC membership from the Ehrhardt group decided to choose a more public avenue to action and produced another paramilitary league called the *Wiking Bund*.[39] By the end of 1922, the Vikings had announced that their political program was the same as that of the Nazi Party.[40] A connection with Nazism was soon to be seen. Alfred Hoffmann, a former naval officer, managed the "General Policy Section" of the Vikings and worked with the Nazis. Similarly, the military-affairs section was headed by Manfred von Killinger, later a high-ranking Nazi official, whose memoirs reveal him to have been something of a war-produced psychopath.[41]

It was Ernst Röhm, who exercised influence beyond others in the shadow land of Free Corps, Defense Leagues and anti–Weimar political conspiracies. The local combat leagues, first formed in an attempt to fight the Left in Munich, were led by a generation of revolutionary-minded junior officers. These younger men had a certain amount of contempt for senior officers, steeped in tradition. Such men formed paramilitary units, not to reinforce traditional militarism, but to enhance their own prestige. Röhm had developed contacts with these men and went to perhaps the best-known of them at this juncture.

Apparently, Ernst Röhm approached Ehrhardt and convinced him to help the Nazi's fledgling paramilitary formation.[42] Ehrhardt had originally refused to have anything to do with Hitler. Despite reservations, he finally decided to give in to Röhm's urgings. It was arranged that someone from the Vikings would be sent to try to provide a more militaristic structure for the SA. The first Sturmabteilung leader became Johann Ulrich Klintsch, a former officer.[43] The Ehrhardt group also contributed Alfred Hoffmann to become SA Chief of Staff.[44] Killinger, after escaping political murder charges, came to the SA. The Ehrhardt people then installed a Nazi version of their marching song for the fledgling SA:

> Swastika on our helmet,
> Black-Red-White armband,
> Storm Detachment Hitler,
> We are named![45]

The SA now assumed more of a fighting stance. On 4 November 1921 the Party's fighters added another element to the Nazi mythology when Hitler's "soldiers" flung themselves "like wolves" on their opponents to drive them out of the Hofbräuhaus.[46] Of course, this account is from *Mein Kampf* and subject to the usual exaggerations. In party lore this came to be known as the battle of the Hofbräuhaus. It was not seen as all that impressive by the police. Nevertheless, it became a lasting part of Nazi mythology. Ever more frequent "hall battles" (*Saalschlachten*) became typical during 1922. In October of 1922, Hitler and his SA went to Coburg on a special train. Some 800 stormtroopers were passengers along with other Nazi Party members assembling to attend a patriotic meeting. It was scheduled in an area known to have a substantial concentration of SPD members. This invasion tactic was often used by Bavarian Right. Near the end of the Weimar Republic it also became a frequent violence-provoking motif used in the industrial centers of northern Germany.

When the party train arrived at the Coburg main station, Hitler and his followers were warned by authorities not to march into the central city lest trouble ensue. The Nazis ignored the order and marched anyway. A street riot resulted. The stormtroopers cleared the streets of opponents and came close to holding Coburg under siege. This act of bravado seems to have emboldened Hitler. He apparently came to believe that he could challenge Bavarian authorities whenever he desired. The Coburg experience became a part of the developing Nazi mythology. For years thereafter, it was common for members to greet each other as part of their ceremonies with: "Were you at Coburg?"[47]

Although the members of the Nazi SA were sworn to render willing obedience to Nazism, the party leadership was aware that some of the ruffians clustered in the party paramilitary divided their loyalties between the Nazis and other segments of the Bavarian Right. Moreover, Hitler and his civilian colleagues began to differ with people like Röhm about the long-term role to be played by the SA. Röhm saw the SA as an eventual part of a new German Army assembled to avoid the restrictions of Versailles. Hitler saw it as a propaganda weapon. Between 1922 and 1923, the SA appeared to exert independence. Hitler believed it to be overly influenced by outsiders. This was unacceptable.[48]

Starting in the fall of 1920, SA members had been on hand at every party rally. They regularly acted as bouncers. These rowdies then extended their activities beyond the meeting halls. Much like contemporary street gangs, they sought targets upon which to vent their rage. Not surprisingly, as they roamed the streets seeking targets, they often sought people who looked Jewish. One of their songs had it: "The Jew, flat footed and hooked nose, and kinky hair, he dare not breathe our German air. Throw him out!"[49] The Munich police did little to counter this. Emil Maurice, who was a twenty-three-year-old watchmaker, directed young stormtroopers to beat a man in the train station who had called them a name.[50] The police scarcely noticed this violence, although some were standing close to it. This reflected a very tolerant chief of police named Ernst Pöhner, about whom more will be offered later, who listed badly to the Right.

By the time Röhm, Ehrhardt, and others began to try and influence the SA, the membership of the Nazi paramilitary proved receptive. Unlike the rest of the party, it was composed of nationalistic students, out-of-work artisans (unemployment was always a force in SA history), distraught white-collar workers, and demobilized soldiers. There were also ex–Freikorps people, although this last was a minor component.[51] Hitler was forced to counter outside influence as best he could, and a good place to begin was with the SA. Klintsch was replaced at the beginning of 1923 with Herman Göring, a well-known war hero. This changed things very little in the short run because the separation between the two wings of the party was already entrenched. It was perhaps to safeguard himself against unruly SA leaders that Hitler built his own Praetorian guard at this juncture.

During March of 1923, a personal bodyguard was formed. This small body of men was

Four. The Infancy of Nazism (1919–1923)

called the "*Stabswache*" and was the ancestor of the future SS (*Schutzstaffel*, or "Protective Squad"). This elite guard dressed differently to differentiate itself from the SA.[52] Hitler's first bodyguard was replaced with a new one in May of 1923, the *Stosstrupp* Adolf Hitler. Its members by and large came from a differing social and age group (older) than the quite young SA. The initial leader of this group was Julius Schreck, a man who superficially resembled Hitler and later served as his double from time to time. These recruits were later described by one of their own: "Hard and rough and sometimes quite uncouth were the customs, habits, and looks of the *Stosstrup*. They did not know ... groveling. They clung to the right of the stronger, the old right of the fist. In an emergency they knew no command.... When ... called to action — to attack right and left — march! march! — then things were torn to bits and in minutes streets and squares were swept of enemies.... Soon we were known in village and town."[53]

Most members of the *Stosstrupp* were from working-class origins and had been involved in their share of beer-hall brawling. Hitler appeared to feel quite at home with these young toughs.

Although this young Nazism had been successful in blending the described paramilitary elements with the civilian wing to produce the dual party, the decision made in 1922–23 to advance on the state with force proved nearly fatal politically. Hitler began to make it known than he desired to seize the state through some sort of coup rather than rise to prominence through the vote. In October of 1922, Benito Mussolini had taken power in Italy by marching on Rome, inspiring much of the Bavarian Right. The question now became: why not follow the Italian fascists' example and march on Berlin?

Hitler, as well as other colleagues on the Right, became convinced that a march on Berlin would in fact work. But there was a practical consideration. Hitler could not hope to take such a step without joining with other paramilitary leagues. On his field of dreams Hitler saw a combined effort of conservative traditional military (in the form of the local Reichswehr contingent) and paramilitary groups. The next part of the vision had it that these forces would unite behind some great natural leader who could come only from the Great War. One such was handy locally in the person of Erich Ludendorff. Most historians believe that Hitler did not yet see himself as the leader to make all of this work. He often used the term the "drummer" when speaking of his part in such an undertaking. Of course, Hitler also showed ambivalence when he wondered in "Christian" terms whether he was just a John the Baptist or the new Messiah.

During this time, the Nazi Party was growing, although not much outside Bavaria. Accounts of early party history appear uncertain about where the first non–Bavarian local might have been.[54] Some have it placed somewhere in Baden during 1921 or in Stuttgart as early as June of 1920.[55] Wherever these locals were formed, SA squads developed for meeting protection. SA growth outside Munich was less impressive than the party as a whole. There were just too many *Vereine* seemingly everywhere in Germany. In Nuremberg, for example, nearly the last paramilitary band to be formed was the quite small local Nazi SA.[56] In Baden, many new local Nazis preferred to stay in other paramilitary formations. The tendency for new SA members to own multiple memberships in a variety of "defense leagues" was seen in many places and that tendency infuriated party leadership.[57]

As the party grew, perhaps six thousand SA men assembled in Munich for the first *Reich* party rally. At this meeting, Hitler called out for a national dictatorship to save Germany from impending collapse. In February, Hitler formed an alliance with other right-wing forces, something that came close to derailing his career. A joint committee was established and Lieutenant Hermann Kriebel was appointed military leader for the "Working Union of Patriotic Fighting Associations." A political role was arranged for Hitler in the formation.[58]

In the following months, as Germany moved from one crisis to another, rumors of an impending putsch intensified. Hitler decided to assert the role of his Nazi movement more forcefully by preventing May Day celebrations of the Left. However, on 1 May 1923, Hitler's sympathizers in the government left him in the lurch. To his considerable embarrassment, stormtroopers, poised for battle on the Oberwiesenfeld, had to return their guns to Reichswehr arsenals from which they had been secured through a ruse. For a time, Hitler, greatly shamed, moved out of the spotlight to remain for a time at Berchtesgaden. Then he returned and participated in a paramilitary rally in Nuremberg (1–2 September). At this meeting a new *Deutsche Kampfbund* ("German Fighting League") was established.

As the *Kampfbund* assumed threatening proportion, the Bavarian government declared a state of emergency. Dr. Gustav von Kahr, former prime minister and reactionary separatist, was given dictatorial powers. His control rested directly on General Otto von Lossow, in command of the Seventh District of the Reichswehr, and Hans Ritter von Seisser, in command of the Bavarian State Police. Kahr immediately forbade all mass demonstrations. At the same time, he conspired to be free of the hated national government in Berlin. In these plans only a marginal role was envisioned for Hitler and the Nazis. But Hitler was not one to stay for long on the margin of things.

With all of this, much of the Bavarian Right devoted the month of October 1923 to military preparations. Beer-hall meetings abounded. In the broad Rightist spectrum there was much intrigue. But there was also mutual distrust and a clear potential for fractioning. In early October, typically, there was a rupture in the *Kampfbund* which caused the *Reichsflagge* to be disbanded and split into separate groups. Ernst Röhm seized control of the rump portion left behind and called it the *Reichskreigflagge* (the "Reich War Banner").

Interpolation II

The Bavarian Paramilitary Scene (1919–1923)

The Freikorps

Before any discussion of the Bavarian paramilitary scene at the time that the Nazi SA was developing, it is necessary to take a brief look at the postwar development of the elaborate network of paramilitary groups that fought for and against the Weimar state. The designation "*Freikorps*" was originally applied to voluntary forces recruited by Frederick the Great during the Seven Years' War in the mid–eighteenth century. Later, Free Corps units appeared at the time of the Napoleonic Wars to reinforce troops of the line. During the wars of unification, little use was made of paramilitary groups by Bismarck's highly developed and efficient Prussian army. The *Freikorps* were generally regarded in the eighteenth and early nineteenth centuries as unreliable for actual fighting at the front—they were used mainly as sentries and for other minor duties.

The concept of the Free Corps fighter was changed greatly by the outcome of the worldwide conflict beginning in 1914. The term began to be used to designate paramilitary organizations springing up around Germany as soldiers returned in defeat to their German homeland from World War I. These men nearly all subscribed to the "stab-in-the-back" myth discussed earlier in these pages. It was briefly described earlier how the Free Corps appeared soon after the war. A fuller account of their postwar activities begins here, starting with that historical juncture at the end of 1918.

The Freikorps movement sprang from a number of historical factors. First, was the fact, already stressed, that many German soldiers did not feel themselves to have been defeated. Moreover, when the war ended, German forces were still on French and Belgian soil. In the east, they were as yet in charge of a sizeable portion of the old tsarist realm and their forces were holding territories in the Balkans. They had no idea that the German High Command already knew that victory had eluded imperial Germany. But the eventual consequence of that situation was an imperial German army which imploded rapidly at war's end. A once formidable force began to dissolve quickly as soldiers surrendered in ever greater numbers.

On the home front there was in Germany an extreme–Left political force at work, taking the form of the so-called "*Spartakusbund*," named after the gladiator who had rebelled against ancient Rome. The leaders of this movement had been greatly inspired by the successful Bolshevik revolution in Russia. They acted at this point to inspire large scale strikes which broke out across Germany. Moreover, that summer, sailors had mutinied against the commanders of a High Seas Fleet in Kiel, which had been bottled up in port for most of the war by a British blockade.

Shortly before the armistice ending the shooting, the German High Command decided to get the best possible situation for the country by ordering the fleet to venture out to confront the British. This action was intended to demonstrate that the Germans still had a powerful naval force. This policy caused navy men to revolt on their ships in reaction to what they saw as a meaningless and suicidal action. On the ships quartered in the harbor at Kiel, 28 October 1918, the crews raised the red flag of revolt. The mutiny quickly spread to other ports like Lübeck, Hamburg, Cuxhaven, and Bremerhaven.

The Social Democrats, a quite moderate political group when compared with the Spartacus League, needed a military force to deal with chaos in Berlin during the first weeks of November 1918. There were many armed men in Berlin, but they were splintered into mutually antagonistic groups. These often engaged in fighting each other to determine who would become ascendant in the capital. On 10 November 1918, Quarter-Master General Wilhelm Groener had offered military support to suppress the leftist rising. However, the field army was still far from Berlin and some groups developed, such as the National Association of Deserters, put together by the Spartacists, which encouraged men who fled the army to enter their ranks and bring about a Bolshevik-style revolution in Germany. The regular army units, troubled by desertions and consequent insufficient numbers, were not able to quell the Christmas disturbances in the capital.

By Christmas of 1918, the SPD had fractionated to the Left, producing the independent socialists (the USPD) who, in December, were led by Emil Eichorn to build a "security police" to attempt an assumption of power in Berlin. In Germany's capital, the "People's Naval Division," with the Kaiser already in exile, had taken over the Imperial Palace to use as a headquarters from which looting forays then issued. The adjutant to the official Commandant of Berlin has left us the following picture of those dark days: "Disorder, insecurity, looting ... had become the order of the day ... soldiers' councils lurked in all the alleys ... worst of all were the barracks. They were full to bursting when it was meal time or time to be paid, but empty when the [Berlin] Command desired [only] a dozen soldiers to perform legitimate duties.... Day and night [there were] senseless shootings.... Berlin lived, danced, drank, and celebrated."[1]

At this stage of events, defeat and revolution had caused the German army to disintegrate more thoroughly. Even where soldiers were still stationed in barracks, there was a good chance that the soldiers' revolutionary councils had taken over. To make matters worse, with the German army in this reduced situation, there were threats in border areas as Poles and Czechs saw the German internal crisis as an opportune time to encroach on German lands. Meanwhile, some nearly intact sections of the German army returned from the front. This army remnant was set upon fighting in Berlin, not to defend a republican government few of them liked much, but, in the words of one of their officers "to fight against the masses ... to fight all physical and psychological opposition [on the home front] ... to become unburdened of all sentimentality."[2]

The returned regular-army force mounted an attack on the occupied palace on the morning of Christmas Eve (1918). The army units responded to their orders by throwing the radical sailors out of the palace. The building was easily taken, but, soon enough, a mob of hostile people, perhaps drawn by the sounds of combat, churned about the armed soldiers. The sailors who had been forcibly evicted took advantage of this situation as some troopers, listening to entreaties from the crowd, went over to the mob. The sailors who had been thrown out of the palace took advantage of this situation and they took people as shields and opened fire on the soldiers still defending.[3]

This was the first and only attempt of the regular army to crush revolutionary forces, and it failed. Thus was provided the backdrop for the initial appearance on the historical stage of a man who would be decisively important in the eventual demise of the Weimar Republic. Major Kurt von Schleicher had begun to move in political circles as a representative of the army. Schleicher suggested that the government recruit volunteers, saying that a volunteer force could stabilize Germany and yet would be unlikely to compete effectively with the army for the position as the preeminent force in the state.[4]

The first Free Corps unit was assembled in Kiel. In an attempt to restore order, Gustav Noske, the Social Democratic minister of defense, had decided that he could right the situation by enlisting voluntary Free Corps units to supplement the regular army.[5] The first Free Corps unit assembled on Noske's orders was called the "Iron Brigade." Then, on the morning of 4 January 1919, Noske and Friedrich Ebert accepted an invitation to observe a parade staged by a former army and now Freikorps general. Ludwig von Maercker had been building his group of irregulars intensively since the previous month.[6] This "Volunteer Provincial Rifle Corps" was now ready to serve under republican authority for the purpose of suppressing revolutionaries on the streets of Berlin.

Maercker's example was soon followed and one Free Corps after another was assembled in the immediate area of Berlin. Quickly, the Iron Brigade moved in from the North Sea ports to help in the assault on the revolutionary fighters. A confrontation soon developed. On 23 December 1918 the Spartacists and associated paramilitary forces began their assault on the republican government. On 30 December the *Spartakusbund* changed its name to the German Communist Party (KPD). This immediate threat from the KPD caused the Social Democratic provisional regime to move in haste in their employment of the Free Corps. This was timely in that a full-scale armed insurrection was ordered by Red leadership on 9 January 1919. The following day, Free Corps groups converged on Berlin to occupy the outlying districts. Beginning on 12 January, Free Corps units were deployed all over the city. They mopped up nests of Red resistance and sought out snipers to eliminate. On 15 January the arrests and subsequent murders of Liebknecht and Luxemburg transpired.[7] On 19 January the new government was voted in, the meetings transpiring in the city of Weimar because the capital was considered to be too unstable to host the event.

Noske had entered Berlin on 11 January, marching with the Iron Brigade.[8] His was the first of a group of fighters to be welcomed joyfully by the citizens of Berlin "all along the way," as the vast majority of the people were up in arms because of the "Communist rule of terror."[9] Soon enough, the revolutionary fires in Berlin had been dampened. They were finally extinguished fully by the end of March. But it was not in Berlin alone that the "freebooters" played an important role. Maercker's rifles moved into the city of Weimar to defend the deliberations producing the polity known from that original meeting as the "Weimar Republic."[10]

During the spring of 1919, there were new *Freikorps* springing up all over Germany. Some were the size of a single infantry company and some the size of an entire division with cavalry and artillery elements. The units were usually built around a core of veterans from the front, but often also included students and other fervent German nationalists too young to have served in the war. It was necessary for Noske to use these forces to secure control over various port cities like Bremerhaven, Cuxhaven, Wilhelmshaven and Hamburg. These had been in Communist hands since the final days of the revolution. These actions involved primarily the Iron Brigade and the Ehrhardt Brigade. After only a few days of fighting, the cited ports yielded to governmental authority.

Immediately thereafter, revolution broke out in the *Ruhrgebeit*. A general strike was called in this industrial heartland. Soldiers' and Workers' Councils moved into support positions.[11] Soon enough, there were violent clashes with the Free Corps as they encountered the so-called "Red Army of the Ruhr." There were a number of these violent encounters, but an agreement was negotiated by the SPD in order to avoid sabotage of the mines by radicals. Such an event would most certainly have had a dire economic impact on Germany.

After that, the wave of insurrections moved on to central Germany. Here Noske relied primarily on Maercker's rifles to quell insurrections appearing among the different industrial areas (although other veteran Free Corps formations like the Ehrhardt Brigade were also involved, as was a German veterans' organization, the *Stahlhelm*). Several of the central German cities had proclaimed themselves autonomous at the end of February 1919. The city of Halle was assaulted on 1 March. During April, Brunswick and Dresden were subdued. In both places Communist governments had been established and their leaders had made public their desire to break with the Reich and associate themselves with the "new Russia" under Lenin. Dresden then fell on 14 April. By 10 May, Leipzig had been conquered. By the middle of June, it was over. One Free Corps member would say later that, at this juncture, "order had been established sufficiently to allow the lifting of martial law."[12]

In Interpolation I, the Eisner revolution followed by the violent and short-lived Red Republics in Bavaria was detailed. It is useful here to turn back briefly to the Free Corps response to those leftist assumptions of power. In Bavaria, the general responsibility for restoring order was turned over to General Ernst von Oven. Shortly, some 30,000 men were sent by him to surround the city of Munich. This force included veteran units like the ubiquitous Ehrhardt Brigade, as well as others. The most important of these others was the "Bavarian Free Corps" under Franz Ritter von Epp and the associated *Bund Oberland*.

The Bavarian Red Army had at some point consisted of approximately 60,000 men. However, by the time the Free Corps began their assault on Munich, the Red fighters had dwindled in numbers considerably through desertions. Soon enough, the "Red Terror" that had ruled in Bavaria for some six months had been ended through the use of decisive force.

During what the Free Corps fighters liked to call the "Battle of Liberation" of Munich, the *Freikorps* leaders reported losses of some 68 killed and 170 wounded. The Red losses were much higher. One report had them at 1,000 to 1,200.[13] That estimate is probably conservative. It is recorded that the numerous undertaking establishments in the Munich area simply could not handle the volume of dead bodies and the decaying corpses which soon became a health menace. In an ominous preview of what the Nazis would do on a larger scale in World War II, the Free Corps men dug shallow trenches, shoved the decaying bodies of their foes into them and covered them over.[14]

The Munich victory raised the *Freikorps* to the heights of their fame in Germany. It was due to them, people said, that insurgents had been defeated in Berlin, the port cities, the

Ruhr, and central Germany. The Weimar state had been established under their protection. Soon enough, they also moved into border warfare to turn back those who would encroach upon German soil.

At the end of World War I, things were going very much better in the east than they were in the west. By August of 1918, the Treaty of Brest-Litovsk had taken Russia out of the war and given Germany large chunks of territory far beyond the eastern borders of the imperial empire as they had existed in 1914. It appeared to many that the old pan–Germanic dream of the "Drive to the East" (*Drang nach Osten*) was to become fact. But the triumph was short-lived. The Western front collapsed and wartime boundaries, however recently established, were said by the victorious Allies to be no longer relevant. In actuality, the new order of things in Europe was not to be settled until well into 1919 with what was called in Germany the "Versailles Dictate."

The Poles refused to wait upon Versailles. They began to move after the armistice, with weapons confiscated from defeated German forces, into the city of Posen (in Polish "Posan").[15] The Germans moved out of Poland without any sort of major incidents. But Germans and Poles were soon fighting for control of territories with mixed Polish/German population which had traditionally been part of Prussia.

The Germans were decidedly unwilling to turn over territory which had been part of the most important state (*Land*) in the Reich. A military command structure was quickly established for the purposes of *Grenschutz* ("border protection") in the East. Unfortunately for the Germans, similar border problems developed in both East and West Prussia. Moreover, there were considerable dilemmas of the same kind in Upper Silesia. The new military command, faced with so many problems at the same time, was forced to turn again to the Free Corps. It was actually necessary to call for more of them because of this problem. An authorization was given to recruit all over Germany. Soon enough, freebooters began to assemble in the East.

At this point tension was rising in Posen and the area around it (sometimes called Pozania). Fighting broke out there at the end of December 1918. This was, of course, within the same time frame that revolutionary upheaval was transpiring in Berlin. Actually, so much fighting transpired across Europe in the immediate postwar period that some historians have dubbed it "the war after the war."

It had appeared in the capital, at least momentarily, that Berlin was about to fall into the hands of the Spartacists. Once the forces supporting the government overcame the Spartacists in the capital, the Free Corps was given the green light in the East. Two task forces of *Freikorps* men were organized and an assault was launched on Posen in February 1919. As the forces moved forward, they were unaware that Polish diplomats in Paris were warning the Allies of a revival of German power.[16] On 16 February the Armistice Commission assembled at Trier to deliberate. The result of this deliberation was that the government in Berlin was instructed to immediately withdraw all of its troops from Pozania. On 20 February 1919 the offensive was halted and the two Free Corps conducting it fell back upon their original departure points.

In the real world of political diplomacy it was apparent that the republican government in Berlin had little choice; they had to follow Allied instructions because they had no rational hope of opposing the militarily superior forces confronting them if any renewed conflict appeared. In the romantic world of the Free Corps desperado, however, the freebooters convinced themselves that they had given away a glorious victory under the force of "cowardly" commands from the central government. Those people in Berlin who had sold them out were the infamous pacifists, spawn of the German revolution. They were the "November traitors" who had seized victory from their hands again.[17]

At the same time that the drama surrounding Posen was unfolding, the German army had occupied the Baltic area. In this case, the Allied response was a bit different regarding German paramilitary activity; as they saw it, any rapid withdrawal of troops from the area might well surrender it to the Russian Red Army. Sending Allied troops would have been unpopular indeed in war-weary London and Paris. The "armies" of Estonia, Latvia, and Lithuania, actually pitifully inadequate forces, were unable to halt the Soviets on their own. For this reason the German Eighth Army was ordered to stay in the region. But this force was as demoralized as the rest of the German army. Quickly enough, another "Iron Brigade" was created out of the German forces remaining loyal in the area. The other major force raised was the *Baltische Landwehr*. It was built out of the German aristocracy, which had formed the landowner class in Estonia and Latvia since the days of the medieval Teutonic Knights. For that reason, the German aristocracy was actually very much disliked by the Latvian population. The Latvians saw the Red armies offering them a way to free themselves of their traditional domination by Germanic overlords.

General Graf Rudiger von der Goltz was made supreme commander of all Free Corps in the Baltic and he arrived there on 1 February 1919.[18] One of the first men von der Goltz met in the Baltic was the nearly legendary Major Joseph Bischoff, who had been ordered to the East in January of 1919. He introduced himself to the general as a "freebooter" and also told him that he had been at war for twelve years, eight in Africa, by 1914.[19] Here in fact was the archetype of the desperado. Bischoff had been placed under orders to help organize Freikorps in Königsberg to take to the Baltic. Due to the help of men very much like him in outlook and methods, by the time of the spring offensive, Bischoff had organized a division which numbered some 14,000 men.

The attack against the Red Army was launched from Libau during the second week of February.[20]

By the end of February, German troops supported by Latvian nationalists controlled Libau. In March, von der Goltz launched attacks toward the east and toward Riga and northward to occupy Kurland (Courland). In the process, the Red Army suffered heavy defeats. Since the Latvian military performance was so poor, von der Goltz displaced the Latvian government. The Western powers protested, but, since they were not of a mind to send in their own troops, von der Goltz was able to continue his agenda. He wanted to control Riga which owned the finest port on the Baltic. On 25 May, Riga was stormed by frontal assault. The Free Corps marched into the city as the Red Army fled.

The news of victory in Riga was received with enthusiasm by the *Freikorpskämpfer* back in Germany. There was talk in desperado circles about the "German Army" still emerging victorious on the field of battle. In fact, the fall of Riga had marked the high point of Free Corps success in the Baltic. German nationalists saw the victory as "illuminating the brilliance ... which is eternal soldierliness."[21]

The Free Corps fighters had actually been too successful for their own good. It soon became evident what it meant to be "set free" by German forces. Some 500 Latvians were shot without trial by them in one town, 200 in another. The excuse was always the same, regardless of the truth: "They were pro–Bolshevik."[22] After the fall of Riga another situation demonstrated that the Freikorps fighters were no longer needed in the East. The poorly equipped and equally poorly organized Red Army, which had moved into the Baltic area from the East, now fled it to return home.

The indigenous Baltic peoples, materially helped by the British, now began to organize armies on their own.[23] From Berlin came the order to Von der Goltz to cut his forces in half. But the general continued campaigning. The expanded Estonian army resisted Von der Goltz's invasion from 21 June. This time the *Freikorps* were defeated. They retreated back to Riga under attack from both the Estonian and Latvian armies. About this time, Germany signed the Versailles Treaty and the British began to pour large quantities of weapons into the Baltic states. Moreover, the Western powers now began to demand that all German troops be withdrawn from conquered areas before the end of August.

The Iron Division and associated smaller Free Corps refused to obey. Other volunteers marched from Germany toward the Baltic. What Free Corps remnants could be gathered under Von der Goltz were offered to White Russian troops in Latvia who still hoped to undue Red control in Moscow. Throughout the previous centuries Russians had ruled in parts of the Baltic and the German-Balts had been loyal subjects of the tsar. The White Russian commanders were quite happy to accept this oddly mixed German-Russian army which was forming during September of 1919. Estimates of its strength ran around 55,000 men, of which 40,000 were German volunteers.[24]

This new army attempted to storm Riga on 8 October as the city had been reclaimed by the Latvians in the interim. As the city was near the point of falling again to a Free Corps onslaught, the British Royal Navy pulled into the harbor and began shelling German forces. This help allowed the Latvians to go on the offensive. From 19 October the Latvians were able to force the Free Corps back toward Lithuania. The Lithuanians, neutral to this point, joined the struggle against the German invaders. The upshot of all this was that the defeated Free Corps fighters actually were forced to limp back into East Prussia, raging at a government that they saw as one working continually to undermine a potentially victorious campaign. And victory, they believed, had been denied because of the lack of proper support from Berlin.

From this juncture, the Free Corps followed two basic lessons they believed they had learned from their postwar military adventures: (1) that their greatest enemy was not some foreign power, but rather republican Germany and (2) that the volunteers need to formulate political goals a great deal more precisely.[25]

Actually, few generals and fewer Free Corps leaders supported the Weimar Republic. The terms of the Versailles Treaty began to be applied from 1 January 1922 and, most important in this context, the army could keep no more than 100,000 men in their ranks. Moreover, General Hans von Seeckt, who was never very enthusiastic about the Free Corps, ordered that they be disbanded.

Not long after, as seen, the Kapp *Putsch* was attempted in Berlin. Though it failed, it had important consequences, particularly in Bavaria. There, on the night of 13–14 March, Bavarian Free Corps elements overthrew the SPD government and gave over power to monarchist politician Gustav von Kahr, even though Kahr was at the core separatist-minded. He had seen the Kapp *Putsch* as simply a "Prussian affair." Before turning to the aftermath of the Kapp *Putsch* and the path of Free Corps refugees to Bavaria's "orderly compartment," it should prove useful at this point to indicate what the usual mindset of a *Freikorpkämpfer* amounted to in 1920.

The Freikorps Mindset

The circumstances surrounding the organization of the Free Corps are important to consider here. When Noske allowed the people who wanted to do so to organize and recruit their own troops to create a personal army, as he himself admitted, his actions reminded some of an earlier tumultuous period in German history. He said as he evaluated the situation that it was "not unlike the days of Wallenstein."[26] Count Albrecht von Wallenstein was an organizer, although certainly not the only one, of the mercenary bands that fought in the Thirty Years' War (1618–1648). One of the distinguishing characteristics of that war was the absence of a centralized, effective military structure to coordinate and keep on a leash the freebooter attack dogs of that time. In that case, all too often, the allegiance of fighters was given only to individual commanders. This sort of situation was reflected in the twentieth-century German freebooters. Often, individual units formed in 1918–19 were named after their own commanders ("Storm Section Rossbach," for example) beyond whom the men of the formation acknowledged no other leaders.

Much as in that decisive struggle of the seventeenth century, each volunteer's loyalty was given to his immediate leader. Interestingly, the leader of each individual unit was often called simply *der Führer* ("the leader"). In this Free Corps idea of command, the leader was set upon a figurative pedestal and it was held that he was, almost magically, an embodiment of all the positive characteristics the volunteer saw in himself.

Another characteristic of Free Corps fighters was that they delighted in appropriating for themselves the worst epithets an enraged citizenry could use to defame them. Among these terms were "traitors," "outlaws," and murderers." But no matter how harsh the labels, the freebooters gloried in them. The term *Landsknechte* ("freebooters"), applied to themselves commonly, was an obvious echo of the Thirty Years' War.[27] And such an epithet showed up eventually in the memoirs of a famous Nazi who had been part of Von Epp's Free Corps. Ernst Röhm called his autobiography "*Memoirs of a High Traitor.*"

Although actually owning no Marxian or neo–Marxian components, the *Freikorps* men liked to think of themselves as classless in nature. The idea was that the whole Free Corps movement was a patriotic upsurge in which all true Germans rose as one to save the nation. In this view, all class distinctions were forgotten as class consciousness was purged in a boiling cauldron of war-originated nationalism. Obviously, this idea had some of its roots in the wartime propaganda of the imperial government which had propagated such a notion. There actually was some class leveling transpiring in the Free Corps, but the movement preponderantly was composed of men who had lower-middle-class, middle-class, and peasant backgrounds. Laboring men did not join the formations in any substantial numbers. Out of this, over time, came a unique feature of Free Corps activism; men of bourgeois origin revolting against that very segment of society from which they had come.

The unique turning away from their own social origins was perhaps rooted in their shared fondness for wreaking total destruction upon foes. And this sort of attitude was totally unacceptable in a normal bourgeois world. Such a movement was bound by its very nature to be set against anything remotely resembling a structured bourgeois, liberal order. And that entity which most appeared to resemble the archetype of the bourgeois, liberal order was the Weimar Republic. These men's view of the new republican Germany was profoundly negative at the core. And at the various junctures when the republican authorities tried to set them aside as no longer needed, this hatred was greatly intensified.

Their numbers consisted of former shock troops, junior officers who often had held only temporary commissions, and university students who had wanted to enter the war only to have the shooting stop before they could take their places in the trenches. It was typical of nearly all the members of the Freikorps that, even after participation in what to that juncture had been the greatest bloodletting in European history, they still spoiled for combat. If veterans, they wished to eternalize the world of the trenches in postwar civilian society. All of the units were also typified by an intense masculine camaraderie. In fact, many of the men in the Free Corps were open homosexuals, as was Ernst Röhm.

At the height of the movement, there were roughly 400,000 men in the ranks of this group of military desperadoes. They were most unlike the average war veteran who had been only too happy to return the quiet and order of civilian life. They were, as seen, very much antibourgeois and hence antirepublican. Ernst von Salomon, who glorified this group of social misfits in his writings, stated openly that the "peculiar experience" of such men had made them turn against the societal values with which they had been raised.

The memoirs left by the Free Corps men are full of hatred for the Weimar Republic. It was a symbol of all they despised. In his authoritative history of the Free Corps, Robert G. L. Waite cites three examples of the intense antibourgeois feelings of the Free Corps desperado. Three memoirs quoted below display these attitudes. The first is that of Peter von Heydebreck, the famous one-armed Free Corps figure who led an organization called the *Wehrwölfe*, who offered: "But my idea was not to husband and preserve my troops until the new state had established itself. On the contrary, it was [to fight] against this state of Weimar and Versailles. War daily and by every means." The second comes from the commander of another Free Corp, the *Eiserne Schar*. He was Rudolf Berthold, who wrote: "I will not forget these days of criminals, lies, and barbarity. The days of the Revolution will forever be a blight on the history of Germany.... As the rabble hates me ... I remain strong. The day will yet come when I will knock the truth into these people and tear the mask from the faces of the whole miserable, pathetic lot." And the last is from a former member of the Ehrhardt Brigade who was later to take part in the Beer Hall Putsch: "Out of the experience of the Revolution came the conviction that our task for the next decade would be: For the Reich! For the *Volk*! Fight the Government! Death to the Democratic Republic!"[28]

It has been offered that the Free Corps was an extreme example of German cultural fragmentation, most of which stemmed from the lost war and its aftermath. Throughout the 1920s, Germany society was unable to find rewarding roles for its young men and women. In consequence, some 4.3 million young people belonged to youth organizations ("Workers Youth," the "Young German Order" on the nationalist Right, "Young Communists" on the Left, and others). Most of these groups were opposed to the Republic and gravitated toward the political extremes of both Right and Left.

It has also been offered that a deep-seated pathology troubled Germans during the republican years. In this view the prevailing cultural miasma developed from a coalescing of several preexisting pathologies. Again the war is an obvious cause in building this construct, desensitizing the public to armed conflict and the brutality emerging from it. But the evidence is also held to be long-term in nature, showing the existence of pathologies in past centuries. They are thus said to reach deep into the past. It has argued that even traditional German fairy tales can be presented as proof of long-term pathological trends.[29]

The folk tales published by the Brothers Grimm, which have been read to generations of children in Germany and indeed the world, do contain all sorts of unusually cruel acts. In one, a queen boils and eats her own children. In another, a pretty young girl is hacked to pieces and thrown into a vat with decomposing human remains. A little boy in another is chopped to bits and made a part of a pudding. And in one tale, familiar to many, Hansel and Gretel were to be roasted and consumed by a wicked hag. Several stories also appeared with the theme of child abandonment featured prominently. As this notion goes, these stories were powerful tools used with the intent to shape the youthful mind. The lesson learned from these stories was, for young Germans, the teaching of obedience to authority. Another lesson was distrust of anything "un–German" (including Jews, Gypsies, and other people who were eventual victims of the Nazis). This definition of un–German was, in some cases, even extended to other Germans, including the deformed and the physically handicapped.[30]

Before one embraces this theory that German fairy tales indicate a generational transfer of pathological symptoms, however, it must be modified. It is necessary to take note of similar tales in other cultures not noted for warlike sentiments or practices redounding unfavorably to one's fellow human. In the words of Maria Tatar:

> It may well be that some of the fairy-tale episodes ... capture aspects of the harsh social climate of past eras. Child abandonment was by no means an uncommon practice [in German stories and] in earlier eras, particularly in times of war, famine, and other extreme situations. Yet even in cultures where child abandonment is supposedly rare or unknown, the theme of children deserted at birth figures prominently in folkloric traditions.... Fantasy, more than fact, seems to serve as the basis for that vast class of fairy-tales in which the central figure is a victimized hero. Such tales can be found all over the world; they are [by] no means limited ... to the texts compiled by the Grimms.[31]

Because of the German nation's submission to Nazism, the Allies after World War II censored some of the bloodshed and torture from folk stories read by German children. It was claimed that, because of the repetition of harmful themes in the fairy tales, these motifs might well have provided models for Nazi torture tactics. It was thus necessary to censor them.[32] This showed an early acceptance in the West of a theory which became part of a social-psychological approach employed by later scholars like Robert G. L. Waite to explain the rise of Nazism. The problem here is that it is too difficult to explain the savagery of the *Freikorps* and the Nazis later by use of this theory any more than the use of the earlier-cited theories of the psychohistorians explain the basic causation for Hitler's actions. If one seeks one cause more than any other that explains the ferocious aspects of the Free Corps mindset, which the freebooters could have bequeathed to the Nazis, it is much safer to return to the ideology of the trenches in which cruelty and savagery were learned close at hand by watching men mowed down in windrows.

The Free Corps Underground

The Right did take power in Bavaria, but elsewhere it was not the same story. Once the Kapp *Putsch* had been neutralized through a general strike, there were Communist riots in

Kiel, Halle, Leipzig, Chemnitz, Magdeburg, and Frankfort. These were put down by local police, but in many cases that outcome was just barely achieved. In the Ruhr, the Red rising was more successful. Again, the *Freikorps* had to be summoned to defend the state. This turned out to be the bloodiest series of events in the long fight between Freikorps units and Communist fighters. A full-scale offensive was launched by the Free Corps on 3 April 1920. By 8 April, the entire area was controlled by *Freikorpskämpfer* and, as in other instances, hundreds of prisoners were rounded up and "shot while trying to escape." Others were sentenced to death by illegal freebooter courts-martial.[33]

Many Free Corps fighters followed government instructions to disband in 1920, for Berlin had ordered that course of action following the final armed suppression of the Left. Others simply refused to disband. Those who did not masked their activities in a fashion the Nazis would use later when they suffered periods of prohibition; they created a variety of organizations, small "political parties," sport-shooting clubs, trucking companies, bicycle clubs, etc. One device often employed was the creation of *Arbeitslager* ("work camps") or *Arbeitsgemeinschaften* ("working societies") in various places throughout the Reich. At these locations they formed the half-military and half-agricultural communities their leaders had only recently been devising to be built in conquered Baltic areas. There is little doubt that this is yet another case in which neo-romanticism prevailed; this was an attempt to establish something which would recall in concrete form the sort of domains ruled over by the medieval Teutonic Knights.[34]

In Bavaria, the relationship between the Reichswehr and such clandestine groups was particularly close. The *Organization Escherich* ("Orgesch"), created to coordinate Bavarian volunteer units set upon overthrowing the Weimar Republic, had brought Kahr into power over that South German state. The local Reichswehr had very good relations with most of the Free Corps movements then residing in Bavaria, Orgesch among them. The von Epp Freikorps, based on their role as "saviors" of the state from the Red Republics, was melted into the Reichswehr units garrisoned in Bavaria. Röhm, as Epp's Chief of Staff, played the role of protector for the various underground and semi-clandestine Free Corps successor units.

As soon as he had taken command of the army after the Kapp *Putsch*, General von Seeckt began the task of rebuilding Germany's armed forces. His plan was to take the 100,000 men allowed him for the Reichswehr and convert them to a leadership army. This army was to be built of highly trained officers, disciplined along the lines set by the classic Prussian pattern. There was no room in an army of this sort for the chronically violent and undisciplined Free Corps man.[35]

The beginnings of the underground Free Corps, the intensification of its building after the Ruhr adventure, and their migration to Munich, which actually began before the Ruhr with the failure of the Kapp-Lüttwitz plot, can best be examined by following the arrival and early activities of the Ehrhardt Freikorps in Bavaria. Following the Kapp *Putsch*, disgruntled freebooters and nationalists found their way to Munich, a center that attracted them, as one of Hitler's favorite phrases had it, "like a magnet attracts iron filings." The reason for this is revealed in the activities of two individuals, the premier of Bavaria, Gustav von Kahr, and Police Chief Ernst Pöhner.

Kahr, a somewhat pompous and pious man, was not the possessor of an imaginative mind. His goal was to make of Munich, and Bavaria more broadly, a safe haven for those who shared his antirepublican views. He also hoped that Munich would serve as a prime mover in a monarchical revival throughout central Europe. He had been placed in power during the following the Kapp Putsch by the Bavarian branch of the German army. The Bavarian military and its associated paramilitary groups (von Epp's, especially) became a *Sammelbecken* (collecting point) of conspiratorial groups scheming to overthrow the republican government in Berlin.

Ernst Pöhner was the chief of police in Munich. At war's end, he was a member of the Thule Society and thus had early contacts with the German Workers' Party of Anton Drexler. In time, he became a Hitler supporter. It was Pöhner who, following the failure of the Kapp adventure, invited Captain Ehrhardt to come to the Bavarian capital. Once in Munich, Erhardt established a new headquarters in the Franz-Joseph Strasse. Ehrhardt's men then enrolled in the Civil Guards to keep their military skills at a high level. Ehrhardt's troopers were largely quartered in farms in the countryside just outside of Munich. If they did not enroll in the Einwhonerwehr, they enrolled in the Bund Oberland.

Following the initial projects on Bavarian soil, various successor organizations began to issue from the Ehrhardt Brigade. One of these was the earlier described Organization Consul, formed in the spring of 1921. It was Pöhner who was the chief patron of the organization.[36] In fact, the chief of police provided its members with false identification papers and allowed them to use his own office for clandestine meetings. In Ernst Röhm's memoirs is to be found the depiction of an episode demonstrating Pöhner's mindset. One day, an alarmed statesman went up to the police president and spoke quietly to him, saying, "Herr President, political murder organizations exist in this country." Pöhner then replied: "So, so, but there are too few" (*So, So, aber zu wenig*).[37]

The murder squads so admired by Pöhner killed all sorts of members of the populace at large. In October of 1920, members of the OC murdered a young servant girl named Marie Sandmeier. She stumbled onto one of the caches of illegal arms which were to be found all over Munich in those days. Since she took the law of the land seriously (in this case, the law of 7 August 1920 requiring all citizens who knew of illegal arms depots to report them to the Disarmament Commission),[38] she believed it was her duty to report this discovery to the authorities. Because of her report, she was hanged from a tree in a Munich park under a sign claiming: "You lousy bitch; you have betrayed your fatherland. The Black Hand has judged you."[39] The actual "judge" in this case was a man named Sweighardt. He was given a false passport, fled to Austria, was extradited back to Germany, and then released because of "lack of evidence."[40]

Once the murder of the man who signed the armistice ending the shooting in World War I, Matthais Erzberger, had transpired, attention nationally was focused on Munich. The city was now seen as a breeding ground for right-wing terrorism. Leftist and liberal elements throughout Germany demanded that the central government in Berlin do something about the continued aggregation in Bavaria of rightist groups. Kahr took the position, in consonance with his overall views as a would-be separatist, that this was interference from Berlin in Bavarian affairs following a pattern already established during World War I.

Beyond Kahr's protestation, General von Lossow continued to be defiant of orders issuing from Berlin and shielded the elements of refugee Free Corps fighters who appeared to get off nearly every train from the north arriving in the Munich *Hauptbahnhof* ("Central Station"). Soon enough, many political groups forbidden in other German *Länder* were openly tolerated in Bavaria. The local Reichswehr unit even gave some of them weapons with the

Interpolation II. The Bavarian Paramilitary Scene (1919–1923)

idea that its mission had changed. Now its goal was believed to be to "break the bonds of Versailles" and to destroy the Weimar Republic.

As the Nazi Party developed in this Bavarian context, the *völkisch* paramilitary bands or parties outside it had far greater numbers than did the fledgling party growing out of the old DAP. The SA of the Nazi Party was viewed by most Bavarians of all kinds as but one of the many patriotic *Verbände*. And these "racist" bands constituted a major force in Bavarian politics apart from emerging Nazism.

One should classify these bands as political-paramilitary formations. They tended to be organized as was the *Bund Bayern und Reich*. And it was a complex of military and political subcomponents. It was their military posturing which gave them whatever political influence they exercised. These native Bavarian *Verbände* shared a common point of origin; they all traced their roots to the formation of the eventually suppressed Red Republics in 1919.[41]

As described, most of the Bavarian *Freikorps* had been incorporated into Reichswehr ranks in Munich. They were thus not as important in determining the nature of combat leagues developing after that point in Bavaria. Among these was the "Home Guard" (*Einwhohnerewehr*) or the "Temporary Volunteer Corps" (*Zeitfreiwilligenkorps*). Those Freikorps members, who for various reasons could not get into one of these two usually enrolled in the *verbände* growing out of these groups and the Free Corps elements arriving in Munich between the Kapp *Putsch* and the Beer Hall *Putsch* (a period of over three years).

The *Bund Bayern und Reich* maintained its unity until the end of 1922. At that point it was sundered by centrifugal forces which could no longer be controlled. What split the movement was a difference in political outlook. In time, the division of the *völkisch* movement in Bavaria was set along ideological lines. There was a Right-monarchist division calling for the reinstallation of the deposed Wittlesbachs in Bavaria and a Right-radical division envisioning the creation of a new racist and patriotic Germany. The Right-radical organizations fell under one of two umbrella formations: "The Working Group of Combat Organizations" (*Arbeitsgemeinschaft der Kampfverbände*) and the various organizations pulled under the Ehrhardt roof after the elements of the Naval Brigade had emerged into the Bavarian scene. Finally, the *völkisch* bands also combined into the "United Patriotic Bands of Bavaria" (the VVVB). This last was organized in the summer of 1922. The most important Right-radical organization to appear during this period was the Arbeitsgemeinschaft. It consisted of the following paramilitary units: the *Bund Unterland*, the *Reichsflagge*, and the "Voluntary Corps of Munich" (also called "Organization Lenz").[42] This acted as the centralizing organization for the radical wing of the *völkisch* movement until it was replaced by the *Kampfbund* in which Hitler was to play a meaningful role.

The *Kampfbund* was a more restricted roof formation. It originally had within it only Oberland, Reichsflagge, and the SA. Eventually, the southern half of the Reichsflagge remained in the *Kampfbund* as the *Reichskriegflagge* while the northern half split away. This "Reich's War Flag" was then placed under the leadership of Ernst Röhm.

The less significant associational division of the paramilitary in Bavaria was composed of various organizations. These were rather loosely integrated and had descended from the Ehrhardt Brigade once it had migrated illegally to Bavaria. The best-known successor formation in this group was the Wiking *Bund* which was banned in the rest of the Reich once it appeared and was actually disliked by many in Bavaria itself. Associated with the Vikings were the *Blücher Bund* (named after a famous Prussian general), *Bund Frankenland*, and a

Bavarian branch of the "young German Order." The *Organization Consul* acted as a connective formation, while only a small percentage of its participants were involved in the infamous murder squads.

There is a tendency in many works on Nazism to see the Nazis as the most important representative of the entire pre–*Putsch völkisch* movement in Bavaria. Within the context offered by this view, the SA assumes an outsized importance. The Nazi Party only provided a small part of that movement and an even smaller component of the total paramilitary mix. For every Nazi SA man there were hundreds of members of various other *Verbände*. It is true that one man often took up membership in many formations. And, soon enough, that began to disturb Hitler; he wanted none of his stormtroopers to own memberships in formations outside his own party. The *völkisch* movement was thus not unified. It displayed deep inner divisions. The deepest of these divisions was between Left and Right. This separation was far more important than any of the very public confrontations between egocentric individual leaders.

It is a mistake to assume that the Free Corps were all drawn in eventually to the waiting embrace of Nazism They were born under revolutionary circumstances and were provisional in character. By far the majority of them appeared in the first months of 1919 and then dissolved by the end of that year. This was generally not true, however, of the largest formations, usually founded by generals and colonels. These were commanded by men who owned no republican sentiments, but displayed relatively moderate political aims.

There is another category which includes most of the Free Corps. This was composed of some veterans and many like-minded civilian volunteers who belonged to units that operated only for a short time and disappeared when there was no further need for them in what were local matters. A third category was one consisting of units led by junior officers. These were the most radical, including diehards who could never accept Germany's defeat. It was they who most hated republican forms. It was this group that most often had the word *Sturm* ("Assault") displayed in their titles. These were, for example, the *Sturmabteilung* Rossbach, *Sturmbataillon* Schmidt, and *Sturmbataillon* Heinz. It was from the Rossbach group that the SA of the Nazi party likely drew its name.

If the SA was not a dominant part of the Bavarian paramilitary movement once so many of this third category of radicalized freebooters had ended up in Munich, then how did it become so important by the time of the 1923 *Putsch*? To determine that, we must return to the person of Ernst Röhm. Röhm belonged to the growing band of desperadoes whose entire existence had been shaped by the war. It was earlier indicated that he had come from a family of traditionalists. Most of its male members had been civil servants who worked for the deposed Wittelsbach monarchy. He reflected his family background superficially by often indicating his staunch Bavarian monarchism. When the Wittelsbach monarchy fell in 1918, however, he put that devotion aside in favor of a leveling nationalism he had learned, as had so many others, during the war.

It has often been maintained that he was far more a true "national socialist" than Hitler ever was. He was an irrepressible conspirator and worked tirelessly from 1919 to build a new secret army. He wanted to form a clandestine force to act as a national militia to be called upon should Germany come under attack. When the civil guards were being built in Bavaria, it was Röhm who contacted men from the various *völkisch* groups like the Nazis to provide candidates for service.

Ernst Röhm often claimed that, from his childhood, he "had only one thought and wish — to be a soldier."[43] He eventually joined the Nazi Party because he saw it as an extension of the old pre-treaty Germany and as a natural means to achieve his own paramilitary goals. Once the Civil Guards had been disbanded, Röhm lost his first Bavarian vehicle for building the German army in secret. With scarcely a pause, he was back at work gathering paramilitary elements to rebuild the clandestine army.

Röhm owned a very large number of contacts on the far Right. Unfortunately for him, these represented formations which mostly were not sizeable, many of which had been driven underground because of clashes with authorities. Röhm had been working with the War Ministry in Bavaria to accumulate weapons to be placed in secret locations throughout the *Land*. He did not have a definite political profile at this juncture and sought simply to rebuild the fighting force of his dreams. As he worked furiously to do this, his arms-collection activities made him known in some quarters as "the Machine Gun King of Bavaria." He clearly had a talent for organization.[44] And he was making use of it to draw together forces to be ready for the overthrow of Weimar.

In the altered post–Civil Guard atmosphere, Röhm became increasingly interested in Hitler and his party. By mid–1921, the Nazis had become a respected and influential part of the extreme Right in Bavaria. Röhm saw Hitler at first as yet another helper to carry out his program. It soon became apparent to the Nazi leader that Röhm had excellent connections in the army command locally, the upper levels of Bavarian politics, and the various paramilitary units under his influence. He used his connections in this paramilitary arena during the summer of 1921 and some veterans were added to the inexperienced men of Hitler's beginning SA. Nevertheless the SA remained little more than a fragment of those organizations Röhm was manipulating. The forces under his influence through 1921 numbered some 30,000. And Hitler's SA counted only 800 to 1000.[45]

Röhm became a closer ally of Hitler in late 1922. By this juncture, the scar-faced war hero had become disenchanted with those leading Civil Guard successor organizations. Röhm had become convinced that nationalist forces had to move soon. He feared that if they waited much longer the Weimar Republic would become more stable. A decisive act was needed and he had to find some leader to guide the movement to "*der Tag*." "The Day" was to be, as he had it, the decisive moment "that would bring liberation [from the Republic]." More and more Röhm became convinced that Hitler was that man.[46]

At this point, Röhm set to work to establish a union of *Wehrverbände* under the political leadership of Hitler. Röhm worked with paramilitary leaders' support from the *Bund Oberland, Reichsflagge*, and other organizations. It was these formations that joined with the SA in the alliance of patriotic associations. The aim of this new group was to create a nationalistic "power group," a striking force for "the Day."[47]

After that the Alliance (*Arbeitsgemeinschaft*) continued to expand. Through Röhm's connections, the member paramilitary units were trained by Reichswehr personnel.[48] The SA was shaped in important ways by this new status. By March of 1923, extensive militarization of the SA had transpired. This pulled it away from its original role as a monitor troop to protect meetings to the point where it could be perceived as another combat league attracting people with greater experience in matters of arms to its ranks. One of the obvious impacts of this was to be seen in the establishment of an SA *Oberkommando* with Hermann Göring at its head.[49] All of this made the SA much more ready for the insurrectionary activity to follow in November.

Chapter Five

The Failed Putsch

Immediately following World War I, the Allies wore blinders and charged that Germany was intentionally ruining itself to avoid reparation payments. Despite requests from Berlin for more reasonable installments, nothing was changed. It was only a matter of time before the Germans were forced to default. They did so in late 1922 on payments in kind (telegraph poles, etc.) The French had long had plans to occupy the Ruhr and, with this default, they acted.[1] On 10 January 1923 the French and Belgian governments announced an occupation of the Ruhr.[2] The reaction generally on the German Right was typified by vows to participate in any sort of undeclared war that the government might launch against France. Secret meetings in Germany involving political leaders and generals produced what came to be called the "Black Reichswehr," consisting of Free Corps and combat leagues.

Once launched, the project's authors had little hope of matching French strength. But the plotters provided the Free Corps and the fighting leagues with a rationalization to continue activities.[3] In Bavaria, the desperado flourished. And the situation there quickly became worse. The economic loss of the Ruhr weakened the mark disastrously.[4] Soon enough, the government in Berlin began financing idle workers by printing more paper money. By the end of October, the mark was rated at 130 billion to one American dollar. Millions surviving on wages and fixed incomes could not keep pace.[5] By December of 1923, a final slowing of inflation was brought through currency reform in Germany.[6] Even though money was again more soundly based in mid–1924, much radicalization of everyday life had already transpired. Both farm and city in Bavaria fared badly, but it was worse in Munich.

Soon enough, there were more protest rallies, some 52 on 14 January 1923. The radical Left appeared on the rise again. Leftists formed paramilitary groups, imitating those on the Right. The Right, for its part, was typified by considerable numbers, but little organization. Under Göring, the SA increased its capabilities and added departments and titles to give the impression of a military formation. But the SA was actually not very militaristic. Nonetheless, Munich's SA unit established a regimental band, a "light artillery unit," motorized sections and others. But the artillery section had no artillery. The motorized sections consisted of a few member's cars and motor bikes. The shortcomings of the motorized unit were revealed by the fact that a bicycle section was created.[7]

The Bavarian Right, with its paramilitary elements, devoted much of the month of October to preparations. The various paramilitary groups (*Verbände*) intensified activities. In potential support of whatever kind of action these groups might take was a collection of weapons secreted in locations around the city. By this juncture, the ersatz military SA was issuing regular orders. Some of these tried, likely without success, to explain a complex paramilitary-political situation to stormtroopers.[8] Then, on 26 October, another order was given to the SA indicating that Bavaria could take one of three courses: (1) passively allow Berlin to "make it [Germany] Marxist"; (2) simply sit like a child and "sulk in a corner"; or (3) follow the desirable option of placing the "black-red-white flag" on top of the Reichstag building in Berlin.[9]

On 7 November 1923 the major leaders of Bavaria's right-wing organizations fully developed their plans for a coup. Although much divided them, including motives and ambitions, they were united against the Republic. The chief *Kampfbund* conspirators were Ludendorff, his personal adjutant, Hans Streck, Dr. Friedrich Weber of the *Bund Oberland*, and Adolf Hitler.

Meanwhile the whole nation, Left, Right, and center, had given voice to indignation over the French occupation. But the government seemed unable to do much to obtain emotional support from the people. Berlin thus turned to passive resistance as its weapon. Consequently, miners would not mine, railroads would not run, and no deliveries were made to the French. The population of the rest of Germany was asked to contribute to the support of those in the Ruhr who did not work. Hitler claimed that these measures were so insignificant as to be tantamount to treason. In his view the most dangerous enemy was not the French, but the republican leaders in Berlin. First deal with the people in Berlin responsible for German weakness and then turn on Paris, he urged.

The German mark, a week before the Ruhr occupation on 11 January 1923, stood at 7300 to the dollar. By September, it was almost ten million to the dollar. Millions of Germans were ruined. People could not purchase fuel or food. Disease, especially tuberculosis, rose alarmingly with the decline in room temperatures and the lack of proper nourishment. The impact of inflation was experienced everywhere. When Minister of Defense Otto Gessler went to dinner at the home of Chancellor Wilhelm Cuno, he was served wine, a little bread, and some hard wurst.[10] In October, a lunch could cost a billion marks. But if passive resistance was to work, the idle laborers of the Ruhr had to be supported. The tonnage of coal delivered to France after six months of occupation was equal to a prewar production of eleven days. As production fell, the economic disaster built. More paper money was produced to be sent chasing a declining supply of goods in order to support idle Ruhr workers.

The French were cruel masters. In Essen they fired on Krupp workers, killing thirteen. Although unarmed workers had been shot down, the official French view, reinforced by a military court, was that the French troops involved in the incident had been attacked.[11] French leaders proclaimed in response to British criticism that this was a matter of defending "our borders against a new rape."[12]

German resistance was not always passive. Some of those who had been opposing the Republic now worked against the French in the Ruhr. Acts of sabotage took place. French sentries were shot by snipers and French troops were stoned. Reprisals always followed. When a Duisburg bridge was blown up and nine people in a Belgian compartment on a train were killed, seven Germans were tried before a French military court and shot. In an Essen hotel, a young German, Albert Leo Schlageter, was arrested, taken for trial, tried, and executed. Despite the Nazis' general dislike of the Ruhr resistance as not being aimed at the proper enemy (the Weimar government in Berlin), Schlageter was adopted by the movement to serve as a martyr for the cause. In 1931, the party raised a monument to him in the Black Forest for propaganda purposes.

German papers reported regularly on French and Belgian activities. Sometimes lurid accounts described German civilians beaten, shot, or raped by occupations troops. Racists in Germany were alarmed because many occupying troops were black Africans. Rumors had it that these troops committed sexual offenses against German women. Actually, most of the colonial troops were miserable, as they were far from their African homes. They ventured into German society very little. Regular French troops were far more likely to be involved in such incidents. In the first six months of occupation, the government in Berlin reported that 92 Germans were killed and 71,000 expelled from their homes in the Ruhr.[13] In the Rhineland cities were yet another category of French colonials, North African Muslims. These colonial soldiers wore brightly colored clothes and turbans. Local inhabitants looked on with astonishment, in places where Christian churches were over a thousand years old, to see followers of Allah pushing Germans off the sidewalk.[14]

The German resistance was heroic, but the cards were stacked against it. The Berlin government could not continue to support the policy of no deliveries from the Reich's industrial breadbasket. The army was powerless to act against the French. Limited to 100,000 men by Versailles, it had no chance of fighting simultaneously in a two-front war against the vast numerical superiority of French and Polish arms. The Poles in fact threatened to invade Upper Silesia in the East.

The commander of the Reichswehr, Hans von Seeckt, told the British ambassador that, if the French tried to leave the Ruhr to march on Berlin, they would do so only by wading through a "sea of blood." This gauntlet was cast down and the French discovered through diplomatic channels that Seeckt meant to defend the whole *Reich* by any means possible. A numerically weak army could not hope to accomplish what Seeckt vowed. Thus, the High Command permitted the clandestine recruiting of volunteers from the great pool of desperadoes. Taken together, this assemblage of Free Corps, *Verbände*, and other groups constituted the "Black Reichswehr." And the Black Reichswehr could have absorbed a great many more groups than it did. A linking with the patriotic groups in Bavaria was possible. But even if an expanded Black Reichswehr was employed, there could have been no realistic notion of armed resistance against the overwhelming forces the French could deploy.

Seeckt was determined to achieve the survival of the German nation. The sole purpose of the Reichswehr was to ensure that it survived. Any talk of a Putsch, like that in Bavaria, tended to leave Seeckt unexcited. He offered his view at one cabinet meeting: "Gentlemen, in Germany no one can make a Putsch aside from myself, and I say to you I will not make one."[15] Seeckt meant to be the representative of the traditional German nationalists and enact their will. Most of the High Command of the Army stood behind Seeckt in his opposition to a Putsch. But not all. A notable exception was the chief of the Reichswehr division stationed in Bavaria, General Otto von Lossow.

Lossow represented particularistic Bavarian interests whenever they clashed with Berlin's. In Lossow's view, as well as Kahr's, the nationalistic formations in Bavaria, including the Nazis, were useful to pressure Bavaria's anti–Marxist movement in the correct direction. Other states might well outlaw a radical group like the Nazis, Bavaria's government would not. Lossow told Seeckt when he visited his commander in Berlin that the "patriotic" units had access to many weapons. Millions of rifles, machine guns, and other wartime weapons had never been destroyed or handed over to the Allies. Enormous stores of them were available in all Germany. Lossow looked upon the stockpiles in Bavaria as an arsenal for patriotic groups.

Five. The Failed Putsch

By the autumn of 1923, the Berlin government had faced crisis after crisis. There were separatist demonstrations in Aachen, Cologne, Wiesbaden, and Trier. It seemed at points that the old pre–1871 separation between Protestant and Catholic Germany was to be resurrected. There also were rebellious Communists in Saxony and Thuringia, allying with moderate leftists to enter state governments. This led many to conclude that Germany's Reds were using their legal status to pursue illegal goals. In the Pomeranian city of Kustrin, a major in the Black Reichswehr attempted a coup to overthrow Weimar. Most importantly for the rise of Nazism, the Bavarian government was set upon a collision course with the Reich government. The Right awaited the call to march on Berlin. While the ruling triumvirate wanted a separatist state centered on Munich, the Right in general (including the Nazis) wanted a nationwide solution to the German "problem."

There was no lack of emergencies nationally. Communists who had entered various state governments took secret instructions from Moscow. It was the view in Russia that an armed rising was only a matter of weeks away and the German Reds were to mobilize all resources.[16] In Bavaria, the Communists posed no threat. Instead, the Right saw its chance to sanitize the Reich and rid it of "alien" bodies. Meanwhile, the Weimar government tried to maintain the Republic against extremists. Seeckt warned that the army was not strong enough to fight both political extremes at once. But this is precisely what the government had to accomplish to save itself.

Reacting to the Reichswehr's hostility, the Nazi press made vicious attacks on Seeckt. One charge had it that Seeckt's wife was actually Jewish. As a result, the Berlin government ordered the *Völkischer Beobachter* to close. Since the paper was published in Bavaria, Lossow was ordered to make sure it shut its doors. Lossow was caught in the middle. He was bound to follow orders both from Berlin and the civilian authorities in Bavaria where Kahr forbade him to carry out his assignment from Seeckt. Lossow decided to obey Kahr. The Nazi paper continued publishing. Lossow was relieved of command from Berlin. In reply, the Bavarian government appointed him "Chief of Armed Forces" for the South German state. The right of any state to do this was more than questionable. Lossow continued down an unconstitutional path by swearing the Seventh Reichwehr Division's allegiance to Bavaria rather than the Reich.

In this manner, the Berlin government was confronted with mutiny in Bavaria and revolution in Saxony and Thuringia. Unable to fight on both fronts with a small military force, Stresemann and Seeckt picked the easier target—Saxony. The chancellor declared it was unconstitutional for a German state to permit Communists in its government. He ordered the regime in Saxony to resign. It refused the order. Communists took to the street where fourteen people were killed. The Reichswehr then marched into Saxony and Thuringia. Order was restored and the governments deposed.

The decisiveness of this action quieted Munich temporarily. Bavarian troops, including some under the command of Ehrhardt, had acted on Kahr's orders and assembled on the frontier with Saxony and Thuringia. Their plan was to kill two birds with one stone, to depose the two Red governments and then march on Berlin. But they had been anticipated. If they had invaded after the two regimes were removed, they would not be in confrontation with the inefficient formations of the Left, but rather the rest of the Reichswehr from outside Bavaria.

Seeckt now issued three communications, two addressed to his troops and one to Kahr. On 22 October 1923 he issued an order of the day indicating that Lossow had acted unconstitutionally. Any soldier accepting a role in the "Bavarian Army" was breaking his oath of loyalty to the Reich. On 4 November Seeckt then told the Reichswehr to obey its superiors and honor its allegiances. Seeckt told his commanders to make clear to their troops that army members who wished to engage in political activity were to leave the service to do so.[17]

Seeckt then wrote to Kahr on 5 November of 1923. Any change of government, he maintained, must come through legal means. He asked Kahr's cooperation in Seeckt's attempt to rescue the Fatherland from the gravest peril.[18] Kahr was no revolutionary. He was a monarchist who wanted to return to prewar days. He had tolerated Hitler and his Nazis, but he had no intention of moving in conjunction with radicals. He would have made use of the SA or any other combat formation, if he had needed them. But he saw himself as a representative of the Wittelsbachs now residing in exile. He therefore followed the communication between himself and Seeckt with a statement forbidding any kind of revolt to take place without orders. Lossow dutifully reinforced Kahr by saying he would use the Bavarian Reichswehr to put down a Putsch.[19]

Kahr called a meeting in the *Burgerbräukeller* for 8 November. In it he intended to unfold his new program. Hitler, for his part, had planned a mobilization of forces near Munich for the night of 10–11 November. They would then begin the revolution by marching into Munich. The idea was to gather like-minded forces and march northward, picking up *Verbände* as they went. But Kahr's announcement of the meeting changed Hitler's mind. With a small group of aides and members of other *Kampfbund* formations, Hitler appeared at the *Burgerbräukeller* on the night of 8 November. Kahr was never to finish his rambling speech in the *Burgerbräukeller* that night. As he spoke, Hitler led his followers through the crowd. He fired a shot into the ceiling to get the attention of the assembled. The triumvirate appeared unable to halt him.

The Nazi leader made a number of pronouncements, most of which were false. He claimed that a national revolution had been launched with the aim of taking over the Reich. He warned that the room was occupied by 600 armed men and no one would be allowed to leave. If the crowd was not still he would have a machine gun mounted on the gallery. The barracks of the army and the police, Hitler lied, were occupied by his forces. The police were said to be already moving toward the beer hall marching under the swastika.[20]

Hitler made more than one speech in the hall that night. After the first one, he forced Kahr, Lossow, and the third member of the Bavarian triumvirate, Hans Ritter von Seisser, to follow him into a side room. He proposed Kahr as regent and Ernst Pöhner, dismissed as police chief for his Nazi sympathies, as the new dictator of Bavaria. He urged an immediate march on Berlin with a force composed of all Bavarian military and paramilitary elements. Hitler argued to secure agreement from the triumvirate. Finally he thought he had their cooperation. He returned to the main hall. He was followed by Ludendorff, who had arrived late. Ludendorff, whatever doubts he might have had about being overshadowed by Hitler, announced that he was certain that "God would bless the enterprise." Then Kahr, who had returned to the main room, rose to say, however insincerely, that he would lead the revolt against Berlin.[21]

While these events unfolded in the beer barn, elsewhere in Munich out-of-control stormtroopers conducted a reign of terror. Social Democratic leader Erhard Auer's residence was broken into by SA men while he was absent, hiding. Hostages were taken throughout the city. The whole Bavarian cabinet was arrested. *Stosstrupp* Hitler vandalized the offices of

Shown here are participants of the 1923 Beer Hall Putsch. Note that all the images show SA men wearing makeshift uniforms. The brown shirts so associated with the formation were not obtained until the mid–1920s.

the socialist daily, the *Münchener Post*.[22] At the same time, back at the beer hall, Hitler made a considerable error by leaving to lead efforts elsewhere to take over barracks. With Hitler gone, the three reluctant hostages persuaded Ludendorff to accept their pledge to abide by the agreement. Ludendorff allowed them to leave the hall. When Hitler returned to the *Burgerbräukeller*, he was appalled to learn that the triumvirate had been set free.

Only one military objective was attained on the night of 8 November. Ernst Röhm and some 2,000 SA, *Bund Oberland,* and *Reichskriegflagge* men assembled at the *Lowenbräukeller* where they received the code word from the Burgerbräu to march in support of the coup. Then a courier arrived who ordered the group to seize and hold Military District headquarters. At the very front of Röhm's formation marched a nearsighted, spindly man named Heinrich Himmler. By this juncture, the Putsch was already failing. Once Kahr, Lossow, and Seisser had slipped away, the plot was bound to unravel. Lossow declared a general alarm and ordered outlying Reichswehr units into the city. Just before 3:00 A.M., the following message went out to all radio stations: "State Commission Generals ... repudiate the Hitler Putsch. Expressions of support extracted at gunpoint are invalid. Caution is urged against misuse of ... [our] names."[23]

This pronouncement was followed by Kahr's local proclamation indicating the same thing. Kahr then ordered the dissolution of the Nazi Party. He also announced a temporary move of the state government to Regensburg. In Berlin, there was a hastily convened cabinet meeting in the early hours of 9 November. Seeckt was vested with absolute authority to suppress the Munich revolt. Berlin now gave serious consideration to marching south to invade Bavaria.[24]

As the morning hours passed, the would-be revolutionaries gradually discovered that they had been betrayed. Hitler might have been a talented propagandist, but he now displayed unimpressive leadership qualities.[25] After some confusion during the morning, the Nazis at the Burgerbräukeller decided to march on the city to rouse the people. They hoped to convince the local Reichswehr to join them for the march on Berlin.

It was approaching noon on 9 November 1923 when a column of about 2,000 men set out for the center of city. One of the marchers admitted later that the column hardly inspired confidence, looking like a "defeated army that had not fought anybody."[26] When it reached the bridge over the Isar, it encountered the state police. The "Green Police," however, were confused by their orders and were overwhelmed by the marchers. This seemed to invigorate the column and it resumed marching. They continued toward military district headquarters.

One commander of the state police was determined to stop the column's progress. A tough young lieutenant, Michael von Godin, set his men to fire if the marchers would not stop. One of the marchers shouted to the police not to shoot because Ludendorff was coming.[27] Suddenly, a firefight commenced. Ulrich Graf, a loyal bodyguard, threw himself in front of Hitler to save his life. Graf was hit by eleven bullets. Göring was hit by a round in the groin, but escaped. Sixteen putschists were killed. Hitler escaped the scene to be arrested two days later outside of Munich. Hitler soon found that he was to be tried for high treason with other putschists, including Ludendorff. The Nazi leader realized that he might take propaganda advantage from such an event. He decided to use his trial ensure his prominence on the radical Right.

The Hitler *Putsch* was hardly a military operation. In fact, it had not been one from the outset. There had been a considerable reliance placed on theatrical demonstrations. And these had not worked as planned. Perhaps most importantly for the future of the party and its SA, the leader of Nazism had been forced to recognize that "political soldiers" were far too amateurish to pull off a coup opposed by professionals like those of the state police. He also had to have become aware that alliances made with egocentric Free Corps leaders treated as equals were not at all worthwhile.

Five. The Failed Putsch

The Beer Hall *Putsch* was part of a pattern seen many places in Europe during what has been called "the war after the war." In the years immediately after World War I, parts of Europe were involved in a kind of civil war. The specter of Bolshevism was raised at the Peace of Paris in 1919 by nearly every delegation. The major defeated powers (Germany, Austria, and Hungary) held that the tales of horror drifting westward about actions taken by the Bolsheviks against their enemies were true. And it was agreed among these powers that this terrible thing called Bolshevism might well sweep over the continent.

Populations responded with an excess of irrational hatreds. In this sort of atmosphere, someone in Weimar Germany who did not choose superpatriotism might well be denounced as a Bolshevik. The spread of this great fear developed an ideal climate in many countries for the military desperado and the putschist. Particularly was this true in Germany. The heyday of the postwar German desperado had ended by the time Hitler went on trial during 1924. In Italy, the desperado had attached himself to Benito Mussolini's fascism. In approximately two years' time, the party he backed had established its initial grasp on power. The corresponding phase in the history of the Nazi movement was 1919–1923. During that period, the Free Corps and/or the Reichswehr had subdued revolutionary factions of the Left throughout Germany. The Nazis remained a provincial party which had mounted an abortive putsch.

On 24 February 1924, the "Hitler Trial" for high treason opened. The defendants, beside Adolf Hitler, included Ernst Röhm, several Kampfbund leaders, Ernst Pöhner, Wilhelm Frick (later to become a prominent Party leader), and Ludendorff. From the outset, Hitler and his colleagues benefited from the fact that the Minister of Justice, Franz Gürtner, was openly sympathetic to the Nazis. They also benefited from the fact that the major witnesses testifying for the prosecution—Kahr, Lossow, and Seisser—had themselves been involved in the earlier stages of the putsch.[28]

The presiding judge was Gregory Neithardt, a fervent nationalist who regarded Ludendorff as a national treasure.[29] The lay judges were blatantly open in their support of the putschists. The defendants became aware that the climate inside and outside the courtroom was favorable to them. The Nazi leader thus took the offensive as soon as the trial opened. Unlike Ludendorff, who tried to prove that his role in the *Putsch* was that of an unwitting participant, Hitler took an opposite tack. He proudly admitted culpability. He attacked the witnesses by claiming that Kahr, Seisser, and Lossow shared his goal of "the removal of the Reich government" and thus had also committed high treason.[30]

Among those attacked by Hitler during the course of the trial, only Lossow had an effective counterargument. He accused Hitler of trying to be a "German Mussolini."[31] But Hitler replied that Lossow was a coward and a "turncoat," causing even this very partial judge to reprimand him for excesses.[32] Hitler was allowed to make closing remarks where, as he had so often in the beer halls, he painted himself as a man of destiny. He pointed out that the *Putsch* had not been a defeat, but rather a stepping-stone to ultimate victory. He tried to speak to those beyond the courtroom by saying that only the "eternal court of history" was fit to pass judgment on him.[33] Hitler then profited from the tolerant attitude of the Bavarian judicial system. Incredibly lenient sentences were handed down. The stated cause for such treatment had to do with the Nazi leader's "pure patriotic motives." He was then sentenced to five years in prison with the almost certain potential of parole within six to twelve months.[34] The bias of the court can easily be demonstrated by a comparison. Shortly before the putsch trial, one Felix Fechenbach was sentenced to eleven years hard labor for making public a telegram that was years old and not damaging to authorities because it had long since been exposed in the press. But Fechenbach was of the Left. The sentences of the other conspirators were equally lenient. Kriebel and Pöhner received terms similar to Hitler's. Others, like Röhm, were given fifteen months, but were paroled quickly. Ludendorff was exonerated altogether. When these verdicts were handed down, there were shouts of "bravo" in the courtroom.

From 11 November 1923 to 20 December 1924, Adolf Hitler was in a minimum-security setting, the prison fortress of Landsberg about fifty miles west of Munich. Imprisoned with him were some forty Nazis. It was a commodious incarceration. There were comfortable cells. Some of them had views of the surrounding countryside. The prisoners were given decent food, beer, and wine. Landsberg quickly became a beehive of Nazi Party activity. Cells were decorated with Nazi emblems and personal pictures. At meals, the Nazis would gather in a common room like a family. Party inmates were given considerable free time to play cards, engage in sports, and take walks in the prison garden. They organized an orchestra, put out an in-house newspaper, and otherwise amused themselves.[35]

In contrast to the leisure-oriented behavior of his comrades, Hitler spent most of his time in Landsberg reflecting on the past and plotting for the future. He had so much time to do this that he later called this experience his "university education at government expense."[36] In fact Hitler responded so well to a prison routine where his fellow inmates made his bed and saw to his needs that he gained weight and had time to write his political testament.

Hitler had always shown great preference for the spoken over the printed word. In spite of his past preference for impassioned oratory, he now appeared eager to establish his "intellectual" credentials. He set out to prove that, despite his lack of formal education, he was a serious thinker. Starting in the summer of 1924, he spent hours every day dictating his thoughts to fellow inmates, particularly Rudolf Hess. Once he began to compile a substantial amount of material he came up with his first title, albeit a long and clumsy one: "Four and a Half Years of Struggle Against Lies, Stupidity, and Cowardice." In time, his publisher shortened it to *Mein Kampf* ("My Struggle"). The book was finished by the time he left prison in December of 1924, but the somewhat inchoate manuscript had to be pruned and corrected by several editors. Some detractors poked fun at the book when it appeared, suggesting it should have been called *Mein Krampf* ("My Cramp"), because of the turgid style.[37]

Because of its stylistic and organizational shortcomings, many contemporaries underrated the importance of *Mein Kampf*. It was verbose, difficult to read, often dull, full of the pseudo-intellectual tricks of the half-educated person.[38] This judgment, while sound, obscures the fact that the substance of *Mein Kampf* became part of the public perception of political reality. And the work is not devoid of content.[39] The style of *Mein Kampf* is intensely aggressive and propagandistic. It was badly written, so badly, in fact, that one expert in the German language has counted 164,000 errors in grammar and syntax.[40] But the book managed an attempt at an articulation of a coherent ideological profile for Nazism.

This profile was constructed of a system of prejudices rather than a philosophy based on principles. The work did become over time a major tool to draw elements of the mass society into Nazism. This was not done directly, but rather through the words of party propagandists spreading throughout the nation to repeat endlessly a few notions drawn from its pages. These constantly mentioned maxims can be summarized as follows:

(1) the Aryan race is both culturally and biologically superior, the cultural superiority deriving from innate racial characteristics;
(2) the discernible design seen in nature, shaping all species, is Darwinistic in character and, for humans, Social Darwinistic;
(3) the strengths and weakness of humankind are based on "blood," qualities such as intelligence rooted in "racial purity";
(4) the human race divides into three distinct and different groups: Aryan culture founders, culture bearers, and culture destroyers; and
(5) Jews have no real culture of their own nor or they capable of creating one, thus being forced to live a furtive existence replicating the norms of the cultures within which their "rootless" people reside.

Hitler believed in common with many of the anti–Semites of his time in a Jewish world conspiracy which was reported in the pages of an infamous nineteenth-century forgery entitled *The Protocols of the Elders of Zion*. Every destructive tendency seen in society was therefore the work of the scheming Jew, whether he be the moneylender, leftist, parliamentary democrat, pacifist, or a Bolshevik. Sometimes his hatred took on sexual connotations as in the case when he held that "bow-legged Jewish bastards" were lurking behind the corners of dark allies, hiding in wait to rape Aryan girls.[41] As were many drawn to Nazism, Hitler was passionate in his conviction that a peoples' historical greatness depended upon purity of blood. The new state, when established, had a mission to "breed" the most racially pure "specimens." After defining who should be in the new state, *Mein Kampf* continued to make clear at the outset that the *völkisch* state had to be based on the principle of solitary authority rather than majorities. The state should be organized from top to bottom like a military command with a person at the apex of the pyramid who decided everything for everyone. What was offered was dictatorship. Effective organizations, whether political, economic, or educational, were to be governed by strong leaders at every level.[42] In the Hitlerian view, this contrasted with decadent Western style democracy and portrayed a true "German Democracy." In this new polity, the leader was to be "freely" chosen by the people to exercise absolute power.[43]

Hitlerian foreign policy ideals were essentially Pan-German. Germany had no future unless it acquired living space. Unlike prewar imperialists who desired colonies in what would later be called the Third World, he sought to create colonial territories within Europe itself. He believed that French policy toward Germany had not changed since the days of Louis XIV. All French statesman desired to balkanize Germany into small states. German foreign policy, in the face of this attitude from its Western neighbor, had always to be controlled by three precepts: Berlin should work to align itself with Italy and Great Britain against France; break the chains of Versailles; and secure *Lebensraum* (living space) in eastern Europe. The political aims enunciated in *Mein Kampf*, in contrast to some of the foggy ideological assertions, were crystal clear.

In domestic policies, the breeding of a higher race of people was proposed. In international affairs, Germany would be elevated to a level of world power by dominating the core of what interwar geopoliticians liked to call the "Earth Island." In most of the conceptions of these theorists, the Earth Island was thought to be all Europe as far east as the Urals. Before all that could be accomplished, however, a successful movement had to be erected built upon the manipulated masses. Propaganda was the primary means to that end. The function of propaganda in the new state was to hammer precepts home by endless repetition of a few unelaborate ideas. It is far more effective to appeal to the emotions than the rational capacities of people. This can always be accomplished most effectively through the spoken word. The masses could be shaped into the proper mold because of the fact that the "people in the overwhelming majority are so feminine in their nature and attitude that their activities and thoughts are motivated less by sober consideration than by feeling and sentiment."[44]

The view of women expressed in these thoughts reflects Hitler's gender bias. He saw females as "weak" and persuaded effectively only when all doubt was expunged. Eventually, it could be said in truth that propaganda, held to be so important in *Mein Kampf*, was the major builder of the Third Reich. It could also be said that it helped to destroy that Reich. The themes described here replaced normal thinking for much of the mass base that supported Nazism. People were urged to react to all matters through instinct rather than rational evaluation. Intellectuals were a source of danger to the new state so they had to be controlled or removed from important positions.

In actual practice the Nazi's crude prejudice that the lower levels of society were "healthier" than the "overeducated apes" without "sound instinct," of the upper orders became a very practical position.[45] The Nazis offered recruitment and promotion to people of the masses based solely on race and political correctness. Entrusted with absolute power, in time, Hitler would follow the blueprint laid down in *Mein Kampf*.

While Hitler created *Mein Kampf* and served his time with his colleagues in Landsberg fortress, the Nazi Party fell apart.[46] Hitler was largely to blame. Behind bars, he hibernated rather than acting through emissaries with whom he had contact to hold his forces together. As long as he could not exercise direct control, he preferred disarray. And this was the state of affairs within Nazism when he emerged from jail.

Chapter Six

The Years of Preparation (1924–1930)

When Hitler stepped out of Landsberg Fortress, the emergence of the masses into Nazism was a remote dream revealed only in *Mein Kampf*. What remained of the party was still tied to its Bavarian base. Actually, the Munich police and the Bavarian government wanted to have the Nazi leader deported to his native Austria as soon as he had returned. In September of 1924, a Bavarian official contacted Austrian authorities and broached the idea of Hitler returning. The Austrians replied that they had no wish to see Hitler reappear. A bit later, officials from the lower administration in Vienna informed Munich that the leader of Nazism, if sent, would simply be put back across the German border.[1] The following year, after a visit to Vienna, Hitler moved to make any attempt to repatriate him to his native Austria an impossibility. He submitted a formal request that his Austrian citizenship be revoked. The Austrian government was only too happy to do this and he became stateless until 1932.

The climate in Munich had changed markedly since the departure of the Nazis in 1923. Kahr had been replaced as General Commisar by Eugen von Knilling and then Heinrich Held. Held remained in control of Bavaria for the next nine years, enjoying a reasonable popularity. The mayor of Munich was Karl Scharnagl, who, like Held, continued in office until the Nazi takeover in 1933.

Along with administrative changes tending toward stability, came the stabilization of the currency through the introduction of the *Rentenmark* in late 1923. Then, in the spring of 1924, the Dawes Plan (named after American banker Charles Dawes) had refinanced German reparations payments. At the same time foreign loans were made available to help the economy. These policies also had an impact in Munich by 1924 and local businesses did better. Throughout Germany, despite the reforms, there existed a lingering malaise. Munich was no different. Too many people had been damaged by inflation to allow for easy recovery. The citizenry had to begin from economic ground zero. There was little capital for investment. In comparison, Berlin had moved ahead more rapidly and this factor caused Bavarian jealousy to surface.

On his return, Hitler did not perceive how much things had changed. Those tactics he and his party used to move the masses behind them came from observations of how the Left had accomplished the building of a lasting membership. The general situation provided a climate unfavorable for that strategy. When Held allowed the Nazi Party to continue he asked Hitler to refrain from attacks on the church and the government. The reply was that Nazism had only Marxism as an enemy. Another claim was that the *Putsch* had simply been General Ludendorff's fault. Held was skeptical but agreed to lift the ban on the party and its newspaper.[2] Almost immediately, Held had cause to regret his decision. On 27 February 1925, Hitler delivered a speech before 3,000 people in the *Burgerbräukeller*. It indicated just how much the Nazis had missed the change in the times. He came close to threatening future violence against the Republic.[3] This Nazi tendency to return to the style of 1923 resulted in a ban on Hitler's speaking in public.

One of the challenges facing the party was whether it should be moved beyond Munich. Hitler was forced to travel outside of Bavaria to appear in public and avoid the speaking ban. But the Nazi leader declared his intention to keep the party headquarters in Munich. That city had borne witness, he maintained emotionally, to the "martyrdom" of the movement.[4]

The decision to remain centered in Munich caused considerable controversy within National Socialism.[5] Hitler's conversations with Held had convinced other like-minded radicals to believe that Hitler was overly inclined to make bargains with officials. Captain Ehrhardt summed up the suspicious feelings many northerners harbored for Hitler by calling the Nazi leader "an Austrian" and, hence, not a "true German."[6]

The *Frontbann*

For old followers like Ernst Röhm, Hitler was in error to abandon the *Putsch* as the path to power. Once the 1923 *Putsch* had failed, the various elements of the German radical-racist Right milled about in apparent confusion. As for the SA, after the *Putsch* attempt when the Nazi Party was declared illegal, the paramilitary wing was also proscribed. The Bavarian state government did not lift its ban on both the party and its SA until 1925.[7] Various bands of paramilitary men tried to fill the gap. Ehrhardt attempted to pull the dispersed remnants of the dissolved *Kampfbund* under his control as part of the Viking organization. He failed.[8] And others were similarly unsuccessful.

The SA was the hardest hit of the paramilitary *Kampfbund* organizations. Not only was it prohibited, but it had severe organizational problems. Its remnants turned to Röhm who began to work with the Sturmabteilung as early as April of 1924 (the same month as his release from custody). In mid May, SA leaders met in Salzburg and Röhm established himself as the leader of the paramilitary remnants of the *Kampfbund*, although he was not officially designated as the occupant of that role.[9] The Salzburg conference (11–18 May 1924) issued guidelines for a reorganized SA. In true Freikorps form, the conferees agreed that regional and local commanders would be given considerable autonomy in their own SA units.[10]

The immediate response to the entreaties of Röhm and others like him was to think again in terms of an overarching formation like the *Kampfbund* to pull in scattered paramilitary elements previously associated with Nazism or the broader racist-nationalist movement. There had already been an attempt in Bavaria to do this sort of thing with a formation called the *Deutscher Schützen und Wanderbund*. It had also failed to replace the *Kampfbund*.[11]

Röhm made several attempts to convince Bavarian authorities that the SA should be legalized. With Hitler in Landsberg prison, after Röhm was released, the former army captain became part of the effort to reunite the broad racist-nationalist movement's Free Corps remnants by asking them initially to swear loyalty oaths to Ludendorff.[12] Röhm's next step was to establish the *Frontbann* ("Front Band"). This was to be a centralized organization covering all of Germany.[13]

Rohm's *Frontbann* was to be a strong military force serving as a support for Nazism when it reemerged from the shadows. Actually, the *Frontbann* was meant to be only a part of a looser organization called the Front Ring, meant to include a division for older veterans and a youth formation. The Frontbann had four regional headquarters in Berlin, Halle, Munich and Salzburg. The Frontbann was also meant to serve, if possible, in secret combination with Reichswehr forces.[14] This was perhaps the most overly ambitious goal asserted and the one which failed most suddenly. Röhm, although a former officer, had not been able to recreate pre-putsch connections with his old army colleagues.

When Hitler initially learned about the building of the *Frontbann*, he doubted the value for Nazism to be found in such a project. After all, Röhm wished to build an organization which was to be, like the Reichswehr, above politics.[15] Röhm was motivated by an attitude developed in the pre-putsch *Verbände*, which was distrustful of politics. He meant to build the Frontbann, including the SA, as a roof formation which could, at one and the same time, serve high political goals even as it excluded political activity in its ranks. He tried at one point to make Hitler, in the manner of the disbanded *Kampfbund*, political leader for the Front Band while Ludendorff would remain enshrined as "leader." This would be the formal face of the Frontbann even as Röhm ran day-to-day affairs. Ludendorff quickly refused to reestablish what was essentially the pre-putsch situation with the potential of leading to another abortive coup. Röhm apparently never saw the apparent contradictions in his proposal. Others did. He continued to make the claim that, in the post–*Putsch völkisch* world, the Frontbann was constructed to serve as a politically neutral formation. But this was not widely believed. Some of the paramilitary leaders refused to join the Frontbann or did join it and began to quarrel regularly with Röhm as soon as they did.

Soon after its formation, the *Frontbann* was troubled by internal strife. One critic claimed that the organization appeared to be dividing internally along class lines.[16] The larger *völkisch* movement of which the *Frontbann* was a part was troubled by internal fractionation. Röhm had hoped to use the Front Band to hold it all together. He failed. The *völkisch* movement collapsed and caused the *Frontbann* to break into northern and southern components.[17]

In September of 1924, Bavarian authorities moved against the Frontbann and began arresting some of its members. As this transpired, Hitler was busy reorganizing the Nazi Party. To him, both Röhm and Ludendorff, if they pursued courses outside the limits for Nazi activities he had established, constituted a liability. Hitler also considered it a problem that whole companies of the *Frontbann*, at Röhm's urging, were adding themselves to the SA lists. Many of the Frontbann leaders, who now also became SA leaders, displayed a tendency which became known over the short term as the "SA spirit." This development immediately drew Hitler's disapproval. This spirit was dynamic, ruthless, aggressive, and anti-bourgeois. This disturbed Hitler at a time when he wished to make inroads among the middle class of Germany.

These men displayed their Free Corps heritage by being ready for action of any sort. They could easily get out of hand and threaten the newly reconstituted legality of the Nazi Party. As Röhm became disgusted with the fractionation of the *völkisch* movement and the sundering of the *Frontbann*, he resigned from both posts in the *Frontbann* and the SA.[18] When Hitler began to reorganize the party in early 1925, he made it clear that the *Frontbann* would play no part in his plans. On 26 February the reconstituted *Völkischer Beobachter* announced the rules and regulations involved in shaping the new SA.[19]

While this transpired, the Nazi leader met with Röhm and offered him the leadership role in the new SA to be constructed completely within the party with no links to any other formation or political organization. Discussions followed concerning the nature of the relationship between the paramilitary and the party. By April of 1925, Röhm was still insisting that the SA be taken under the roof of the *Frontbann* and that the Front Band should enjoy independent status in the movement. Hitler would not brook independence. Among other potential problems, an out-of-control paramilitary could have led him and his party back into the world of the putsch, a realm he had learned to avoid after the debacle of 1923. Röhm then left the *Frontbann* and SA behind him. A number of young officers followed his example and what remained of the roof formation after that fell apart. According to party sources, however, the *Frontbann* was active as late as August of 1925 and there were still Nazis in it. One party history of the SA reports a clash with the Reichsbanner of the SPD on Berlin's Kurfurstendamm. In this instance one Nazi, a man named Werner Doelle, was reportedly killed.[20] Whether this is an accurate accounting of events or not, the reorganization of the SA did not rank highly on the party's to-do list and was left low on the party-planning inventory until 1926.

In sum, what had happened was that, as it became legal to reestablish the SA, Hitler insisted it be loyal to the party only and that it cut links to any other paramilitary formation. Röhm rejected this position and resigned from the movement, although he would return to it a few years later. In the short term, he was a salesman for a time and even worked in a factory. He then accepted an invitation to join other former officers on a journey to Bolivia where they acted as advisers charged with demonstrating for local commanders how the Germans made war.

Despite the fact that Hitler wanted the *Frontbann* to be detached from the Nazi Party in 1925, because he saw it as a continuing hindrance to gaining political goals, membership in it was later commemorated by the Nazis. In 1932, the so-called *Frontbann* badge began to be awarded to Nazis who had been members in it. Most of these by this time held SA leadership positions at various levels. However, when the SA was purged in 1934, it was no longer authorized for wear.[21]

The Nazis' Potential Schism

At this point, there appeared something of a North-South split in Nazism. In the North, Gregor Strasser, a former pharmacist from Landshut, was placed in charge of a party now organized nationally into districts (*Gaue*). The most notable among the district officials at this point was Joseph Goebbels. Strasser, backed by Goebbels, thought that the Nazis ought to take the "socialism" part of National Socialism more seriously. Strasser had in mind ushering the masses into Nazism through a combination of Nationalism and Socialism, developing an appeal like the SPD. But, it was hoped, the Nazis could go beyond the SPD by using nationalism to draw in patriotic workers.[22]

With historical tides deemed to be running in favor of the Republic, the ban placed on Hitler's speaking was removed. He could now make speeches in Bavaria where the far Right maintained a hard kernel of followers. But its leadership in Bavaria was divided and acrimonious. The infighting among those who wanted to dominate the entirety of the Right was bitter. And the Nazis were quickly drawn into an intense competition.

While Hitler had been in prison, Alfred Rosenberg, the weakest and least threatening person to Hitlerian dominance over Nazi affairs, was allowed to keep the Party together in something called "The Greater German Peoples' Community." Soon, this organization was proclaimed the National Socialist Freedom Movement. The most important leader of this new substitute organization was Gregor Strasser, although Ludendorff gave his name to be used as a presidential candidate. It was this rightist faction which, by the end of 1924, could only draw just under three percent of the vote in a national election. After this debacle, Ludendorff quit the movement in 1925.

The party had an image problem. Many on the Right were still traditional monarchists. Both the radical and traditional Rights saw a need for full-scale change. It appeared that none of these *völkisch* factions could tolerate opposition, as all owned a full-blown ideological stance. For all on the Right you were a foe if you did not agree totally with their views. There was also something of this tendency briefly within Nazism as it developed factions. The more "bourgeois" elements of the Right behind Hitler were arrayed against the Left of the party behind Strasser and Goebbels. This reflected in many ways the broad division nationally between traditionalists and radicals on the Right. It also gave the lie to the notion that only the Left splintered into factions.

Within National Socialism, acrimonious storms raged over policy issues. Goebbels, for example, denounced Hitler as a "little bourgeois" who ought to be expelled. As *Mein Kampf* revealed, Hitler's views on the future of the Soviet Union were negative. But Goebbels and Strasser had a more benevolent view, liking the utopianism of the Russian leadership. Strasser actually desired an alliance with Russia against the French and British. Nazism was thus divided in many ways during 1925. The main point of contention had to do with whether or not the property of the former princes in Germany should be taken without compensation. The Communists and the Social Democrats had drafted a bill in 1926 calling for confiscation. A petition signed by more than 12.5 million voters was presented in favor of a referendum on the issue. But that proposal was defeated in a popular vote. The left wing of the Nazi Party, including Strasser and Goebbels, also wanted the land confiscated for public use. But Hitler did not agree.[23]

Hitler was backing the traditionalist position for a practical reason. All politicians need money to stand for election. The old Right was a far better source of money than any radical element. He therefore revised the party's position to side with paid compensation for the aristocrats. Goebbels was enraged. When Hitler spoke at a party meeting in Bamberg during February 1926, Goebbels asked in his diary what kind of Nazi Hitler actually might be. Was he not a true National Socialist, but simply a reactionary? He had heard Hitler speak of destroying Bolshevism. Hitler had spoken on property rights, holding that even those of a former German prince should be inviolable. Goebbels went so far at that point to demand Hitler's expulsion from the party.[24]

Goebbels had derived his economic views from men like Gregor Strasser. Strasser was a man who believed much more in class warfare than did Hitler. In a rough sort of way, Hitler had once been closer to this view. Nazism was, in its origins, a movement designed to replace the old order with a sense of community. In the new community, birth and money would be meaningless. The problem now for the Munich leadership was that there were still too many who took the socialistic side of National Socialism seriously. Gregor Strasser's idea of the Nazi community to come was one where birth and money would not be decisive.

Hitler had invited his dissidents to Bamberg on 14 February 1926. He meant to use the meeting to reconstitute his dictatorial control. Although the dissidents did not cave in to Hitler that day, their opposition faded soon after. Goebbels appeared particularly impressive to Hitler and he went to work to draw him away from their ranks. He wined and dined him. He let him speak at party meetings. By April, he had made him into a devoted follower.[25]

Only Hitler could resolve the contradictions in the party. Without Hitler's centralizing control, there existed too many extreme and contradictory views. For his part, Hitler could change course easily, in the manner of many politicians. This was to be seen in his views on private property. When the "unchangeable program" of Nazism had been declared in the 1920s, in it was the leftist-sounding idea that land not put to "productive" use should be taken from its owners. In 1928, the NSDAP wooed Bavarian peasants. An "outdated" platform was a liability. Hitler switched. Like the princes, the peasants should be able to keep their land no matter how they used it. Private property as a basic right was restored in the Nazi program, raised to the level of sanctity. Hitler now reinterpreted point 10 of his "Unchangeable Program." It was not meant to be an attack against all dealing in real estate, but only "Jewish speculators."

Hitler had learned much from the failed *Putsch* of 1923. He had learned to speak softly to authorities, especially when one could not back a challenge with force. The National Socialists were able now to win some recruits, with internal quarrels moderated. It was still a problem, however, to keep followers' revolutionary sentiments under control and their utterances in public within the bound of decorum. There was, for example, a Berlin meeting where such disorder ensued that the party was banned in that city for nearly a year. This brought with it, even though he was not at the meeting, a decree forbidding Hitler to speak in Prussia. Actually many of Hitler's speeches were less decorous than those of his followers. But because of the public bans, he had to make them in closed meetings.

Once he was free to speak again in Bavaria, Hitler returned to public meetings, but he did not draw the expected crowds. The 1927 situation caused the Nazis to return to the tendency seen among political factions before the putsch; the numbers of people at meetings were inflated in the party media. At the annual rally in Nuremberg in 1927, for instance, it was claimed that some 30,000 Stormtroopers and a total of 100,000 party faithful were present. As far as the SA was concerned, police estimates of its strength at the rally were around 9,000. This revealed clearly that the party could not justifiably claim the numbers it often did. It was growing slowly, remaining just below the 100,000 mark for the nation. This situation ensured that it would not fare well in national elections during 1928, receiving only a minor percentage of the vote.[26]

The Weimar system was one where voters were scattered among thirty-one political parties in 1928. The so-called "Automatic Procedure," in use since shortly after the war, meant that any party could receive one seat in the Reichstag for every 60,000 ballots cast for it. Many parties obtained only one seat or two. There were very small parties on every ballot whose aims had little to do with shaping the government. Some parties were splinters of splinters. Only on larger issues like the foreign policy of reconciliation practiced by Foreign Minister Gustav Stresemann could a majority be formed in the Reichstag. These majorities were unstable alliances that held only if there were no major problems.

In the May 1928 elections, the vote cast for the Right generally and the radical Right specifically dropped sharply. It was a typical Weimar election. There was a moderate drift in most of these from Right to Left or the reverse. This time the shift was toward the Left. The Social Democrats and the Communists made decent gains. Typical of Weimar politics was the fact that a government could be built only through a broad coalition. This one was a particularly fractious combination including Democrats, Centrists, the "Peoples Party," and a mix of middle-class and labor parties. It was certain that it would have a difficult time if differences arose. Despite this, the so-called "Grand Coalition" stayed in power for two years (1928–30). And this was longer than any postwar government before Hitler was appointed chancellor in 1933.

Despite the somewhat better times reflected in the short-term stability of the Grand Coalition, underlying problems persisted. The losses of the inflationary year (1923) had never been made good. Germany had been living the last few years on borrowed money. If the Republic suffered any kind of financial crisis, many short-term credits would be withdrawn. Germany would be bankrupt. In a press conference, Stresemann said Germany was "not only militarily disarmed" but "financially disarmed."[27]

Whatever underlying problems existed, on the surface the Republic appeared in reasonable health. Accordingly, events did not work out well for Hitler and his party. Articles appeared in the press proclaiming the demise of Nazism. The Nazis, after participating in the 1928 elections, could count just twelve delegates in the Reichstag. The German nationalists could elect only 73 with a more traditional Rightist message. Much more electoral strength was demonstrated in the center and the Left.

The electoral shift to the Left transpired as voters remained unaware of the economic danger signs on the horizon that Stresemann had identified. But these were certainly in evidence. Agriculture was doing well in some areas, but not in others. The debts of East Prussian landowners and farmers rose some 80 Presidat million marks in 1927. All interest rates for bank loans were high. Taxes were burdensome. President Hindenburg and those who advised him set out to help. Long-term credits were proposed for farm holdings. Lower taxes and cheaper shipping rates were proposed. These were installed for troubled areas Another soft spot in the economy was increasing unemployment. Only in 1925 had it fallen beneath a million. In January of 1926 and 1927, the number had risen to over two million. It reached some three million in early 1929. But on the whole, production had been rising steadily. Real wages for the first time reached their prewar level of 1913–14 in 1928. Per-capita income was the highest it had been. But large segments of the working electorate were still dissatisfied. The increased Communist vote reflected this lack of satisfaction.

On the Right was the sizeable veterans' organization, the quite substantial *Stahlhelm*, associated with the nationalists. The *Stahlhelm*'s political stance was revealed in a manifesto published in October of 1928: "We hate with all our soul the present state structure, its form, its content, its development, its nature." The manifesto continued to enumerate Republican defects and called for building a "strong" state. The *Stahlhelm* remedy for changing the state structure was not a putsch. Their answer was a plebiscite on the constitution.[28]

The *Stahhelm* presented a problem for Hindenburg and he did not reprimand them for taking a stance against the Republic he served. They were still bound to the Kaiser by oath. But Hindenburg appeared capable of reconciling their devotion to the old fatherland, which he shared, and his duty to Weimar. In his thinking, they were not precisely the same thing.

Hindenburg would always feel himself close to the *Stahlhelm,* an association of his old veteran "comrades in arms." On receiving assurances that the organization intended no action against the Republic, he remained a member.

Hindenburg did not bend easily. When nationalists attacked him for accepting the Locarno pact, he paid no attention, even though it was a treaty he also disliked. In sum, bristling problems remained for the Weimar Republic. The German state was not yet rescued from its past illness, but it was clearly in remission. As long as this state of remission lasted, the Nazis could not become a major player in the politics of the Republic.

The Nazis continued the work of building their movement. By the summer of 1926, Hitler had regained complete dictatorial control of the party. Between 1926 and 1928, Hitler and Gregor Strasser imposed a uniform structure on Nazism by dividing the nation into *Gaue* (districts), solidifying top leadership positions, and moving into cities in the north and west. Hitler chose to ignore the Left of the party as it continued to desire actions against capitalist sources the other side of the party wished to expolit.[29]

Under the so-called "Urban Plan," the organizational and electoral focus was concentrated on the industrialized Ruhr, Berlin, Hamburg, and Thuringia-Saxony. These were areas where the Left was strong. The weakest links in the Nazi organizational chain were in Berlin and Hamburg with their concentrations of leftists. In both cities the Nazi effort was in disarray. To attempt the penetration of the Left's hold on Berlin, Hitler made Goebbels *Gauleiter* of the city. He was to transform "Red" Berlin into a party bastion for the Nazis. Goebbels' "Battle of Berlin," however, was marked by too much extremist propaganda and the use force with the brawling local SA the instrument. When the party became overly menacing, a seeming threat to public safety, it was banned by the authorities.[30]

Goebbels, whether the party was under ban for short periods or not, began to spread the party message through *Der Angriff* ("The Attack") where he simply put his stump speeches on paper.[31] It is in this paper that one can find the clearest exposition of where Nazism stood on the Weimar Republic. In Goebbels' thinking: "We are an anti-parliamentary party and we reject for good reason the Weimar Republic.... We go into the Reichstag in order to obtain the weapons of democracy.... We become Reichstag deputies in order to paralyze the Weimar mentality with its own help."[32]

The Nazi Party of the late 1920s has been the subject of a great many differing interpretations. Until fairly recently, most historians have agreed with the early social analysis of Nazism; it was a "lower-middle-class amalgamation of small shopkeepers, teachers, some professional people, farmers and craftsmen." Actually, this formulation is just about as old as the Third Reich itself.[33] More recent studies of voting patterns have revealed a broadly based populist party forming during this period. Such a party was something of a novelty in German history where political parties catered to narrow interests. The Nazis appeared to have drawn people of differing classes by means of organizational effectiveness. And it was this organization, with this new umbrella movement, which would, during the Depression, help the masses emerge into Nazism.

By 1928, without an outside stimulus having been provided, this concept of a party had not helped the "Urban Plan." It was now abandoned after the dismal election showing. The party switched to a rural scheme. Most Germans still lived in villages and towns in 1928. They tended to be more nationalistic than urban dwellers. With a smaller expenditure of energy, money, and time, these people could be pursued effectively. In 1925, the Nazis encouraged an "organic" development of *Gaue* in those parts of Germany where strong organization could gather a following. The term *Gau* derives from an old German custom of dividing land and people into specific regions. After the party's abysmal showing in the election of May 1928, Hitler decided to revamp the organizational structure in order to reach his electoral goals. The *Gaue* were then more closely aligned with the electoral districts of Germany.

The organizational ideas of 1928 appear to have been modeled on what Nazis believed was the medieval-feudal relationship between knights and vassals. In return for his bestowed *Gau* (fief), the *Gauleiter* (knight) owed specific fealties to his Nazi overlord. These normally were recruiting, raising money, and educating people.[34] Provided with considerable autonomy within his region, the *Gauleiter* was the personal agent of Hitler. Whatever organizational changes transpired, the party was still multi-form in nature. For example, it increasingly developed a modern bureaucracy while never losing what one might call the "bureaucratic romanticism" seen in the feudal models upon which it depended. This romanticism was also seen in the officially charismatic nature of the party. It developed a personalized style of leadership wherein the "Leader" (Führer) demanded homage based on his "myth figure" status.

To some extent this multi-form party of 1928–29 was also modeled on governmental institutions. There was a Reich Directorate commanded by Hitler and his secretary Rudolf Hess. There was a treasurer, Franz Xaver Schwartz, and a secretary-general, Philipp Bouhler. Gregor Strasser directed electioneering. The institutional mechanisms by which the party could, once in power, transform itself and Germany were assigned to Colonel Konstantin Hierl, a former Free Corps leader. One can, in fact, look at the 1928–30 organizational chart and envisage the future leadership of the Reich. There was Otto Dietrich, the future press chief; Hans Frank, chief of the party's Legal Affairs Office; and Walter Darré, an agricultural "expert." Not involved in the daily operations were Hermann Göring and Wilhelm Frick.

Göring had been absent for almost four years, in exile in Austria and Sweden. He returned to Germany to resume his party activity. Without any money of his own, Göring soon established himself in Berlin as a sales representative for BMW. Finally, in 1928, he became one of twelve Nazi Reichstag deputies. His rise to power within the party had begun. Frick had been involved in the 1923 putsch, but was able to escape a prison term by moving into an "immune" Reichstag seat in 1924. In 1928 he won a Reichstag seat again. In 1930, he became both interior minister and education minister in Thuringia. In his job as education minister he inveighed regularly against "nigger" and "jazz" (obviously French) music and cultures. Between 1928 and 1929, the Nazi Party also expanded its ancillary organizations.

The aim of ancillaries was to draw every German into some facet of the party's activities. The youth organization was expanded and became the "Hitler Youth" (*Hitlerjugend* or "HJ"). This organization had branches for both boys and girls. A Nazi student league (*Deutscher Studentbund*) was established. The leadership of this youth section was entrusted to Baldur von Schirach. Specific professional organizations were established. Included among these was a "Teachers' League," a "Physician's League," and an association of Nazi lawyers. The image meant to be portrayed was of a disciplined and uniformed force, resolutely led by Hitler. This image was to be fixed in the public mind with marches, uniforms, and party congresses. In 1927, the first of the Nuremberg party congresses was held. These mass meetings involved orations, marches, torchlight parades, and chants. Stormtroopers were also out daily reminding everyone of the party's determination and power.

Now the stormtroopers wore brown shirts as the party had been able to secure never-worn colonial uniforms which became available at war's end when Germany was stripped of its imperial holdings. Between 1926 and 1928, the SA underwent significant changes. Hitler appointed an ex-army officer, Captain Fritz von Pfeffer, as Reich leader for the SA (OSAF). He had served on the Western front. After the war, he founded his own Free Corps. He had been drawn into the Kapp Putsch. In 1923 he was active in the Ruhr against the Left and, in 1925, joined the Nazi Party. In short order he became a *Gauleiter* and SA leader for Westphalia. Pfeffer was asked to rebuild the SA shortly after Röhm left.

As with Röhm before him, there was a question with Pfeffer about whether his paramilitary force could be properly subordinated to the party. Hitler remembered 1923 when he was more or less dragged into the world of the putsch behind a paramilitary which, from its institution, had never been under his control. In practice, the SA became a grassroots formation allowed to develop relatively independently under a leader who was given latitude. With some doubts, but aware of his own shortcomings in administering the paramilitary wing of the party, Hitler was forced to act as he had in the period before the putsch and turn to a man with a paramilitary background.

Pfeffer was hardly distinguishable from the other Free Corps leaders. He wanted to establish a disciplined army of political troops of the line. Pfeffer was allowed to restructure the organization pretty much as he desired.[35] As leader of the SA, Pfeffer was also in charge of the *Schutzstaffel*. The SS was at this time still a token force and Pfeffer paid it little attention. Pfeffer quickly went to work reorganizing the Sturmabteilung. The Free Corps remained his model.

The SA was, like the military, divided into various units. The smallest was a *Schar* (band) composed of three to about a dozen men, followed by a *Trupp* (troop), a *Sturm* (storm), a Standard and a Brigade. It was decided that only party members could join the SA. The SA then began to grow. The smallest party local could form its own stormtrooper unit. For many young German men, left fatherless because of the war, the SA became a surrogate family.

The SA avoided the German army's consciousness of rank and instead allowed its men to enjoy an easygoing camaraderie. Considerable decision-making was allowed even in the lower ranks. However, top positions were filled only by former army and Free Corps officers. The SA was a formation combining youthful idealists, militants, asocial bullies, and, in cities like Berlin, former criminals sporting underworld nicknames. The youth of the SA rank-and-file was demonstrated in Berlin where some 70 percent of the members were men under 26 years of age (1929).[36] Between 1926 and 1929, the SA grew steadily. Its visibility on the streets made seeing it a part of the daily experience and it came to appear as an almost normal part of German life. Over 30,000 noisy stormtroopers appeared at a Nuremberg party congress in 1929 to listen to Hitler.[37]

By 1930, with the development of what Hitler loved to call "machinery," the drawing of the masses into Nazism was closer to becoming a reality. An exceedingly large number of auxiliary groups were developed to draw people in. It might be proper at this juncture to observe the old adage: "Two Germans, a conversation, three Germans, a club." In many ways the SA became a kind of club of the nation. It is instructive to observe that many of the party's auxiliary groups were SA subsidiaries. One such was the Nazi automobile club, which often used vehicles provided by members to convey stormtroopers from one demonstration to another. A women's auxiliary, with a name borrowed from the Red Cross, appeared as

Six. The Years of Preparation (1924-1930)

Various party activities are shown here from the period 1924–28.

the "Red Swastika." Its primary charge was to care for stormtroopers injured in street brawls.[38]

The party had thus grown to the point where it compared with the KPD by 1929. Of course, both political extremes were far behind the SPD in terms of numbers in the ranks of followers. But young unemployed men flocked to the SA as much if not more than to the

Communists. The earlier trends continued and, by 1930, two-thirds of SA members were under thirty-five. The majority of the *Sturmabteilung* members arrested in Munich were under thirty. Nationally, the Nazi Student Union was formed to draw in university men who were then urged to also become members of the SA.[39]

The Storm Detachment of National Socialism eventually was elaborated to where it could fulfill the earlier dreams of people like Röhm, massing would-be desperadoes behind the Nazi banner. What was needed at this juncture was an incident or incidents, overlaid with a general pattern of societal malaise, to act as a prime mover. That came with the Great Depression. By the summer of 1929, the Nazi Party had been successfully reorganized. Its image as a failed band of putschists had disappeared. Two events would transform the Nazis into a formidable threat to the Republic, the nationalistic agitation against the Allied nations-promoted Young Plan and the coming of the Great Depression.

In 1924, the Dawes Plan had been put forth as an interim solution to deal with reparations. In 1929, reparations had to be confronted again. The Dawes Plan of 1924 was only meant to serve as an interim solution, and its conditions, the payment of 2.5 billion gold marks in reparations a year, could not be borne by a shaky economy indefinitely. In the summer of 1928, German and Allied representatives began the discussions that would lead in March 1930 to what was believed to be the final solution of the reparations problem — the Young Plan.

The Young Plan was worked out under the chairmanship of an American business leader, Owen D. Young. It was approved in January 1930 when the economic decline had gained momentum worldwide. The plan did put a ceiling on the total of reparations where one had been absent. Stresemann had died, but earlier he negotiated a conclusion to the Locarno Pact — securing mutual guarantees of the German-French frontier in 1926 — and German entry into the League of Nations, and turned to the task of evacuating the Rhineland. Still occupied by French troops, final evacuation was connected with the Young Plan. Stresemann had convinced the French they should withdraw their troops in exchange for German adoption of the Young Plan.

Meanwhile, on 9 July 1929, *Stahlhelm* leaders had formed a national committee to push for a plebiscite against the Young Plan. The committee was headed by Alfred Hugenberg whose nationalists gathered most of the Right to oppose it, saying reparations should be canceled completely.[40] Hitler joined the anti–Young effort. Its other members were acceptable to most Germans, thus conferring an aura of respectability by association on the Nazis. The National Socialists could no longer simply be dismissed as that "band of racist fanatics" from Bavaria.

Hugenberg, a mass-media mogul, put his substantial communication resources into high gear. This included wire services, the Universum Filmgesellschaft (UFA), and newspapers. Using all of these outlets, the leader of the nationalists unleashed a campaign of chauvinistic intensity. The Nazis were delighted to be involved. It gave the party a national forum without cost. Despite this imposing array of nationalistic forces, only slightly over four million signatures were obtained. This was about 10 percent of the signatures needed to submit an anti–Young referendum to the voters. The failure to attract a larger number of signatures had several causes. Perhaps the most important of these was President Hindenburg's opposition to point 4 of the referendum. This point, in demagogic style, insisted that any governmental representative who rendered Germany liable to further payment of reparations would be guilty of treason.

The progress of the bill continued. Since it had been rejected by the Reichstag, it had to be submitted to a plebiscite in which it needed to gain over 50 percent of the voters. It failed badly. Although the nationalists had unleashed a propaganda blitzkrieg in support of their referendum, the Reichstag had defeated it decisively. This defeat was in truth a victory for Hitler as much as for the Weimar government. For almost five months Hugenberg had given the Nazis much publicity through his media. This opened the way for Hitler to contact influential people in conservative circles.[41]

Three weeks after Stresemann's death, the Wall Street crash of 1929 interrupted and ended Weimar's period of relative tranquility. Without the world depression, there might have been continued short-term problems in the German economy. But with the Great Depression, the existing problems turned into catastrophe. Once there was a disaster in New York, the dependence of the Germany economy on the health of the American stock market was such that the Wall Street crash was experienced immediately. Investors who had deposited short-term funds in Germany since 1924, in the form of notes easily recalled, withdrew their investments. German industry, deprived of its financial support, suffered. Innumerable firms declared bankruptcy. Production levels in others lowered rapidly. It was certain that all this would produce high unemployment and it soon did. The national fund which was meant to provide benefits for the unemployed quickly proved to be inadequate. The cost in terms of human misery was beyond measure. The political response took the form of further disaffection with Weimar. The whole anti–Republican spectrum tried to exploit the precarious economic situation. The Nazis set out to harvest the disaffected. This they did quite well.

Chapter Seven

The Reichstag Elections of 1930 and the SA

It was described how, in the early days of Nazism, the movement needed a ring through which to draw various threads emerging on the other side in a merged strand of the masses entering Nazism. In those initial days, the party had not been able to pull together the various Right-radical groups which had made Bavaria into something of a rightist armed camp. That ring merging the threads was now to be provided by the Nazi electoral surge of 1930. The Nazis had been working through the years just before the Depression to build an umbrella party, leaping across age and class boundaries in a novel fashion for Germany. Finally, the old idea of a roof organization to cover diverse paramilitary elements was realized in the SA.

For most of the Weimar years the greatest right-wing opposition to the Republic had been the German National People's Party led by Alfred Hugenberg in 1930. Most of the middle classes voted for a variety of parties, the most important of these was the German People's Party (DVP). The DVP was also nationalistic. But it was moderate, it tolerated the Republic, and its leaders led it to participate in coalitions. Members of the Weimar coalition had to contend with the forces of the Right cited above and the undemocratically inclined radical Left as well. The German Communist Party (usually called the KPD) rigidly adhered to an orthodox version of Marxism and exploited crisis with the idea of building a critical mass of revolutionary fervor to mount a Bolshevik-style revolution. The Nazis had recovered, after arduous effort, from their dismal showing in 1928. They benefitted from a spontaneous tremor of fear running through Germany's middle class. Many had not fully recovered emotionally from the stressful times experienced during the 1923 inflation only to now be confronted with a worldwide depression. Many believed that a prolonged economic crisis, like the earlier one in 1923, would mean the loss of jobs and homes.

Small businessmen now felt themselves hemmed in and made less relevant by the growth of large corporations, on the one side, and labor unions on the other. Resentment was harbored on the part of the lower middle class, particularly white-collar employees. There was a sudden political impact of all this. Most of the middle-class electorate quickly lost confidence in the DNVP and DVP. It was yet to be proven, but the Nazis had benefitted more from the old Right's problems than had other parties. Into 1930, the Nazis had made efforts to enlist members and sympathizers from the unemployed. For some years the chronically unemployed had trickled into the party, mostly joining its SA which remained over the years the Nazi Party's most accessible organization. With the Depression, the middle-class unemployed came in greater numbers. The SA offered shelter in "barracks," abandoned warehouses, and similar places. Within these stormtroopers could eat from a common stewpot and escape idleness waiting for assignments.

Of decisive importance was the fact that the worsening economic and social conditions established a deadlock within the government. The Grand Coalition described earlier had been anchored in the DVP and SPD. Suddenly, under new pressures, the coalition split along class and economic fault lines. By March of 1930, the coalition was sundered. Emerging at this point was a presidential system. It became necessary, in the absence of a working majority, to depend upon the constitution which had allowed government by decree. President Hindenburg, without legislation forthcoming from parliament, began to so govern.

Given the experiences with governmental problems from 1919 through 1923, during which time President Ebert had been forced to use executive decrees, most Germans were willing to trust in strong presidential action to help them in this new crisis. Heinrich Brüning was the first chancellor to lead a presidential government. He quickly tried to push through a barely functioning parliament a series of unpopular measures. He was rejected. But his government did not fall as it might normally have. He continued with the blessing of the president. Elections were then scheduled as Brüning hoped to achieve a supportive Reichstag.

It was a mistake to hold an election in the middle of an economic crisis. The campaign became one of the most intense in German history. When Germans went to the polls in September, they provided a breakthrough for the Nazis. Suddenly, the Nazis rose from the obscurity of 1928 to become the second largest party in the Reichstag. On the other political extreme, Communism moved forward. Presidential government continued out of necessity.

The SA had played a substantial role in attracting the masses into Nazism in this decisive election. From 1927 to 1929, members of the Front Generation emerged into party leadership to organize propaganda and use violence as a weapon.[1] The SA was useful because it was violent. Stormtroopers followed orders better than Nazi "civilians." Actually, the average SA man *was* a civilian who saw himself on his personal field of dreams as a soldier. He thus did not really have much in common with a Freikorps desperado who might well have served as his superior at a substantially higher level in the party.

This new stormtrooper took pride in his faithfulness, his obedience, his aggressive behavior, and his comradely spirit. In his view the civilians of the party (the "PO," for "Political Organization") owned none of these "heroic" traits. This widespread attitude in the SA helped to build an inner-party tension. The belligerence of what often was little more than a very large street gang was there to be developed and party leaders used it after 1928.[2] The drawback to making extensive use of the SA was that its leaders repeatedly asked of their superiors that they be given more military training. Hitler and others in Munich wanted the brownshirts to be used only in electioneering. Refusals to grant training caused complaints about Nazi *Bonzen* ("bigwigs"). And this exacerbated inner-party crisis situations.[3]

Often enough, the SA leaders, as in Berlin, interpreted their political activity to be an unending series of street brawls.[4] There were many who believed that the SA could be used more productively than simply as a band of thugs roving the streets looking for "Reds" to assault. It appeared that little profit could be taken from that kind of simple turmoil.[5] In fact, SA disorder in Berlin had led to a prohibition on its illegal activities by the capital city's authorities.[6]

As indicated earlier, the Nazi Party entered the year 1928 following an urban scheme.

Beset by financial problems, they moved forward at a slow pace. They were often unsuccessful in arranging meeting places. This caused them to turn to open-air marches. Party performance was also hampered by local inner-party corruption.[7] Growth was slow during this period, but growth there was. There were a few local electoral victories in 1926 and 1927, and there transpired a passing of the old high membership watermark of 1923 (55,000). This had happened despite the fact that the party issued a statement at the official annual membership meeting in 1927 that its growth had been retarded by lack of funds.[8]

The urban scheme behind them, suddenly the watershed election of 1930 focused media attention on the Nazis. In turn, the media attention helped draw in more members and contributions. It also defined the role of the SA in shaping the new mass appeal of the party. An optimum use for the *Sturmabteilung* meant putting aside old ways. The most important lessons that came out of the period before the 1930 election, as far as the SA was concerned, had to do with the Nazis' part in the referendum against the Young Plan. It was the public demonstrations against the plan and slogans mouthed by stormtroopers on the march that set the pattern. The sloganeering approach to exploiting economic distress and charges of governmental betrayal helped to set *Sturmabteilung* patterns used in boosting the 1930 vote. Moreover, the impact of the Young Plan campaign was a steady source of Nazi growth into December of 1929.[9] Much of that growth was in the Storm Detachments. Before the national elections, the Nazis tested their new strength in the state of Thuringia's *Landtag* election of early 1930. The result of the election was a tripling of 1928 totals to make the Nazis the third strongest party in that state.[10]

During 1930, the National Socialists had occupied their new party headquarters (the "Brown House") in Munich. There Franz von Pfeffer as *Oberster SA Führer* (OSAF), was given special status. He reported directly to Hitler and was given his own separate chain of command.[11] The organization Pfeffer led was young, even younger than the rest of the party as it prepared itself to enter the lists for the upcoming election.

The growth of SA as part of the youth movement reflected a phenomenon seen in Depression Germany. The most radical elements of Right and Left everywhere, but particularly in urban situations, were those young workers receiving the lowest wages. Similarly, the largest group of unemployed men prominent in the SA was constituted by the youthful. In 1930, approximately 52 percent of those receiving benefits were under thirty.[12]

Working-class youth experienced the impact of the Depression almost immediately. The normal pattern would have been for young people to leave school at about fourteen to enter an apprenticeship leading to a job. The pattern now became for them to be jobless once they left apprenticeships. Middle-class young people were faced with a hopeless outlook as well. Secondary school teachers were not needed. There was an overabundance of legal graduates. Other normally open bourgeois professions offered similar outlooks.[13]

For the disenchanted young people of all classes, an important place to discover an outlet for frustration was the Nazi SA. Unlike the Red Front Fighters, the Nazi brownshirts seemed to be developing, like the party as a whole, into an organization superseding class. Most now drawn to the SA seemed to be between nineteen and twenty-two years old, serving under a leader at the Storm level only a few years older.[14] As indicated earlier, the police noted in Munich and surrounding areas that SA men arrested for violent activity were invariably under thirty. Moreover, about one-third of those taken into custody were not yet twenty-six years of age.[15]

This picture of a young SA membership, too young to have fought in the war, negates one of the common assumptions made about the Sturmabteilung; it was not an updated Free Corps. The highest Storm Detachment leaders were, as indicated, from the Front Generation. But the rank and file was overwhelmingly from the next generation. These frustrated young people were sufficiently angry to be drawn into violent activity. Their anger was with a society which had no place for them. The result of this was very much like activities seen in contemporary American street gangs fighting "turf wars" in urban centers. Only there was a paramilitary twist. Young SA men called the doorways of Nazi-frequented taverns "outposts" and roaming the streets looking for brawls was "going on patrol."

In terms of party strategy, this youthful membership made it easier for the party to transform stormtroopers from soldiers-in-waiting to electioneering and propaganda activists. Young stormtroopers were used between 1928 and 1930 particularly to enhance the circulation of the *Völkischer Beobachter* by peddling subscriptions door to door.[16] It was during this same period that the Nazis developed the technique of constant campaigning. This meant that the whole party strength was brought to bear on one local or regional election after another. The SA was a very important part of this, because, with their high rate of unemployment, they could campaign daily without going to a job.

The basic idea was to let Germany have no rest. A proper propaganda approach was defined as holding some 70 to 200 rallies in the same district in a period of seven to ten days. After SA men had gone about nailing up posters for a time, it was estimated (by the party) that an additional 70 to 150 villages would become aware of the party. Rallies also often spawned SA recruitment sessions.[17]

During the spring of 1930, the party turned further away from its exclusive activity in the city to the countryside. Again, the SA was at the center of activity. Every weekend the uniformed SA would, as it had in the years before, ride on trucks into the smallest villages of a district. Propaganda marches would then be held. Only now the extent and amount of these "out-marches" was much greater. Commonly, local party groups were founded in such areas, where none had existed before. Because the Nazi media was not read everywhere in 1930, the propaganda marches and rallies remained the principal way for reaching the masses. When word of the Reichstag dissolution came in mid–1930, Hitler lost no time in beginning the election campaign with a speech in Munich's Zirkus Krone.[18] It was soon decided that "proper" opposition to the Young Plan would be presented as a key campaign issue, a tactic employed by the nationalists as well. During the month of August, that campaign reached a fever pitch.[19]

Hitler made impossible demands of his campaign workers. During the two days before the election itself, in Berlin alone, the National Socialists put together twenty-four major demonstrations. Once more their posters were pasted on walls and fences. The city appeared to have been papered over, red-white-black. The Nazi Party newspapers, both the *Völkischer Beobachter* and various local party sheets, were produced in huge numbers and sold to members for a pfennig. The papers were then each to be distributed door to door or outside factories. The new Nazi electoral tempestuousness contrasted with the dull, routine ways established parties mounted elections, the party faithful attending rallies to listen politely while dry speeches were given. At local levels, efforts of this sort by the older Weimar parties carried little conviction. Many unsatisfied potential voters, bored with politics as usual, moved over to enroll in the Nazi party. As indicated earlier, parties located on the Right, lingering in the political spectrum from the heyday of the *völkisch* parties along with one major party, the nationalists, were most likely to lose their following to Nazism in this manner.[20]

The Nazis' radical methods of spreading propaganda made it possible to raise money at an elevated level. Nazi activities now began to penetrate provincial towns where political campaigning was a novelty. There they staged noisy, exciting demonstrations and aroused local interest. Those attending often had to come up with an entrance fee, and these cash collections were carried out by the SA. Unlike the poorly organized "middle-class" parties of the Right, the Nazis continued to draw funds in substantial amounts through a variety of devices. This made them much less dependent on business-interest patronage than "respectable" opponents.[21]

All the frenzied activities of the SA reached a climax in September of 1930. Because of the lateness of the election announcement, the Nazis, with their continual campaigning, were the only ones ready.[22] In nearly all *Gaue*, uniform propaganda themes had been established. These had been issued from Munich by Goebbels. In almost all districts there were mass rallies and individual roles for stormtroopers. For example, SA men were told to appear at party headquarters. There they were met by Nazi officials or members who owned automobiles and motorcycles. They then worked together to provide transportation to bring people to the polls.[23] This is hardly a novel technique in terms of today's electoral campaigns, but it was unique in the Germany of 1930.

These SA techniques had been taking shape since the relative failure of the party in the 1928 elections. Throughout 1929, before the Depression, support at the state and municipal levels had been growing. Of course, some of these successes had to do with Nazi participation in the referendum against the Young Plan. Those factors that influenced the shaping of the Sturmabteilung in 1930 can best be described by looking at a tendencies appearing in Nazism more broadly. Among them was a developing strain of anti-capitalism.[24] How much was transferred to the rank and file to act as a motivator is hard to determine. But there were some who began to see lower-middle-class, non–Marxist anticapitalism emerging in the SA. This view appeared best to have been expressed in organized demonstrations against Jewish shops and various small businesses.[25]

More important than ever was the stormtroopers' paramilitarism, used repeatedly in protests against "exploitative" economic concerns. This paramilitarism strayed from the original model used in the Free Corps. It was instead a kind of common-man street gang's reconstruction of German militaristic traditions. It was true that much of the SA tendency toward violence was learned from leaders who had perfected their craft in the trenches or the Free Corps.[26]

Emulation of Free Corps fighters ended at that point and the rest of the model for behavior was provided by the idea of the "propaganda soldier." By 1930, stormtroopers surged out into the street on political missions regularly. These were young men who knew little of how things were really done in the military.[27] Such youths imagined that something like throwing rocks through the window of an opposition newspaper was in fact an attack on a military objective.

SA rank and file in 1930 was primarily composed of unemployed workers and ex-students. The Depression caused these young men, who would perhaps in more normal times have entered the workplace, from developing the usual political affiliations. This meant that, unlike the rest of the party, the SA of 1930 was likely to be confused about its proper attitude

An SA "march-out" is shown here from 1930. Hitler and Goering appear in the lower right and in back of them are the typical Deutschland Erwache (Germany Awake) banners.

toward other political-paramilitary organizations like the KPD/Red Front. Once directed against a target they often attacked without a rationalization. As author Joachim Fest has it: "Above all in the big cities a permanent underworld war was carried on between the SA and the Red Front (RF), in which both sides made use of low taverns as bases ... with frequent desertions from the SA to RF."[28] This appears to indicate that these men, like Free Corps members before them, lacked clear ideological profiles. On the few occasions when the two enemies cooperated it was almost always in the big cities and joint action was anti-republican in nature. This likely happened because a similar socio-economic background was shared by both urban Communists and stormtroopers.[29]

This political-ideological confusion in the cities caused many contemporaries to attribute a semi-conscious "socialism" to the SA.[30] This concept of a Red-like Nazism was in fact, something more like the so-called "third way" between socialism and capitalism developing in the nineteenth and early twentieth centuries.[31] By 1930, the SA was so diverse it was difficult to categorize it so easily. The differences among its segments were many: between city and countryside, between generations, and between different areas of Germany.

As one searches for a common theme in the party and its SA, the notion of a catch-all party of protest is useful. The idea subscribed to in this view is a negative one. The shared antipathy for a system seen as not willing to provide more for them was the vital cement holding the party and its SA together. Of course, one thing that seems to have shaped the actions of all Nazi organizations was anti–Semitism. One witness at the postwar Nuremberg trials provided his view of the influence of anti–Semitism on the SA. He testified as follows: "The concept of the 'master race' was never fostered in the SA; that would have been contrary to reason, for the SA received its replacements from all strata."[32]

This witness was Max Jüttner, a former official of the *Stahlhelm* who moved to the SA after 1933. Since his testimony contradicts other early interpretations of the SA, it should prove useful to evaluate it in terms of the 1930 elections when the Nazi paramilitary arm was taking on its shape for those last dark days of Weimar. The generally bad economic conditions of the Depression were exploited more successfully by the Nazis than any other political party. Within Nazism, it was the SA that was most stirred by hostility against the well-off and well-educated, much like it was in the KPD. Among the new proletarians, a hatred grew of those employed.[33] In one collection of party biographies is the story of a stormtrooper who complained about observing the well-to-do waiting at taxi stands, people who could afford a form of travel beyond his means. In a reflexive expression of party ideology, the same man estimated that 80 to 90 percent of the customers he saw and envied were Jews.[34]

This is a highly unlikely estimate for any number of reasons. Obviously, there was no way for the observer to know whether all these people were Jews. Perhaps he saw a long nose or another physical characteristic common to many people. But it meant to him that he was looking at a Jew. Despite examples like this, this set of biographies is flawed with regard to the amount of anti–Semitism in the SA. Submitted in an attempt by the collectors to construct a profile of Nazism, these autobiographical essays came primarily from people who were in the party before 1930 and were of an age group and a socio-economic strata where anti–Semitism was nearly always present. In 1930, as historian Conan Fischer has it: "Anti-Semitism might have been general among stormtroopers ... but this was not entirely so."[35]

Many stormtroopers, especially in the cities, continued buying equipment from Jewish firms. This caused Viktor Lutze, the commander of SA Group North, to complain that "an SA man who buys from Jews demonstrates that he has not grasped the meaning of National Socialism."[36] Even after the "seizure of power" in 1933, the stormtroopers were ordered to stop buying from Jewish establishments. Some stormtroopers attacked Jews indiscriminately. But some went so far as to protest the discrimination against Jews because those few they knew personally were often patriots. For yet others, "Jewishness" was just one more way of identifying enemies. And Jews differed little for them from Leftists.

Moving into the Depression years the sentiments that most typified stormtroopers were anti–Semitism and hyper-nationalism. Of these two by far the most important for the newest 1930-and-after joiners was nationalism. It is apparent that many from this period indicated that they could not become KPD or SPD because they had been raised in working-class homes where nationalism was ascendant. The ideological profile of the SA after the onset of the Depression and the flooding into it of unemployed youth is much more muddled than before 1930. Action for its own sake often appears more important than ideology. As in urban street gangs in our own time, marking the target was essential. Of all the targets, the preferred one for the Depression-era SA was the Red Front, for the Communists were always ready to take their war to the street.

Much work has been done on the social composition of the Nazi Party. Most significant here is the conclusion that a significant percentage of nonunionized workers were among those providing the increase in Nazi supporters for the elections of 1930.[37] In fact, the growth of numbers of unemployed workers in the Reich continued to correspond closely after September 1930 with the increase in Nazi Party membership.[38] Moreover, between 1929 and 1933, more workers left both radical and moderate "Marxist" parties to become Nazis. This situation was clearly less typical of workers in the countryside than those in urban-industrial settings.[39]

Conversions from radical Left to radical Right continued because of simplistic motivations. Some formerly leftist workers admitted that they had done this because they were confused and simply did not know what their political destination ought to be. Many held that they had heard too many meaningless slogans stressing international ties to Communism. In many cases, these people had been members in youth organizations which had stressed nationalistic themes. This made them tone-deaf to messages from the KPD. Some saw the KPD as "cowardly" because it had gone on the "defensive" beginning with the 1930 elections. They thus decided to move to the more "heroic" SA. Obviously, with workers and unemployed young men of this sort, ideological messages meant little. They appeared to have scant grasp of ideology except in relatively meaningless outline. What happened was that these refugees from the Left came to the Nazi Party attributing to it "populist emancipating attributes" that the Nazis actually did not display to any degree.[40]

The taste of these people who enrolled, many from the Left, was for action and they had picked the SA because its ideology was actually far less precise than that of the KPD.[41] The SA offered a kind of a fill-in-the-blanks view. Taken together, the relative unimportance of ideology and the considerable importance of target identification caused the SA to be useful in the party approach to the elections of 1930. The 1930 election strategy depended on using greatly increased numbers of campaign workers. New unemployed SA members took up those tasks. They were nearly always available. In 1930, and then in subsequent electioneering, Hitler raced back and forth across Germany by air.[42] When Hitler arrived to speak in any locality he was driven in an open automobile into the heart of a town. As he rode into the *Stadtmitte* he was accompanied by an escort of "SA Rider Units" on motorbikes. When he arrived at his destination, massed stormtroopers were waiting. Then, in pseudo-military style, the SA passed in review in front of the leader before his speech was presented. After his speech, he left quickly with SA escort to go to the airfield. He boarded his plane to move to the next speech where all this was repeated.[43]

Before Hitler appeared for his speeches, the Nazi local or national press carried detailed accounts of how stormtroopers were to participate in the local appearances by the *Führer*. The various party sheets provided times, notice of a signal to be used, usually a siren, to sound when Hitler had entered the outskirts of a municipality. Added were instructions for stormtroopers who were to line the streets to shout "Heil Hitler!" when he passed. Where possible, usually in rural areas, SA "cavalry" units appeared with Hitler. All of this was novel in German politics, impressing people with the strength, energy, and size of the movement.

The above described activity, if somewhat vulgar by traditional German standards, was essentially nonviolent. But the politics practiced by Nazis often encouraged considerable hatred and thus engendered violence. The ideology and political style made violence acceptable. Party leaders like Goebbels wanted to incite violence for propaganda purposes. Goebbels wrote: "The SA man wants to fight, and he also has a right to be led into battle."[44]

Violence was often cited by contemporaries as a major aspect of the SA appeal. Stormtroopers were painted as the defenders of "Germanism" against international Marxism. The Nazis were able in 1930 and after to come up with what might seem an odd mix of appeals, drawing both those displaying violent instincts and those which were more "respectable." Such contradictions are built into the Anglo-American umbrella political parties. But this mix was novel in Germany. The National Socialists were thus able, particularly after the turning point in 1930, to propose "a restoration of order and conservative values." Simultaneously, they proclaimed a "readiness to challenge the Left on the streets."[45]

From almost the beginning, and particularly after the onset of the Depression, the SA was involved in turf wars with the Left. By the time that Hitler became chancellor in 1933, SA violence had spread from large city to the smallest hamlet. This violence was embodied in the SA slogan calling its members to "clear the streets" for the brown-shirted armies. The rising tide of this widespread violence was primarily limited to street brawls. This could be seen in growing calls for SA-sponsored insurance help. These jumped upward to just over 100 claims in 1927 to over 14,000 in 1932.[46] At about the same time that SA violence in the streets leaped upward, there appeared some stormtrooper terrorism.

The party by 1930 was obviously dual in nature; there was the "Political Organization" (or PO) and the SA. But the PO was much more completely middle and lower middle class than was an SA full of unemployed youth. Generally, the young unemployed of 1930 poured into both the KPD and the Nazi Party. The KPD had behind it the social cohesion of working-class districts in cities like Berlin and Hamburg. And in such cities they had for some time stressed paramilitary activism in absence of gainful employment. But much working-class radicalism was channeled into areas where socialist or Communist organizations were weak. And the Nazi SA gained more than the KPD in these locations.[47]

All such discussions of demographics and class division do little to portray what life was like for the radicalized young men who were stormtroopers in 1930. For that, we need to turn to a contemporary observer. Konrad Heiden was one of the Nazis' earliest and most articulate opponents. In 1923, the leader of a small democratic organization at the University of Munich, he was part of activities designed to stop the spread of the entire rightist movement. In 1934, after combating the growth of the Right throughout the republican years, he left Germany as political refugee. He eventually came to the United States. Once in America, he became a professor and published works detailing the rise of Nazism and Adolf Hitler. Some of his conclusions are outdated, but one thing remains certain, there is no other work better at describing the electric and frightening atmosphere of those days.

Seven. The Reichstag Elections of 1930 and the SA

Heiden describes how unemployed miners in the winter of 1930 lived in unheated rooms and sometimes broke down the fences of nearby inactive mining operations to steal coal for heat. In the summer of 1930, gas broke through the walls of a mine in Silesia and hundreds of miners were asphyxiated. And yet, out-of-work miners petitioned the government in Berlin to open the mines, some of them cited as death traps, indicating their willingness to suffer peril to eliminate the hunger of their families. As this happened, tent "cities" arose around Berlin where the unemployed who could not pay rent lived and ate in community kitchens. In nearby fields, peasants stood armed guard over their crops as "potato patrols" came out from the cities to carry off produce. Often, the peasants were powerless as desperate marauders rushed them in broad daylight to crush through their defenses.[48]

All over Germany "Storm Centers" were established. Often they were warehouses belonging to party businessmen and standing empty because of the Depression. Most often they were back rooms of beer halls. As Heiden has it in his discussion of the Storm Centers: "There sat the unemployed in their coarse brown breeches and discolored yellow shirts for many hours of the day over their empty beer mugs; at meal times they were fed ... from a great iron kettle.... But when the whistle blew in the back room of the beer hall ... these men rotting in activity sprang up ... marching off. For wherever they might be marching, "it could only be better."[49]

Interpolation III

Battleground Berlin (1925–1933)

The city in which weariness with a seemingly impotent Republic and the impact of the Depression provided the greatest access for the emergence of the masses into Nazism was Berlin. The Berlin described in this section is not solely the city of numerous parks—the Tiergarten, the Charlottenburg gardens, and the Bellevue Park. Nor is it solely the city of parades down the Unter den Linden, the museums, concert halls, theater, and opera houses that, before the war, made it an example of the gilded age. It was also a city devastated to some extent by pressures from a lost war. It was the seat of a government hardly ever popular. Permanent changes were set in motion there in the period immediately following the Great War as part of the turmoil surrounding the Republic's birth.

Historically, Berlin came to greatness much later than Paris, London, or Rome. These others were well established in the Middle Ages. Prior to 1871, there had been no Germany and, hence, there was no capital to act as a focal point.[1] Berlin was to become that focal point after unification. But there was not much in its history before that juncture to indicate future greatness. It developed relatively late in East Elbia. It was not founded on a great river like Cologne was on the Rhine, but on an insignificant artery, the Spree. The twin city of Berlin-Coelln was established there in the mid–thirteenth century.[2] The site became a marketplace, providing merchants traveling the East Elbian area with a place to stop and rest. In time, the rising settlement became involved with Hamburg and other Hanse cities in trade. Eventually they joined the Hanseatic League.[3]

In 1415, Friedrich von Hohenzollern received Mark Brandenburg as an imperial fief. The twin city of Berlin-Coelln then felt the strong hand of princely authority. The new ruling family forced the city to cut ties with the Hanseatic League and, after resistance from the local population, established firm and lasting control. During the Reformation, Lutheranism spread to Berlin, although it was opposed by the rulers. Yet, Berlin (as the city came to be known while "Coelln" was dropped) was not a center of fervent Lutheran belief. It thus did not play an important role in the revolt against the Church of Rome.[4]

Hohenzollern history centered on Berlin does not become significant until the beginning of the seventeenth century. At that point, the Hohenzollerns made claims on two inheritances: the Dutchy of Prussia in the East, formerly organized by the Teutonic Knights in the late Middle Ages, and the other in the West (the small duchy of Julich-Cleves). In order to press the claims, the ambitious monarchy allied itself with the young Dutch Republic, becoming

Calvinist in the process. But the state, under Frederick William, the "Great Elector," granted religious freedom to its subjects. Its residents thereafter were both Calvinists and Lutherans.

From the Great Elector forward, the driving force in Prussian politics was dynastic ambition. Under Frederick William I, who became king in 1713, the process of creating a Prussia centered in Berlin was furthered by the establishment of a garrison state. At the time of this ruler's death in 1740, Berlin was still an average-sized city in Germany. Some fifty years later, after the rule of Frederick the Great, the urban center was one of the most important capitals in Europe. This was because Frederick the Great made it his political capital from which he managed to enlarge Prussia through war. Moreover, he continued earlier plans to make Berlin an architectural show place. At the close of Frederick's rule, Berlin was one of the larger German cities.

From 1795 to 1805, there was a great intellectual flowering in North Germany. This was disrupted in 1806 when, in a single day, Napoleon defeated the vaunted Prussian army made famous by Frederick the Great. The humiliation of the once proud country was complete as the French ruler imposed an indemnity and chipped off chunks of its territory to help remake the European map. At this point a new generation appeared on the Prussian political scene. Many came from other parts of Germany, believing that Prussia provided the best hope of expelling Napoleon from the Germanies. Led by the Baron vom Stein, these new members of the kingly bureaucracy transformed Prussia from an old-style absolute monarchy into a modern state. The transformed state existed in terms of an understanding between the king and his people and a centralized power based on Berlin.[5]

By this juncture, the city had a population of about 160,000. But it was such a government-controlled city that even local courts and the police force remained under state control.[6] A few years later, the Prussian army became a vital part of the expulsion of Napoleon in 1814. After the end of the Napoleonic Wars, Prussia emerged from the Congress of Vienna once more a power, with its territories enlarged. Soon after, the Germanic Confederation was formed, consisting of 39 states.

Prussian king Frederick William IV began his rule in 1840. By that time, there were internal enemies of the regime. Many of them met at a local coffeehouse in Berlin called the *Konditorei* (which in time became a general title throughout Germany used to indicate places with coffee and pastries). Some of these mostly young men discussed the articles appearing in the *Rheinische Zeitung* written by another young German man named Karl Marx.[7]

In March of 1848, revolution convulsed the German states. These "revolutions" or "revolts," depending upon the interpretation, were put down. Violent activity in Berlin was similarly suppressed. During the turmoil, promises were made from above that democratic changes would be made. But, once made, they were made under duress. They were almost universally not fulfilled once the revolutionary dust had settled. As is so often the case, a period of reaction followed the revolution. An assembly, formed during the revolutionary months of 1848–49, was elected by a reactionary three-class voting system. The Prussian state adopted a new, more realistic attitude which received a name in 1853, *Realpolitik*.[8]

Political repression coincided with an upsurge in economic activity, bringing a lengthy wave of prosperity to Prussia and Berlin. Such circumstances helped the city population grow to some 658,000 inhabitants by 1865. By then, Germany had entered the period of unification. The central actor in all of this was Otto von Bismarck. The story is well known. In a series of limited wars in 1864, 1866, and 1871 Germany was unified.

First, Berlin began as the capital of Prussia, then of the North German Confederation (lasting only from 1866 to 1871), and finally of the unified imperial Germany. Thus was the Second German Empire established (the first being the medieval Holy Roman Empire). The powers of the new all–German parliament (Reichstag) were limited from the outset.[9] A new constitution was written and it included no provision providing ministerial responsibility. The chancellorship became the fulcrum of power as the person occupying that role was simultaneously the prime minister of Prussia and the foreign minister of Germany. This was as extensive an overlapping of state portfolios as one was likely to see in that era.[10]

Once Germany was unified, its capital experienced a lasting boom in real estate. In 1871, Berlin was still restricted to a rather small area. The city limits had been marked by a wall, somewhat like the cities of medieval and early modern times.[11] There were villages and estates in close proximity to the German capital where real-estate speculators began to become active in the initial year after unification. Thereafter, Berlin's urban area grew rapidly, if in a helter-skelter manner. There was no city planning. Growth was not designed by urban planners, but by capitalists who bought land and transformed it by placing houses on it. This expansion left working-class districts basically untouched. The housing conditions of the working classes, as in so many other European cities, left much to be desired. Many were forced to live in damp and unhealthy basement apartments, little better than dungeons. This produced waves of sickness of all sorts, ranging from rheumatism to tuberculosis. Public and private sanitary arrangements were inadequate. And there was often no separation of the sexes, a situation leading to incest, illegitimacy, and venereal disease.[12]

The eastern and northern sections of Berlin remained for years the home of the working classes. It was notable that the capital's police headquarters (*Das Polizeiprasidium*) was located on the fringes of working-class districts. From there it was only a short journey into the conglomeration of factories and working-class slums. The Berlin of 1900 was thus the result of wild and undisciplined speculation. When the real-estate bubble burst, small investors rationalized personal economic setbacks with anti–Semitism. Anti-Semitism was linked to disliked liberalism, and second-rate writers like Rudolf Meyer and Paul de Lagarde provided slogans for the anti–moderate and anti–Left cause. Liberalism (interpreted in this case as demands for greater constitutional freedom, less economic giveaways to the favored classes, etc.) was declared to be a part of an international conspiracy. Liberalism was held to be dangerous because of its lack of proper nationalistic ties to the Fatherland.[13]

By 1914, the Berlin described here had expanded even more, rivaling London, Paris, and other "world cities." There were many public services provided: schools, parks, public gardens, and more. But by far the greatest number of Berliners made their livings in the city's factories.[14] By this time, a constant rise in the vote of the Social Democratic Party produced fears in the upper classes. Some might call it a fear bordering on hysteria.[15] When World War I began, proletarian brotherhood was sundered in Berlin. It was overwhelmed by the deceptive unity of the whole German people, proclaimed by the national government. It was not long, however, before a great schism of Social Democracy began which fractionated the SPD and produced independent socialists and Spartacists by the end of the war.[16]

Berlin in the 1920s was, first and foremost, a place for the interchange of ideas and social experimentation. The dynamic impulses in Berlin created the illusion of a powerful metropolis, a real fountainhead of ideas. The competition of intellectuals was more intense here than elsewhere. Berlin became a target in Germany, a scapegoat for nationalistic grievances, as it appeared involved in Left radicalism, sinful degradation, and the embrace of modernism. Such attitudes were, in time, to be embodied in Nazism. In the city itself, there was much tolerance on the surface, but beneath that there was a welter of contrasts. Modern auto traffic grew. English sports became popular. And, uniquely, women began to emerge into politics. Against basic change was the traditionalism held onto securely by large segments of the population longing for the imperial past.

Despite all the social and intellectual changes, postwar Berlin differed little physically from the prewar city. One obvious change was that, following the collapse of the monarchy, the omnipresent German army receded from public view. Prewar Berlin had been the scene of nearly daily parades, court festivities attended by the military, and general martial pomp. All this was gone after 1918. Deserted barracks, in what was once a garrisoned city during the rise of Prussia, reawakened memories which grew fainter with time.[17] The Berlin police now held authority, without the army, over 552 square miles.[18]

Until 1929, the most troubled area in this urban sprawl was the so-called Carpathian region. This area in Neukolln was a center of political unrest. Neukolln and Kreuzberg had been the scene of numerous street brawls between stormtroopers and their foes. During the May Day "uprising" in 1929, Communists came out of tenements to oppose authorities (in the Nazi view "like rats out of their holes").[19] Radicalism was not limited to the working-class districts of Berlin alone. The economic dislocation of the Depression came as a greater shock to the lower middle class than to the workers. Soon enough, apartment houses in these areas also carried a smell of poverty. Here, however, young men dreamed not of a Soviet-style Germany, but of the Third Reich.[20]

Other bourgeois sections also had enclaves of political unrest. In Wilhelmsdorf, there were recurring Red-Brown clashes near meeting halls. There was an area in Charlottenburg called "Little Wedding." It was the location of an underworld stronghold. It also played the role of a "terror zone" for the Communists to approximate as closely as they could "true" revolutionary unrest until 1933.

Some of the bourgeois danger zones also saw confrontations between Nazis and Leftist intellectuals or artists. A frequent participant in these rows was the Stahlhelm.[21] Thus, many parts of Berlin by 1930 displayed scenes which, when looked at in microcosm, were typified by violence bordering on revolt. A useful way of looking at Nazism during this time is by viewing the career of Joseph Goebbels, who was put in charge of *Gau* Berlin. The Nazis often proclaimed that Berlin was "the reddest city [in Europe] after Moscow." That was a typical Nazi exaggeration. But it was the headquarters of the SPD and it owned a well-organized Communist party. The greatest part of the intelligentsia there was located on the Left. Moreover, the Jews had a considerable share in Berlin's spiritual and intellectual life. Many Jewish writers, scientists, and others came, after various stays here and there, to take up residence. One such was Albert Einstein.

The dissolution of the German Empire had greatly stimulated the development of Germany's Jewry. Whatever remained of the feudal society which had been discriminatory against the Jews on the basis of their religion had disappeared. Many members of the Berlin Jewish intelligentsia reached responsible positions in leftist political parties where they became fighters for progress. Yet, nothing could have made the Left more of a target for the Nazis in Berlin than this Jewish presence in their ranks.

Goebbels moved into this Red Berlin in November of 1926. He discovered a party there which showed the results of the Nazis' failure with the urban plan. His powers as *Gauleiter* were exercised over a local district that owned scarcely a thousand members. Goebbels' task was to conquer Berlin for Nazism. In his writings, Goebbels outlined the situation he confronted. Quarrels among leaders were endemic. Actual fistfights between members were a daily occurrence.[22] The Nazis had received less than a thousand votes in Berlin during the most recent Reichstag election.

At the first meeting of the party in Spandau, a Nazi stronghold, Goebbels warned that no more inner-party fights would be allowed on pain of expulsion. Violence was to be directed against the Reds. He quickly made the decision that one SA brawler was worth three PO members. The local SA was under his direct command. Officially from the PO, his situation was unique among district leaders. In time the Berlin SA was to become the most notorious in all Germany.[23]

By 1 January 1927, the party had moved into new headquarters. By this juncture, Goebbels had welded together a small but active fighting group. Soon Goebbels decided that the time was at hand for the first assault on Red Berlin. His initial public meeting was fixed for 25 January 1927. It was held in a Spandau *Festsale* and lasted over two hours. Apparently, although one must allow for Goebbels' exaggerations and falsifications, Communists invaded the meeting to brawl with Stormtroopers.[24] This is verified by the Communist press (the *Rote Fahne* or "Red Flag") which soon charged that the Nazis were converting their Spandau meetings into "bloodbaths."

Soon after that first public meeting, Goebbels flooded the city with enormous red posters indicating that on 11 February of 1927 a meeting was to be held in the Pharus-Hall. The Red posters formed a direct challenge to Berlin's Left. Moreover, the Pharus-Sale was situated in the heart of the Wedding district. It was a place previously used for KPD meetings. The walls of surrounding houses had posters pasted on them by stormtroopers. These were warnings against unwanted visitors coming into the hall. A direct provocation to the Left was issued, threatening to beat Red visitors "to a pulp."[25]

The Pharus-Hall meeting led to the expected battle with leftist opponents. Following a brawl lasting about ten minutes and resulting in the expulsion of opponents, Goebbels had the bruised SA men bandaged and placed on stretchers at the speaker's platform. He gave a speech to the crowd while standing over a man on a stretcher. At the end of the speech he pointed at the man and coined a phrase which became famous; his finger jabbed at the bandaged man as he ascribed greatness to this "unknown SA man."[26] During World War II, Goebbels supposedly recounted to a circle of friends that his "unknown SA man" speech had been prepared in advance and that very few of those placed on stretchers had been hurt at all.[27]

What the Pharus-Hall meeting accomplished for the Party was what Goebbels sought. He received public notice. The whole Berlin press carried accounts of it. From Goebbels' point of view, his conquest of Berlin had commenced. When he reported in his diary that the SA looked forward collectively to the next brawl he was likely correct. What was happening was that a form of street-gang turf warfare had begun. So much publicity was realized out of the Pharus-Hall incident that Goebbels decided to do it again. This time he concentrated on the outlying Tetlow District. There he had built a gigantic burning woodpile near a mill. The SA men grouped there took an oath of allegiance. They then returned on the train to Berlin the following day. They were meant to march across Berlin upon arrival. According to Goebbels, Red Front fighters were on the train and another brawl ensued. Far superior in numbers, the SA triumphed. On returning to the city, they staged the march. Some SA men then beat a Jewish passerby and invaded a cafe known to be a meeting place of intellectuals.[28]

In Goebbels' view of all this, for the first time, the SA "ruled" the streets in Berlin. But the Nazis were still not strong enough to do what the KPD did regularly; they could not confront the armed police of Berlin. The Communists still had the massive support of a portion of the Berlin populace and could, if they wished, stage open rebellion in various working-class sections. For that reason, Goebbels pointed out in his published *Instructions to the SA-Man* (1927), "Presently, all resistance against the police and the state is senseless, because you will always be weaker than they. No matter whom is correct, the state has the power to retaliate. When there is no other way ... submit ... to strength and remember that the day of reckoning will arrive."[29]

Goebbels asked Hitler, who was for the time being banned from public speaking in Prussia, to come to Berlin and address a closed meeting of party members. Hitler came. By Goebbels' design, he arrived on May Day, the annual workers holiday. He delivered his address in the Clou, an old amusement hall in the center of Berlin. The hall was filled. But the press took little notice. Goebbels was outraged. Soon after he called a mass public meeting. His speech given there became a poisonous diatribe against the "Jewish press" and other papers both "liberal" and "Catholic." According to his own account, there was a personal insult from the audience. Then, he maintained the individual refused to sit down and continued in a loud voice. Two SA men grabbed the heckler, slapped him, and expelled him.[30]

A very different report of the incident appeared in a Berlin newspaper. It revealed that "Goebbels began his speech reading out press commentary on Hitler's 1 May 1927 speech, calling the editors 'Jew pigs and swine.'" A Vicar Stucke of the Reformed Church had risen to object to the terminology used concerning the Jews. At that point, stormtroopers sitting near him jumped up and hit him with beer mugs. Covered in blood, Stucke staggered outside.[31]

Goebbels, who appeared always to be creating a sensation or trying to invent one, now had his publicity-grabbing incident. But there was a price. The Stucke case, torn from its political context, could simply be depicted as a common crime. The press did so. The police banned the party in Berlin. Goebbels left briefly for a Nazi meeting in Stuttgart and when he returned he was greeted at the station by a crowd shouting a slogan that would be used from time to time by Nazis in all Germany: "Despite the ban [we are] not dead" (*Trotz Verbot Nicht Tot*).

During the prohibition of the party, Goebbels founded a newspaper called *Der Angriff* ("The Attack"). Also, in a long-established Nazi tradition, various organizations were formed as covers. There were bowling clubs (full of SA men who seldom bowled), swimming clubs, walking clubs, and fishing clubs. This was a Nazi version of the German associational tradition. In this manner, activists were kept close to the party, but were ostensibly nonpolitical. The SA was assigned tasks of going to the main thoroughfares of Berlin to assault Jews or Jewish-looking individuals. This broad target designation caused them, somewhat embarrassingly for the party, to commit violent acts against such people as the officials of South American embassies. As a result, as early as May of 1927 which was shortly after the ban, a local newspaper demanded an end to the *Kurfurstendamm* outrages.[32] Soon thereafter stormtroopers began to be arrested.

By 1930, some of the Berlin SA formations could hardly be distinguished from professional gangsters. One Wedding troop proudly called itself "the Robber Band." Goebbels drew martyrs from these groups (about one a week or so killed in street fighting). He buried each one with impassioned oratory for the newspapers, although he later admitted to friends he could scarcely remember their names. One name he did remember. The most celebrated of all party martyrs was a twenty-one-year-old student named Horst Wessel.

Horst Wessel had broken with his family (the father was a Protestant pastor) and had descended into the Berlin slums. Once in Berlin, Wessel took up residence with a prostitute and became her lover and pimp. He also led his neighborhood Storm Troop. He drew upon some musical education and wrote a marching song for the SA. One day in 1930 he became involved in a confrontation with another pimp as they argued over who should benefit from the services of the prostitute. His antagonist had also lived with and pimped for the same woman before Wessel had taken up this task. The whole situation could not have been less political in nature. As the argument continued between pimps, both men pulled pistols and discharged them. Wessel was wounded and taken to the hospital where he lingered near death.

Goebbels quickly involved himself in the Horst Wessel matter and issued daily bulletins on the physical state of his new Nazi "hero." Since the rival pimp had belonged to a Communist gang, Goebbels painted the quarrel over a "lady of the night" as political terrorism. When Wessel died after lingering for weeks, Goebbels staged a spectacular funeral. The Horst Wessel song became the official Nazi anthem. Wessel became, as one author states, a "hero in Valhalla."[33]

All that has been discussed thus far is not meant to suggest that Berlin was totally convulsed by street fights during this period. Berlin was a very large city, much like London or New York. These were times when each city had many newspapers. And a goodly number of these were sensationalist sheets. A prominent feature in some of these was normally Red-Brown brawls. But it was rare to find anyone who had actually seen a street fight. One American, who had lived in both New York and Berlin compared Germany's capital to the urban United States. Dr. Margaret Mueslum said, "It's the same here [New York] because you hear of fighting in Harlem, but one doesn't see it in on Seventy-second Street."[34]

Berlin street fighting, as in New York, stayed within boundaries. The socialists were acutely aware of the borders of their districts and did not cross them. The Communists were less aware, but still did not venture far from home base. The Nazis tried to move into borderline areas and encroach on Red districts, street by street. But all the action remained far away from the more comfortable and removed middle and upper classes.

After the 1930 elections, the Nazis in the Reichstag who were also SA members were determined to show off their uniforms in the chamber. But this was against the rules. They therefore smuggled their stormtrooper garb into the building and changed clothes in the washrooms. Once assembled before the speaker in full SA garb, they enjoyed parliamentary immunity. The Nazis used this situation to turn every debate into a scene typified by shouted insults and threats of violence.

Nazi membership burgeoned. By 1932, the Nazis could mount a meaningful threat to those who held power in Berlin. In Berlin, as in most of the rest of Germany, the Nazis launched a saturation campaign in 1932. Thousands of rallies blanketed Germany with propaganda shaped for every group.[35] In March of 1932, there was a presidential election. Hindenburg did not secure an absolute majority, thus necessitating a runoff contest against his

The burial of Storm Leader Horst Wessel is shown here with massed SA in attendance. This staged propaganda event made him a "Group Leader in Valhalla."

closest competitor, Adolf Hitler. The SA membership (now some 90,000 strong in Berlin according to some estimates) confidently expected Hitler to win. That Hindenburg was a German hero of almost legendary status did not dissuade brownshirts. Hitler would win and move into absolute control over the German state. Since this was a "given," the stormtroopers nationally, but especially in Berlin, expected the Communists to launch a coup when Hitler won. On the eve of the election (13 March) the SA was mobilized in meeting halls awaiting the call to action.[36] But their marching orders never came. Despite the intense campaigning, Hitler lost to Hindenburg. Shortly after the election, the Weimar government moved to ban the SA.[37]

In the late spring of 1932, there was increasing chatter in Berlin about the possibility of a Rightist putsch. There were various demands made in fear of the other end of the political spectrum, some from inside the Prussian government, that the ban on the SA be lifted so that a Communist coup could be suppressed with Nazi assistance. These demands were made even though the reappearance of stormtroopers in the streets was certain to mean a resurgence of violence. As it was, the Prussian government could hardly maintain order in all Prussian cities. But it was worse in Berlin.[38] Police Chief Albert Grzesinski had a Jewish deputy, Dr. Bernhard Weiss. Weiss, who was a quite competent official, became the constant target of Nazi insults.[39] Goebbels wrote in his propaganda sheets of the man he and his stormtroopers called "Isidor Weiss." In his diary on 14 July 1932 he wrote: "The time has come to finish him off. I have fought him for six years.... When he goes the [Weimar] system will not survive much longer." The government of Prussia actually did remove both Grzesinski and Weiss soon after, not at Nazi urging, but on grounds that they had failed to preserve law and order.

What happened with the police administration in Berlin as well as other notable achievements for the Right were all the result of the so-called "Papen coup." Closely following the presidential election of 1932 in Germany, there was a state election in Prussia. By it, the Nazis became the largest party in the Prussian *Landtag*. The Nazis and Communists immediately became strange political bedfellows, joining to vote no confidence in Prussian premier Otto Braun, a Social Democrat. But, of course, these two political extremes could not agree on a successor. Therefore, the Social Democrats patched together a caretaker regime to carry on to the next election. The chancellor was at this point Franz von Papen, scion of an aristocratic Westphalian family. Papen was a willing tool for a group of traditional conservatives around Hindenburg. He was appointed a minority chancellor on a recommendation to Hindenburg by the traditionalists surrounding the president. Papen quickly dismissed the Reichstag and called for new elections. He also lifted the ban on the stormtroopers, likely because the people around him had promised this to Hitler for momentary toleration of his regime.

When Papen looked closely at Berlin, he found the city in a state of near collapse. More than six million of its inhabitants were unemployed. Red-Brown street fights were now a daily occurrence. Having dissolved the Reichstag, Papen decided that he could best defend his unpopular regime by also ordering dissolution of the SPD caretaker government in Prussia. Instead, Prussia would be ruled from the chancellor's office.

Prussia had been a fortress of Social Democratic strength since the beginning of the Republic. It stretched from feudal estates in the East to the factories of the Ruhr in the West. It contained three-fifths of German territory and two-thirds of its population. Papen had drafted for Hindenburg a presidential decree to seize the Prussian government. All that was needed was a pretext. It came on 17 July when stormtroopers staged a march in an industrial suburb of Hamburg, Altona.

Since the Hamburg-Altona "march-out" was a legal parade, under new rules set down by Papen the police had to do their best to protect the SA marchers. But Reds replied to the invasion with gunfire from rooftops. When it was over, seventeen were dead and over a hundred wounded. Three days later, Papen took power over Prussia to keep "peace." Papen used the opportunity of "Bloody Sunday" (a press label), to make himself "National Commissioner." The Social Democrats protested, but they believed that the only possible weapon they

This is Goebbels' montage of battleground Berlin in the early 1930s. At the top center of the page is an image of Dr. Bernhard Weiss, a Jewish deputy to the chief of the Berlin police department. Goebbels liked to call Weiss "Isidor Weiss" and he saw him as his foremost enemy in Berlin.

could have used, a general strike, was now unreliable. They might well face the German army under imposed martial law. But even more important was the fact that six million unemployed were available who might well act as scabs and take any job that was open.

The Social Democrats took their case to the German Superior Court. However, by the time the court ruled against Papen, his own regime was already doomed. Germany continued under appointed chancellors. But the result in Berlin of the Papen coup was a changed city police, no longer working diligently against the SA. Nazi sympathizers began to appear openly among the police. A ban on joining the Nazi Party on the part of policemen was lifted for them on 29 July.[41]

The police still interfered in Nazi activity when they caught stormtroopers openly breaking the law. Just as often, they looked the other way. Following a gunbattle between the SA and the Red Front Fighters on 6 September 1932, police arrested Nazis and Reds alike. But stormtroopers were released at the police station while Communists were taken to cells.[42]

All of this was part of Berlin's rapid transformation. As the city gave in to Nazism, there were signs that it was losing the leading role it had played in Europe since 1871. An exodus of artists and intellectuals began. Architect Walter Gropius had resigned as early as 1928, hoping a successor would be less controversial in managing the world-famous *Bauhaus*. Neither Gropius nor his successor overcame the general antagonism of the political Right to modernistic architecture. Author Arthur Koestler left Berlin for Russia in July of 1932. Marlene Dietrich, an actress famous in Germany and the United States returned briefly to Berlin in 1932 and took a look around. She went back to Hollywood for good. Albert Einstein also took flight to America. Other well-known artists and intellectuals stayed. In time many would be persecuted.[43]

On 30 January 1933, the night of Hitler's appointment to the chancellorship, massed Nazi marchers, mostly stormtroopers, poured through Berlin streets to the Brandenburg gate, waving torches and singing. They moved on past the Reich Chancellery where Hitler and Hindenburg stood on a balcony. Now the exodus began in earnest. Playwright Bertold Brecht left quickly for Vienna. Kurt Weill and Lotte Lenya, of "Three-Penny Opera" fame, fled to Paris. A number of conductors and composers fled to Switzerland or America. The unique, feverish, turbulent, and recklessly hedonistic Berlin of the twenties was gone.

Chapter Eight

The Shape and Meaning of the Depression SA

Although the SA had replaced most of the old paramilitary formations by the time Hitler occupied the chancellorship, that fact does not mean that it was similar to those organizations. The old Free Corps mentality desired, if vaguely, to save Europe from Bolshevism, resist French and/or Polish encroachment, to avoid returning to an imperial Germany in favor of a new kind of polity, and to devise a framework of reference including anti-bourgeois and revolutionary ideals.[1] In some ways the SA mindset was a continuation of those notions; in other ways it was a distinct departure from them.

Nazism was able to mobilize large segments of society to support it after the Depression began. This situation has been treated until fairly recently as a direct result of a middle class cut loose from its societal moorings by economic catastrophe. By this interpretation, in this new political domicile, the distraught were able to oppose and attack vaguely identified enemies "responsible" for their shared socio-economic agony. Nazism, in this view, offered to these distraught people a real contrast with Communism; it offered patriotic "responsibility." The most apparent manifestation of the discontented masses' mobilization was to be observed in the SA.

This interpretation both hits and misses the mark. It does not really address by itself the problem of why the SA would appeal so widely in 1931–32. If only discontinuity because of crisis is emphasized, then a one-sided view is produced. This perspective ignores the fact that, from at least the nineteenth century, a tendency had cut across class lines to take common action in a broad range of nonpolitical organizations. In many ways the formation of the SA in villages, small towns, and smaller urban centers reflected a considerable continuity of traditional organizational life.

Long before Nazism appeared on the historical stage, many German towns owned a considerable mix of *Vereine* or *Verbände*. In fact, most local address books published in such towns carried an extensive section on *Vereinsleben*. Deep-seated associational tendencies existed, beyond those seen elsewhere in Europe. These were well established by the mid–nineteenth century in the ranges of the middle class.[2] After mid-century, other socio-economic groups beyond the parameters of the bourgeoisie were also driven to organize on the basis of vested interests. One such was the trade unions formed in connection with the SPD. In fact, the SPD was the first political party to take extensive advantage of the associational tendencies in German life. It had an elaborate institutional structure within which there were diverse cultural organizations, media outlets, workers' clubs formed in association with bars and pubs these men frequented, sporting clubs, and an educational apparatus.

All of this was not lost on Hitler and, when he began building the Nazi Party, he expressed admiration for the "machinery" of the SPD. At the same time, he wished no one to be mistaken concerning his hatred for the ideology expressed by the Left. He wanted primarily to see the Nazis have their own "educative" mechanisms, newspapers, clubs, and other organizations designed to spread the message much like the SPD had. In time, this would become the case.

During the nineteenth century, Hitler's eventual reaction to the SPD was foreshadowed by the establishment of a large number of associations among farmers, white-collar workers, shopkeepers, and others aimed directly at limiting the influence of the organized working classes.[3] Simultaneously, there continued a seemingly never-ending expansion of social clubs of all types.

The coming of World War I established a kind of moratorium on associational development. The war did, however, cause some organizations formed in the prewar associational boom to develop further and become more intensely patriotic.[4] With the war ending in ignominious defeat, there was another explosion of organizational life. The era of the Weimar Republic was a period of diminished governmental authority. One by-product of this diminution was a burgeoning of all kinds of associations, among them paramilitary units.

Diverse associational life was damaged by the great inflation of 1922–24. However, associational activity was to flower again soon. Many organizations in this burgeoning group were now militaristic *Vereine*. And almost all of these expressed dissatisfaction with some aspect or the other of Weimar society. To some extent, participation in associations substituted for participation in the Weimar political system.

After the Depression began, the Nazis moved out into the widespread network of associational life by establishing under party auspices many similar, but more highly politicized, substitutes for memberships already embraced. While Nazi propaganda trumpeted the myth of a seamless societal amalgam called the *Volksgemeinschaft,* Nazism actually became a vast roof association. Under this roof familiar German organizations were replicated with National Socialist titles.

Similarly, the SA provided a roof for combat-league members. As the old leagues dissolved, they discharged paramilitary orphans. These men then could move under the roof of a vast SA club of the nation, more broadly diversified and thus more appealing than any of the old leagues had ever been. Moreover, by awarding pseudo-military titles, bourgeois-like status was provided for men outside and beneath middle-class ranks.

The NSDAP itself was a "*Volkspartei,*" if in a distorted fashion. It attracted some lower-class (almost always nonunion) workers, but could not easily penetrate the paradigmatic milieu represented by the SPD or the Communists.

The SA offered itself as something of a seamless amalgam also. In reality it was by the advent of the Depression a roof formation of the sort Ernst Röhm had once wanted the *Frontbann* to become and remain. It was far larger than the old Kampfbund from the putsch years. It managed to bind together, sometimes tenuously before January of 1933, a great variety of disparate elements. By 1930, the Depression had so altered political circumstances that the idea of belonging to such a vast organization, one which often offered socio-economic support in a manner a small combat league could not, had considerable appeal.

Eight. The Shape and Meaning of the Depression SA

One of the reasons the SA club of the nation was so attractive to men of the old paramilitary *Verbände* was because so many of the units in it were led by semi-independent former Free Corps leaders. It should be remembered that it was possible in the late Weimar years to begin an SA unit simply by submitting the fact of its existence and its name to "Munich Central." In this way, a leader rose of his own accord to join the SA extension of the participation revolution and found a squad that could bear his own name "for all time." The SA thus developed an appeal leaping across class boundaries to include people who were both downwardly and upwardly mobile.[5] This was unique in postwar German paramilitary history.

The enrollees in this Great Depression era SA formed a second generation of political soldiers. This generation followed desperado leaders in brown shirts from the first generation of politicized soldiers. This new generation also followed the leaders into surrogate battlefields in German streets which supposedly replaced the wartime trenches. In these circumstances, the fact that the SA lacked narrow combat-league traditions turned out to be an asset. The SA could pull in its diverse membership because its associational framework was so much looser than the strictly paramilitary model seen in the old combat leagues.[6]

The various associational shapes of the SA — the club of the nation, a new plebian "school of the nation" (aimed at supplanting the traditional role of the Reichswehr), and an offered organized route to "adventure" within a drab Weimar setting — formed a very important part of the SA attraction. But there were other attractions as well. One of these was the so-called "SA Home," a direct Nazi answer to the economic deprivation, mentioned briefly earlier, which had spread over the country. These were key locations for the activities of SA groups, providing rooms for group meetings and training sessions. They also acted as safe houses for stormtroopers targeted by the Red Front Fighters or authorities.

Similar roles for the SA *Heime* were played by so-called SA *Lokale*, taverns where SA units congregated. Both the homes and the locals provided tactical advantages for the SA to serve as "command posts." But, most important, the homes served as barracks where out-of-work stormtroopers could sleep and eat meals from a common stewpot.

Those born around 1910 came of age when economic chaos had thrown thousands out into the streets. The youngest applicants found it hardest to compete for jobs. Many young people simply could not start a vocation, as traditional paths to achievement were closed. In the absence of a path to follow, some choose a criminal life. Others simply drifted. These were societal outsiders who suddenly became societal insiders when they became residents of an SA home. Once in the home they could be radicalized by desperadoes and by slightly older but still youthful men who had already embraced Nazism.

With the coming of the Depression, the first SA homes were built or made out of already existing structures — abandoned warehouses, the upstairs floors over taverns, etc. There were some twenty-five of them in the Berlin area by the end of 1931. Some were SA youth hostels. But the SA employed the usual party romanticism by calling them all "Storm Centers." Food for the unemployed in the homes came from an auxiliary organization, the SA *Hilfswerk*, supported by donations from sympathizers or the occupants themselves who contributed to the common stewpot.

A closer look at the SA homes is provided by a series of Prussian state police reports in the Captured German Documents housed in the National Archives. In mid–1930 the Police Presidium in the Westphalian city of Hagen began reporting the existence of three local SA homes. One of these was fairly elaborate, including a "day room," kitchen, and sleeping quarters.[7] By November of that same year, more installations had been added, some holding as many as 120 men.[8] Soon enough, these installations were discovered to have been centers from which radical activities were launched. The authorities placed severe restrictions upon these installations, ordering that no stormtroopers remain in any one home for a period longer than forty-eight hours. It was apparently the authorities' hope that this would restrain the stormtroopers' ability to mount hostile actions. These strictures appeared ineffective. Hence, from early 1932, the Prussian Ministry of the Interior issued orders closing SA Storm Centers in Hagen and elsewhere in the expansive Prussian *Land*.[9]

From the ministry's point of view, SA homes served as "regular guard details" to be "placed on alert status whenever there was a need for them to be called into action." Steps taken in Hagen and elsewhere against the homes were commonly justified by SA beatings of opponents in the city's streets. And, it was added, the SA men were rather unselective in that they often pummeled political innocents.[10] There soon followed closings of taverns condemned as "SA hangouts." It was part of the SA romanticism of the military life that such places as the recessed doorways of these taverns were often referred to in SA files as "observation posts." Once the closings of the homes and taverns were ordered, the usual difficulty involved in keeping the brownshirts from violating prohibitions was observed. Stormtroopers readily and brazenly stole back into the prohibited locations, hardly masking their presence.[11]

The closings were protested in court by Nazi Party attorneys. Wilhelm Römer, former Free Corps member and Hagen *Gauführer* of the Association of Nazi Jurists, filed a great many briefs in protest of the Prussian state action. Römer also defended SA supporters such as Johanna Lösenbeck, owner of an "observation post" (actually a Nazi Party tavern), who had cited the "obvious injustice" and financial damage done to her by the closing of her establishment. She claimed that, in this way, her livelihood had been placed in peril.[12]

The battle over the closings ran on into the fall of 1932. At that juncture, Nazi *Landtag* deputy Wilhelm Schepmann (during World War II to become Chief of Staff, SA) rose in the Prussian Diet to denounce the anti–SA campaign in Hagen.[13] The Hagen situation was still being reported in the press as 1932 ended.[14] Only days before Hitler became chancellor, Carl Severing was still defending the actions of the Prussian state police taken against the SA homes.[15]

The existence of the SA homes provides one indication of why the Nazi paramilitary was so much more effective and popular than the old combat leagues had been. Young Germans, cast out of their own homes by circumstance, were there, as were young men grown to adult life without fathers because theirs had died in the war. Many others found a purpose in life through the Storm Centers. This circumstance was cited by one man writing of everyday life in his Magdeburg Storm Center during 1930: "Because of the unemployment, the SA men remained in their customary abode surrounded by Marxists day and night.... A kitchen was established to prepare food.... Rooms were established where they could sleep or become warm."[16]

Somewhat more difficult to evaluate is the nature and functioning of an SA mythology. What impact might the homes have had on young men concerned with sheer survival in a harsh and politicized world? In matters of belief, nothing rebuffs analysis as much as the basis for concepts held illogically. As Reformation historian Roland H. Bainton had it, "Nothing is so interior as faith."[17] Without attempting to understand individual beliefs we can at least examine the fact that the Nazi SA's membership was presented with a substantial body of mythology, perhaps helping them to channel their convictions for the benefit of Nazism. There were, for instance, considerable numbers of stormtrooper Siegfrieds who had slain their dragons or "ascended to Valhalla" when killed. This kind of mythical fabrication was waiting in the *Heime* for the unemployed when, alone and distraught, they came in out of the cold. They were presented with the notion there that they too could be "heroic" in a movement where myth-figures in the SA pantheon like Horst Wessel were presented to them.

Wessel's case was examined earlier. It is sufficient to point out here that he was one of those young men made fatherless by the war who came into Nazi ranks (in his case in 1926 before the Depression). His father had died during World War I while serving as an army chaplain. Wessel, too young to have served in the war, like Heinrich Himmler and many others, entered the world of the combat leagues soon after.[18] Having joined the SA early, he enjoyed considerable vertical mobility as was then common in a *Sturmabteilung* just developing. He quickly came to be the leader of Storm Five of the Berlin stormtroopers.[19]

After the sordid events involved in his death, he was quickly installed in the ranks of mythic Nazi heroes with a mass propagandistic funeral.[20] From that juncture, Goebbels took an ordinary SA brawler and transformed him into the nationally known "Group Leader in Valhalla."[21] At the center of this myth, Wessel was misrepresented as the idealistic student who left behind him a respectable home to die for Nazism.[22] He became the archetypical "unknown SA man," whose duty it was to contribute his life for Nazism.[23] In the view of historian Jay W. Baird, Wessel provided Nazism's most effective myth, one with pseudo–Christian overtones. This was "the blood myth — which featured the death of a noble warrior, his resurrection, and ultimately his spiritual return to the fighting columns of Brown Shirts."[24]

Any young man entering the SA in the early 1930s could not have avoided the Wessel myth. Moreover, he was also likely to have been confronted with a pantheon of lesser mythic heroes. These were men like the supposed "immortals" who died in the 1923 Hitler putsch. Later, at the beginning of the Third Reich, they would be joined by those killed by the last great outbursts of street fighting at the end of 1932, like "martyred" SA man Hans Maikowsi. Also offered was a composite, the idealized Storm Leader. He was pictured as a strong yet primitive figure. He supposedly could speak to the workers in their own tongue. He was simultaneously profound and simple. He owned great physical courage. He led SA men into the proper "primitization of politics."[25]

The "primitive" SA hero was very much like a figure found in the *völkisch* novel of the nineteenth century. In these works German peasants were idealized as "those closest to the soil" and hence "the most genuine human beings."[26] Such peasants were good men who always vanquished evil ones in the pages of these works. But to vanquish what the novelist depicted as evil they had been endowed with "ferociousness" and "even cruelty."[27] The best known and most widely read of these novels, *Der Wehrwolf*, was published in 1910. In it, Hermann Löns wrote of men who had accepted that the brutality of the Thirty Years' War was a fact of life and that its nature had made cruelty a positive virtue.[28]

The primitivized image of the stormtrooper presented in party literature was very much like the notion of Löns's peasants. The idealized stormtrooper also embraced violence as a positive virtue. It would be too much to assert a direct connection between the *völkisch* literature of the nineteenth and early twentieth century and the idealized SA man presented in the propaganda spread by the Party. But the typologies are sufficiently similar to indicate something about an adeptness within Nazism to pick up useful elements present in German culture and add them to a body of propaganda. In that body nothing was truly original but only skillfully modified to suit Nazi purposes.

It is true that the Löns book was standard reading for those in the middle-class moving into the Free Corps after the end of World War I. And the idealized accounts of Free Corps leaders, the direct ancestors of idealized images of SA men, were also quite similar to those of the Löns's work. Taken in this light, the Freikorps may well have acted as a conduit to bring these notions into the SA.

The notion of a Storm Leader primitive, "uncouth" yet "a splendid fellow," who could be trusted with "all one's money,"[29] obviously was aimed at influencing the blue-collar or semi-skilled laborers the SA wanted to win over for their ranks. Many such workers liked the idea of a simple and straightforward man who contrasted with what they saw as the guileful members of the bourgeois order. This presented primitive was crafted to fit nicely with the Nazi attempt to win over laborers in Berlin or the Ruhr. And there is evidence to suggest that the SA tapped the strength of the Left sufficiently to help fill its own ranks in 1932, as Ernst Röhm had stated they would.[30] Obviously, workers thus attracted could merge with other class elements in the SA, but understandably with some friction between them and middle-class members.

Throughout the works on Nazism, and particularly those centering on the SA, conflicts between the SA and PO have been cited. This recurrent antagonism can be looked at on a functional level, emphasizing Hitler's purposive creation of a dual party. It can also be offered that the difference between the two-party wing's functions helped the SA, desperado-like, in its frequent maintaining that its members were part of a militarized world set apart from the doings of ordinary men. But it is also important to note that the SA-PO schism may have rested in part on the class and age differences between the two elements. Another possible factor shaping this difference was the dissimilar rates of unemployment based on these two factors. Was there in fact a social chasm opened between the SA and the rest of the party based on the differential impact of the world economic crisis on differing categories of Germans?

A determination of the class and occupational picture of the SA to answer the question just posed presents a difficult task. Most assumptions about class structure have generally been made for the party as a whole, then "logically" extended to the SA. As early as the pioneer writings on National Socialism of Konrad Heiden, as observed, it has been asserted that the whole Nazi movement was basically lower middle class.[31]

After Heiden, for some time, works on Nazism repeated this generalization. Eventually, this view gave rise to a contrary assessment of the SA as a possible radical advance guard of a lower-class revolution against a modern capitalistic society. In this view the SA was made up of those who often yearned for a return to pre-capitalist guild structures.[32] More modern assessments of the party as a whole have also made Heiden seem less relevant in his assessment of the Nazi Party's class levels. They have shown the years immediately before and after 1933 to have been a period when manual workers did increase their "share in the Party," although, as historian Michael Kater has stated, they were still underrepresented when compared with the lower middle class. It is difficult to ascertain the extent "to which these class proportions were the result of economic disenchantment with Weimar, socio-cultural alienation, anti–Semitism, anti–Marxism, etc."[33] made a difference.

The traditional lower-middle class definition of the party as a whole, more recently refined by historians like Michael Kater, contrasts with views of the SA also developed more recently. These sometimes point out that Röhm and his leadership cadre canalized SA attitudes in a leftward direction by the use of a definite socio-revolutionary bias not seen in the rest of the party.[34] This kind of view is countered, often angrily, by Marxists who see the SA rabble as violent men working in the service of monopoly capitalism and thus a sworn enemy of the Left and "all workers."

The problem with such positions as these two is that they attempt to categorize the SA within the limitations of a single generalization. That is quite difficult, since the Depression SA may have had as many as 700,000 men in it by the time Hitler became chancellor in 1933. Since this mass paramilitary force was nationwide and diverse as early as 1931, a better approximation of its structure can be discerned by comparing and contrasting different areas within Germany.

In Berlin, as described to some extent earlier, the local SA went through transformational stages during the mid to late 1920s. At that time it came under the leadership provided by a former Free Corps desperado named Kurt Daluege.[35] When the Depression came to the capital, unemployed people poured into various local units of the SA. Walter Stennes, an SA group leader, reported on Berlin to party headquarters on 28 February 1931 that some 67 percent of local SA men were unemployed.[36]

As the unemployed moved into the Berlin SA, both a discernible worker connection and a criminal connection grew. As far as the criminal connection was concerned, police records in Berlin show that many individuals with documented criminal pasts began to enroll in Brown ranks. Perhaps in part because of this infusion, the struggle between the SA and Communists took on something of the aura of prohibition-era Chicago. One Storm called itself "the Robbers," and another the "Pimp's Brigade." Individuals took names for themselves like "Bullet Müller" or "Revolver-Shoot Schmidt."[37]

In addition, large numbers of manual laborers entered to expand the SA opening to the workers. One report from the Berlin SA as early as 1930 cited "the pleasingly large numbers of proletarians" taking up the paramilitary life in service of Nazism.[38] Samples of SA units drawn from the Weimar period support the fact that, in some industrial centers like Berlin, naturally hit harder and earlier by economic distress than more rural locations, the SA actually did draw well among factory workers.[39] It was also in Berlin that the financial and welfare assistance schemes of the party, like a stormtrooper insurance scheme, appeared most needed.[40]

The rush of proletarians into SA ranks was not seen as sweepingly in some other urban centers. In Munich and Frankfurt there were fewer workers than one might expect from examining the evidence of the Berlin case.[41] Similarly, there was underrepresentation of workers among the SA membership in East Germany. This was an area where farmers and artisans dominated.[42] Yet there were some towns even in this area where the SA managed to offer itself as more proletarian. One such was Eutin. But it appears in the Reich more broadly that there was little doubt that the blue-collar workers were more likely to be in the SA than the PO.[43] But even here there are exceptions. In contrast with places like Berlin and Hamburg, the SA was closer to the occupational and class structure of the broader party in Nuremberg. Both the PO and SA were drawn from the middle class in Nuremberg. Manual workers made up more than half of the unemployed male population in Nuremberg, while they only provided an insignificant portion of the SA men there.[44]

It should prove useful at this point to indicate what categorizing the unemployed into workers and nonworkers might mean. If the usual assumption is made that workers are lower class, this raises the possibility that the SA was perhaps structurally as much, or nearly as much, lower class as it was middle class. It has been common also to divide the working classes in terms of skilled, semiskilled and unskilled workers. Also useful, given the way stormtroopers saw themselves as political laborers "of the fist," a meaningful distinction is that made between manual and nonmanual categories in between-the-wars German society.

If working class is defined also in part as incorporating unskilled agricultural workers, they should be placed in the class category as well as some urban factory employees. It is true that the SA was very popular between 1930 and 1933 with young farm laborers. Yet, it is best to keep in mind, as did former SA leader Heinrich Bennecke, that clear pictures of SA occupational-class structure are difficult to obtain, because some workers (classified by many as "skilled") were in some cases undertrained or partially trained and thus forced out of lower-middle-class status into the proletariat. Such workers may have seen themselves as more proletarian than the label many have provided would indicate.[45]

The tentative conclusion reached after viewing several of these structural assessments of the SA is that the organization drew men from nearly all levels of German life, but that only some urban areas had really high concentrations of blue-collar workers who could serve as potential recruits. These new members of the Nazi army thus often had working-class backgrounds, contrary to what early theories of Nazism stressed — middle-class character of the party as a whole.

Moreover, these workers did not all fit into any one category; they were factory laborers, artisans, farm helpers, etc. And they reflected in occupation and attitude the areas from which they came. In the SA, at least to some extent, blue-collar workers merged with master craftsmen, merchants and shopkeepers. But these last were present in lesser numbers than the "urban proletariat." This is not surprising for they were far less numerous in the German economy as a whole.[46]

The picture of the Depression SA that emerges, therefore, is much more like other organizations based largely on "workers of the fist," as was the SPD Reichsbanner. The major difference displayed by such workers is that they were never able to escape the hyper-nationalism stimulated by war and despised postwar treaties. Like the Reichsbanner, leaders not drawn from the desperado remnants were men of the middle classes. Because of their education, these people more easily accomplished bureaucratic duties.[47]

The fact that the SA was to some extent a melting pot of the classes, at least more than the party as a whole, indicates that it was necessary to use a different ideological approach to the membership than that of the PO. One example of this differing approach can be seen in the testimony at Nuremberg of Max Jüttner, a man who had come to the SA from the *Stahlhelm* to become, eventually, deputy chief of staff in 1939.[48] Jüttner testified, "The concept of the 'master-race' was never fostered in the SA; that would have been quite contrary to reason, for the SA received its replacements from all strata."[49]

This ideology reflected within the SA, given the somewhat differing composition of the formations, had therefore a differing ring to it. Some of it sounded more than a little neo–Marxian.[50] Röhm himself was not adverse to providing pseudo-revolutionary statements such as: "The narrow-minded petit bourgeois may discover that my attitude is imprudent, but that does not trouble me."[51] Such comments from the party desperadoes could be taken by workers as representative of a true class bias. Actually, that was not what it was, but rather something more complex.

During an era when the Bolshevik Revolution of 1917 loomed over Europe like a giant specter, the terminology of many from the radical Left and radical Right, or from those who simply wanted to shock people, slipped into the Marxist style. When Röhm denounced the petit bourgeoisie, he was probably concerned with drawing distinctions between front-fighters and civilians. The kind of middle-class person he despised was one who sat comfortably at home while men had fought and had died in the trenches.

In the PO, as well, one found crossover people. There was Goebbels, for instance, who because of his close relationship with the Berlin SA in the 1920s and early 1930s loved to sound in public like a born-again radical. He often wrote and spoke in public in Marxian-sounding ways, perhaps following Hitler's lead in taking from the Left what was useful when he tossed out terms like *Lumpenproletariat* ("the lumped-together masses") or the "overly bourgeois Weimar regime."[52]

Even if the use of pseudo–Marxist terminology was common in the party, it is probably useful to separate the origins of the kind of rhetoric used by Goebbels and other propagandists and that of the SA, although it normally may have come out sounding much the same when uttered. Röhm, for instance, explained how the desperado surmounted class barriers by pointing out that all soldiers "speak the same language" and thus it mattered not whether a combat soldier was a Marxist or not. Any trooper on the line was capable of reaching out "beyond all differences of class, rank, and political worldview" to join with others of his kind.[53] Goebbels and his ilk were, in contrast, primarily trying to shock people.

One thing appears especially certain about the Depression SA. As indicated earlier in connection with the SA homes, unemployment was high throughout. Between 1929 and 1933, German unemployment was just about the worst in Europe.[54] What was severe for the entire German nation was catastrophic in the SA. Typical surveys place it as high as 60 or 70 percent.[55] SA morale reports in 1932 from various locales consistently rate their own out-of-work rates somewhere between 50 and 80 percent.[56]

Figures drawn from the Abel collection of essays, a group of writings sent in to win a contest at the same time that valuable research about Nazis was collected, indicate that the unemployment rate among Nazis joining the party during the 1920s ran somewhat lower. According to this survey, there is an indication that "a good one-third" of those answering the request for essays were unemployed. These estimates, of course, were for the Nazi Party as a whole and the SA men included among them were more likely actually to be of Heiden's lower middle class than those flooding in to become brownshirts after 1930.

It is apparent that only those with sufficient educational background were likely to answer an appeal for an essay. So many other of the evidentiary sources often show nearly illiterate SA men appearing in units with unemployment rates of 60 percent or more. The educational level of men enrolling in the Depression SA causes one to wonder how most of these new recruits could ever have been deeply influenced by the propaganda sheets so regularly handed out in the Storm Centers. It is likely that in most instances they waited for inspirational remarks from their own leaders who could interpret the handouts.

The SA was also overwhelmingly young by 1931–32. For the most part, the age of a stormtrooper ranged between eighteen and forty-five, with the figure heavily weighted toward the lower end of the spectrum. Around 75 percent were under thirty.[57] Most stormtroopers had gone through some sort of training, usually involving a three-year apprenticeship. But, if Bennecke is to be believed, many did not even finish that before entering the ranks of the unemployed. It thus appears that a number of brownshirt recruits left formal education at about age seventeen only to find that there were no jobs. There were others, not quite as young as those graduated from an apprenticeship, who had migrated from their initial apprenticeships to part-time jobs without ever entering full-time gainful employment. In sum, the majority of SA men were out of work and a good many of them were too young in 1932 to even remember the Great War with any degree of clarity if at all. For them it was often only an idealized myth.

Was unemployment, reinforced by a natural yearning for action among the young, the major reason the rank-and-file members of the Depression SA joined? Various historians have provided different answers. Peter Merkl, using the Abel file almost exclusively, has offered the notion that unemployment was likely not as important as an already existing fascist "direction" each man had been provided by his "political socialization at home or in a youth group, long before economic adversity struck."[58]

This may well have been true for those respondents in the Abel file. But as Merkl himself admits, there is a bias in the Abel file[59]; it does not really represent the mass membership obtained by 1932 in significant part because of the existence of attractions like the SA *Heime*. The bulk of Merkl's sample is taken from people who came into the organization before 1930 and thus were less motivated by economic deprivation to join the Storm Detachment of National Socialism.

The continued expression of frustration about unemployment recurring in the body of SA morale reports (not used in many other works accentuating the Nazi paramilitary, with one notable exception),[60] can not be easily dismissed. The most balanced conclusion that can be drawn from all this would have to stress the diverse social and occupational structure of the *Sturmabteilung* of 1930–33. In the total organization, middle-class elements may well have drawn on their earlier social political conditioning to make them ideologically aware Nazis. But the numerous working-class, skilled, and semiskilled elements in it were more likely to use the organization as a vehicle within which they could canalize frustrations about joblessness without deeply committing to Nazi ideology.

Lastly, some Americans, who live in a society where workers since 1945 have seldom been radicalized and have instead relaxed in suburban complacency, have assumed that only the United States owned a working class not driven in some measure by socialistic thinking. But the Germany of the Depression era had many workers similarly not drawn to socialism.

Should the extent of material well-being be the primary causational factor explaining why a worker should be Right-radical instead of Left-radical? There was in fact no compelling reason why many workers in a country like Germany, where a leveling nationalism had long been offered as a positive virtue and was thus offered again during the Great War, should feel any categorical imperative to seek the international linkages of socialism. Particularly was it easy for a patriotic worker to be drawn to the SA. Within its ranks he had a chance to be both nationalistically and socially (rather than "socialistically") radical at one and the same time.

An Above-Class Organization?

As indicated earlier, imperial Germany was to some extent composed of socio-political blocs typified by mutual hostility. Such antagonisms had passed through the portal provided by war into interwar society. The Nazi movement was more efficient than others in joining descendants of these blocs on the Right together in their radical version of the participation revolution. The mastery over competing blocs and a radical Right riven by differences derived from the Nazi use of a dual strategy. First, the Nazis attempted to lure in various social groups by making promises to dissimilar social elements at differing societal levels. These promises to one element often could not be kept without damaging the other groups to which similar entreaties had been offered.

This process of dangling similar carrots before diverse groups is not unfamiliar in the United States. But it was novel in Germany during the early years of the Depression. Moreover, the media of that time did not allow for the immediate awareness offered by today's coverage of events broadcast almost before the events have even ended. The Nazis rationalized all this by offering the notion that conflicts of interests based on class differences were no longer valid, obviated by the appearance of a Nazi movement which stood above normal class conflicts.[61]

The argument that the Nazis had forged an above-class movement without being Marxian was a telling one with workers in jobs without status and with the unemployed. It probably even had some impact with disgruntled white-collar employees who resented traditional social elites, but, at the same time, shared those elites' fear of Marxist revolutionary activities or even substantial electoral change. Such people commonly saw threats which could dislodge them from their precarious perches on the status ladder to tumble down into the proletariat. Generally, Nazism had great success in merging intermediate social segments by promising to eradicate fractious class struggle and replace it with a vaguely defined "truly German working order." SA propaganda followed this theme throughout the early Depression years, insisting that "workers of the fist" had merged in Nazism with "workers of the mind."

One facile manner of explaining the continuity of a dual party, supposedly riven by class and/or factional differences, is to emphasize the workings of charismatic politics. Works that emphasize this tendency in Nazism rightly point out that, unlike movements of the Left where very real divisions over theory have led to extreme factionalism, fascistic movements possess ideologies generally so fuzzy that they cause relatively few major splits. It is, of course, apparent that the vagueness of the Nazi "worldview" allowed vastly differing conceptions of what in its essence Nazism actually happened to be.[62]

Works attempting to explain the somewhat easy subduing of ideological or factional controversy in the Nazi movement do so by looking at Hitler's role as "the primary source of group cohesion, the focus of loyalty, and the personification of the utopian idea — in short, a charismatic leader."[63] One sort of charismatic interpretation thus concentrates on the structure of the Nazi Party and the relationship of that structure to the supreme importance of Hitler.

It is natural enough in cases where charismatic interpretations are the issue, to return to that ultimate German authority on charisma, Max Weber. Weber explained how charisma becomes a legitimate source of authority in place of legal or traditional officials. Weber believed that potential "subjects," given extraordinary circumstances, deed the right to rule to one person because of that individual's special characteristics. In these often dire situations, which promote an intensely unusual search for security, charisma assumes its own special legitimacy.[64]

Hitler came as close to playing the role Weber described as anyone in German history. The leader owned a unique charismatic override allowing him to rule over a Nazi Party which, in the words of Zevedei Barbu, "like a river, moved right to left, to collect the waters from all over the place: from here a dynamic group of ex-officers, from there a ... circle of intellectuals, an enthusiastic youth organization."[65]

In Hitler's movement, the campaign to achieve power was completely identified with the *Führer*. Hence, within the charismatic-overlordship construct, a faction had little chance of survival, if survival meant remaining within the confines of a party where the program was absolutely identified with the leader. Hence, the quarrels resulting from the functional and to some extent structural division between PO and SA could be overridden by Hitler's charismatic authority.

In a slightly differing fashion, some of those who use the psychohistorical approach to explain Nazism also make a charismatic argument. This charismatic argument cites the generational relationship between veterans of World War I and the Depression era. It emphasizes the fact that, as Peter Lowenberg has it "the new adults who filled the ranks of the SA and other paramilitary organizations ... were the children socialized in the First World War."[66] The argument proceeds by indicating that those coming of age during the Depression were influenced overwhelmingly by World War I, although in "vastly differing ways."[67] This view presents a youth cohort haunted by childhood hunger and privation existing across a broad societal spectrum. Fatherless children, driven by the intense memories of privation and the lack of parental guidance, were ready for submission to a glorified charismatic substitute father, "distant" yet "idealized." This substitute parent, in this view, was none other than Adolf Hitler.[68]

How can such a view be reconciled with the atomistic and desperado-informed tendencies be seen in the SA? How can it be merged with the views of historians who tell us there was much that was feudal and thus decentralized in Nazism, particularly in the SA? In fact, decentralization during the Weimar years was often to be noted in the SA where group leaders were like "barons" over their satrapies. Why should they not be the distant and removed fathers offered in the psychohistorical approach?

As far as a thorough review of the German documents indicating the nature of SA groups at their lowest levels in urban areas are concerned, they show an urban Depression-era Storm Detachment where, if any father figures are to be found for young men reared by mothers only, they are to be seen in the slightly older Storm leaders in the individual Storm. In this way the SA of these decisive years appears much like a modern urban street gang where fatherless young men give their devotion to the "elders" of their own local group, although such a man may be only five to ten years older. And like the SA in urban areas of 1930–33, these young men are assigned violent acts to establish their credentials within the peer group.

To understand the charismatic-structural view of Nazism and its SA, one must first comprehend that this view usually concentrates for proof on such inner-party crises as the "Stennes revolt" and Hitler's ability to overcome such events with relative ease. In the spring of 1930, Walter Stennes, Berlin SA leader, led a revolt against the PO. It was particularly aimed at Joseph Goebbels as *Gauleiter*. Stennes demanded freedom of action without the intervention of the heavy-handed Goebbels. He also brought up one of the ubiquitous demands that leaders like him be granted higher salaries, as well as asking for more money for the ordinary stormtrooper. This was only an ordinary revolt against party bureaucracy and the *Bonzen* who ran it. There were few ideological overtones, but instead much talk about how the party's bigwigs led lives of luxury and corruption.

Eight. The Shape and Meaning of the Depression SA

The situation in Berlin continued to deteriorate and Goebbels was forced to call on Hitler to come save the situation.[69] The Prussian state government's report on Hitler's technique describes Hitler bolting "from section to section." In dealing with the stormtroopers in Berlin, as Ernst Ludecke, an early Hitler supporter has it, Hitler moved from unit to unit, "promising, beseeching, upbraiding," until the waters were finally calmed.[70] Such incidents as these are thus often cited in the charismatic-structural view as evidence that, because of his established stance of his charismatic legitimacy, Hitler was able to restrain all factionalism as the "ultimate arbiter."[71]

In the process of reconciling the charismatic view with the feudal-atomistic perspective, it should be noted that the decentralization of the SA did not damage Hitler's charismatic legitimacy. Hitler's rather mystical stance was above and beyond the party as a whole. Had the party's leadership functions been based on traditional bureaucratic authority, Hitler's exercise of control would have been more difficult. Hitler's displayed tendency was to intervene reluctantly only when a crisis was dire. If the descent of the myth-figure from his Olympian perch to act as referee had been more common, then the overlordship myth might well have been damaged. But given the way that Hitler's nature apparently made him act and the broad umbrella-like character of the party as a whole, the roof of the SA club of the nation was sufficiently removed from direct Hitlerian control to allow the necessary latitude for a degree of atomism.

SA structure had become feudal under Pfeffer. When Pfeffer resigned and Hitler became "supreme leader" himself, he was so distracted as commander that feudalism and atomism were not reversed. In part, the SA Stennes revolt was settled as easily as it was because the Storm Detachment structure was so feudalized that the contagion could not spread from one region to another easily. If the SA leaders nationally would have allowed themselves to be influenced by the spirit of rebellion, they would have had to look about elsewhere for a roof under which they could act out atomistic paramilitary impulses. But there was no other paramilitary locale where men of their bent could have gone to operate. It served the independent SA area commanders well to maintain their faith in a distant Hitler who would not interfere in their domains beyond generalized political direction. And it served some of them to distance themselves from Röhm, once he was appointed Chief of Staff at the beginning of 1931, in favor of a removed and enshrined Hitler.

At this juncture, it should prove useful to return to another aspect of the Weberian view of the charismatic leader: "[c]harismatic authority is ... specifically outside the realm of everyday routine and the profane sphere. In this respect, it is sharply opposed both to rational, and, particularly, bureaucratic authority.... Charismatic authority is specifically irrational in the sense of being foreign to all rules."[72]

Irrational charismatic authority vested in Hitler was rarely used with respect to the Depression-era SA. It was also ideally shaped to allow a more fluid SA organizational form. Had the SA been shaped by Weber's "rational and traditional" authority, as was the army, its structure would probably have been sufficiently rigid (and hence brittle) for the cracks of defection beginning with the Stennes revolt in Berlin to spread rapidly.

The psycohistorical-charismatic argument as crafted by Lowenberg can only be reconciled to a partial degree with the actuality of feudalism and atomism in the SA. The psychohistorical-charismatic view tends to put too much emphasis on Hitler's role in the pre-power SA. Thus, a distorted view of a movement which was composed of thousands of component parts is shown. The result is a view of Nazism in which the party and SA are marching inexorably forward in tandem to control Germany. It has been observed how Hitler can emerge from this argument as a substitute, though removed and distant, for a father fallen in the war. It has been mentioned also that a thorough review of SA records demonstrate that a father substitute, if there was one such, was likely more normally found within a young stormtrooper's own *Storm* or *Schar*. Taken in this light, the only strength present in the psycho-historical view is its emphasis on generational relationships, not the summoning of Hitler as a magical parent. Perhaps the fact that young men of the Depression SA were socialized during the war and what historians have often called "the war after the war," a tumultuous period from 1918 to 1923, did shape their development in lasting ways.

This last will necessarily have to remain unproven. But one of the things that is most certainly obvious about the Depression SA is that it was overwhelmingly young, probably more likely with its younger members to have been socialized during the "war after the war" than any other party segment. Fully one-fourth of its members were fifteen to twenty-six years of age by 1930.[73] And the proportion of young men to older ones in this group rose markedly after 1930. These young men were caught up in an all-male machismo cult, enshrining the street fight as an imagined afterglow of trench warfare. As it turned out: "[T]his machismo cult was often closer, in terms of its basic characteristics, to American or European street gangs and American "outlaw" motorcycle bands [of the later twentieth century] than veterans of the trenches."[74]

In the SA, teenage stormtroopers were motivated to carry out violent acts through peer pressure applied by slightly older comrades. Such peer pressure was reinforced at higher bureaucratic levels by the generation-older desperadoes who devised in general the schemes for violent attacks on political foes. What seems to have happened is that fatherless and rudderless young men followed the patterns established by juvenile street gangs in many cultures emphasizing that the gang (as in the case of a stormtrooper youth gang) provided substitute familial relationships and a role model for those in the need of such models. When the image presented by the role model is evident, then violence becomes the price of acceptance within the gang and the badge of performance each member must wear.

One example of these tendencies can be drawn from the Depression-era Silesian SA. A nineteen-year-old and fatherless stormtrooper named Ernst Hannich attempted to shoot and kill a designated target, a local labor leader and opponent of the Nazis. He failed at that, only wounding his victim, but he did faithfully follow instructions given within an SA Storm Center located in the town of Katscher. His shooting incident followed the Storm unit's sending a written warning to the target that they meant to place his head "on top of an electric-light pole" and put "his bowels out to dry."

Hannich had frequented a low tavern called the Inn von Schluss which was designated an "SA command post." There he came under the influence of an older brawler named Johann Cyfka. Cyfka was fond of shouting between rounds of drinks his version of a famous Hitlerian quote: "Heads will yet roll in Katscher!"[75]

Cyfka bragged to police after his arrest following the murder attempt that he had organized a "sacred ring" in a back room of the Inn von Schluss. A ceremony of his devising was carried out there to inspire young SA men like Hannisch. It was there also that he had followed the ceremony by providing a list of targets for his men. He denied culpability, indicating that he gave no specific orders for anyone to shoot one of these individuals designated.

They were simply to be the targets of propagandistic attacks and attempts to invade meetings where these men were featured. But Cyfka did not mention to his interrogators something he must have known; that young men in groups such as these were simply waiting for a chance to prove their worth to the group by an effective and simultaneously symbolic act.

It should be noted here that this is an example of the gang-like and club-like structure of local SA units. In such units, a stormtrooper who committed a "heroic act" like Hannich became an instant figure of admiration for his brown-shirted brethren. And this phenomenon is common in such groups. His deed was "not a misdeed, not a normal murder attempt," but the heroic act of an ersatz "frontline combat soldier."[76] His special badge of accomplishment was to be worn proudly. In many other places and times during the twentieth century violence-prone youth gangs have burgeoned. In these, the sort of peer pressure and role models typical of the Depression SA also developed, particularly in industrialized societies beset by long-term unemployment. Such a phenomenon was noted in the United States by some social scientists during a severe economic recession transpiring during 1981 and 1982. Usually, such youth gangs operate independently. The unusual thing about late Weimar Germany was that they commonly shared the same political bias and were connected to each other by a political structure. And these gangs did not reside on the Right alone. The Communists also had their own street-fighting groups which were also little more than urban gangs.[77]

In Depression Germany, violent youth groups which are often independent or are simply attached to organized crime in other industrial societies, were often likely to coalesce under the vast roof provided by the SA club of the nation. Compelled by a number of imperatives, among them personal psychological inclinations, frustrations deriving from unemployment or marginal unemployment, peer pressure, desperado role models, and even (although likely to a lesser extent) by the charismatic overlord Hitler, these street gangs roamed out from their Storm Centers to commit terroristic acts.

Terrorism in the SA

During the 1970s, international terrorism increased alarmingly. In various parts of the world airline terminals were attacked, bombs exploded in public places, hostages were taken, and big-business or government figures kidnapped. The question of terrorism became increasingly prominent in international relations. As this happened, attempts to define what terrorism actually *was* multiplied in number. Quickly, it was decided that the term "terrorism" had "no precise or widely accepted definition."[78] It was offered with some frequency that this modern terrorism was nothing more than the old crimes— murder, arson, etc.— carried out with the calculated intention of causing panic and disorder. The eventual aim of the mayhem was normally something like the production of a "properly altered social structure."[79]

Other definitions broadened to include terror by the state aimed at building a new order. Once in power, it is offered, the state in such cases establishes terrorist control over society through "the prostitution of the courts, the narcosis of the press," and the practices of murder and subversion.[80] This type of state terror is associated with Nazism and was typical of the period 1933–45 when Hitlerian power over Germany was consolidated and maintained.[81]

The kind of terrorism seen in the SA before January of 1933 contrasted directly with state-originated terror from above of the kind Nazism would establish once in power. It was what has been called "rebel terrorism." In this kind of terroristic activity, the "rebel" conducts terrorist campaigns for revolutionary purposes. This sort of terror has its origins in the French Revolution of 1789, as does also state terrorism, which draws its origins from another stage of the same revolution.

Terrorism in the rebel context was not meant to destroy individuals, although individuals were always casualties, but to bring to an end an established and despised system. During the French Revolution, a new principle of legitimacy was established: "The will of the people." This principle did not simply absolve its agents from adhering to moral and legal rules long accepted. In many case, it obliged them to abjure such principles. The act of the terrorist then became the carrying out of an idea (which became an emotionally transcendent entity) that can not be subjected to the rules of life in the ordinary sense. Hence, state and rebel terror are different expressions of a common terroristic ethos originating in the French Revolution, but they are clearly not the same.[82]

The kind of terrorism appearing among stormtroopers during the last days of the Republic was thus clearly rebel terrorism aimed at destabilizing the existing order. It was the threat of violence, actual violence, or widespread campaigns of violence (as in the Silesian SA during 1932) meant to install pervasive fear. SA terrorism was to some extent, as in more recent similar phenomena, violence for effect. Some portions of it could be classified as acts committed because people (and particularly representatives of the media) would be watching. SA terrorism was also aimed at other objectives. Some of these were simple tactical targets as in the case of a single political enemy. But far more were aimed at publicity for the cause and the subsequent demoralization of disapproving societal elements.

The victims of initial rebel terrorism were highly visible symbols of the "system's inequities." It was generally believed that the deaths of, or injury to, these people would inspire hopes among the masses that insurrection could happen. Indeed, it was held that it must be so if such people could die at the hands of common men. Hence, the image of the terrorist in the nineteenth century was often one of a radical ready to hurl a bomb in an assault on the existing order.

Systematic terrorism of the kind practiced by the SA in the first half of the twentieth century first appeared in the late nineteenth century. And the phenomenon is intertwined with the emergence of the masses. As many of the conditions faced by the downtrodden masses came to seem intolerable, movements of armed protest arose. The "high tide" of terrorism in Europe before war came in 1914 was the era of the "propaganda of the deed" in the 1890s and after. Most of this terrorism was true to the earlier cited form in that it involved attacks on leading statesmen. In that era it was a phenomenon seen coming from the more radical segments of the Left. After World War I, systematic terrorism was mounted by an emerging radical Right as well.[83]

After the Great War, terrorism went through a period of adaptation. In the immediate postwar period, highly visible public personalities were commonly still targets in the hope that their deaths would reveal and somehow alter the system's unliked tendencies. During the early years of the Weimar Republic, such terrorism was initiated by rightist clandestine organizations like the Organization Consul. Terrorist cells, often connected to paramilitary formations, emerged in the European postwar radical Right generally. Similar groups were seen in Rumania where the fascist Iron Guard created terrorist cells called "nests." Members of the nest agreed upon the idea that "a political crime committed by a private person ceases to be a crime when it is based on higher views and dictated by a clear notion, even if it is mistaken, of saving the state."[84]

Similarly, the Hungarian "Arrow Cross" fascist party spawned these groups, all with like characteristics.[85] The memberships of the Organization Consul, the Nests of the Iron Guard, and other similar organizations in varying national situations were not all exactly alike. But their individual terrorism was commonly held to be of lesser importance than mass acts designed to stimulate terror in the populace for propaganda advantage.[86]

The Nazis practiced what has been called since the 1950s "general terror" or "mass terror" where the object of terrorist acts is the "entire people."[87] The SA, of course, carried out the "general terror." By late 1932, there were mass SA "march-outs" to any location where a violent clash would ensue, thus focusing the attention of the national media on the cause. A favorite target in Berlin was the Karl Liebknecht House, Communist Party headquarters. Once arrived at that location, the SA could have its violent confrontation and reap the publicity benefits of what they themselves called "terror versus terror."[88]

Despite the seeming preponderance of mass terrorism in the SA, "propaganda of the deed" retained its place. One location where it remained prominent was in Silesia where the SA was under the direction of Edmund Heines. But it operated under a slightly altered blueprint.[89] By the time that SA Depression terrorism appeared in places like Silesia, prewar individualistic terrorism aimed at high-profile targets had waned. It had been replaced by the tendency to pick softer targets. These targets were more defenseless people who had less value as symbols. But the aim of going after these people was to cause governmental instability. The idea behind attacks was to cause the Weimar government to oppress citizens in retaliation. It was hoped that the citizenry would revolt or, as was more likely in the Weimar state, demonstrate against the government's inability to stop terrorism and protect its people. Once the second of these was demonstrated, the Nazis could offer something stronger to provide that protection. Perhaps paradoxically, in Germany this something stronger became a regime founded by the agents who had themselves authored much of the terrorism in the late Weimar Republic, the Nazis.

Almost certainly, the surge of terrorism in late 1932 was rooted in the Papen government's decision to decree prohibition of all political rallies and mass demonstrations until 10 August. In this way the preferred process of generalized terror was forbidden for a time.[90] The earlier prohibition was followed by the antiterrorist decrees of 9 August.[91] This second governmental step to restrict terrorism inspired for a time a more OC-like approach to the assault on Weimar.

Heines constituted an obvious link with the old OC, in which he had been a participant, and the Depression SA. He was one of the most fervent neo-romantic terrorists within Nazism. He shared with other romantic terrorists from times past a tendency to idealize death in service of a cause.

Before hesitating to use the word "romantic" to describe terrorism, let us remember with the prominent historian of ideas Arthur Lovejoy that the word romanticism should be used "in the plural." There are and have been many romanticisms. It is possible to romanticize the most gruesome or threatening set of circumstances as it is the most lofty of ideals. To romanticize and idealize death for a cause is not far removed from creating the ideal of the cause itself.

Common to almost all romantics emerging in the nineteenth century was a "sense of striving," the idea that the energy present in "one's being" could be concentrated on the achievement of a perfected state of existence.[92] This romantic sense of striving also applies to men of the Heines mindset. Among such desperadoes it emerged as a communal expenditure of emotion aimed at recreating the front life. Heines' romanticism yearned for the desperado utopia. The death and dying looked upon so positively by Heines had to be part of an idealization of the war where so much of that dying had in fact transpired.

In February of 1931, not long after Röhm had assumed his responsibilities as SA chief of staff, Heines wrote to him, setting forth the notion that the death of stormtroopers in brawls and firefights was "a virtuous dying." It had intrinsic spiritual merit and it also had a practical benefit of making the "dead Storm member," fallen on a political killing ground, "useful to the movement." Heines continued describing how photographs of the stormtroopers should be taken where they had fallen, then again at graveside. Storm flags carried by various units should be emblazoned with the names of those fallen in the line of duty. Hence, when one romantically recreated the "front-life," propaganda needs of the party were met. Heines held that "dying for Nazism was essentially desirable."[93]

Heines' Silesian SA was likely more strongly influenced by the traditional "propaganda of the deed" than was the usual SA region. What had happened in late 1932 was that the units of the *Sturmabteilung*, from locale to locale, had arrived at a style of terrorism that was very close to the "Ishutin Solution." This technique of terrorism was named after Moscow revolutionary Nicholas Ishutin In 1866, Ishutin developed a scheme to disrupt tsarist government in Russia. Tshutin wanted to build a party owning first a "political arm" which would do the work of "insurrectional agitation and propaganda." And there was to be another secret arm of his movement devoted to carrying out assassinations and other violence to destabilize the established order.[94]

Without conscious knowledge of the Ishutin tradition's nature, Heines and others of his ilk developed their own secret arms for the Nazi Party. From his headquarters in Breslau, Edmund Heines sent out instructions to subordinate-officers to organize clandestine terror campaigns. For example, on the night of 9–10 August 1932, in the city of Görlitz, midway between Dresden and Breslau, squads of SA men hurled grenades at the homes of Reichsbanner leaders or SPD offices. They shot at individuals, threw rocks through the windows of Social Democratic installations, etc. All of this brought retaliation from Nazi foes. Under police questioning, SA man and gardener Helmut Engmann signed a confession implicating the whole Silesian SA command structure.[95] It was determined by the city attorney's office that, on 10 August 1932, a local SA battalion had sponsored some twenty-five terrorist acts to create "unease in the people."[96]

It is likely that whatever these violent Silesian SA acts might have owed to tradition, distantly to Ishutin, and more directly to the patterns established by the OC, the more direct inspiration in the symbolic sense was probably the "front life." The SA participants in such acts thought of themselves as "going out from the Storm Centers" on killing patrols after briefings from "commanding officers." As noted by historian Robert Koehl, "the comradeship of street combat was invested with the mystique of the trench brotherhood with the majority of young [stormtroopers]"[97] It is likely, according to Nazi Party "historians," that, once the SA was finished with its violent acts, it returned to the barracks where all the men felt a glow of satisfaction. They assumed that they had proven themselves while "acting for Germany. " All this transpired while the "comfortable *Bürger* [was] lying in bed."[98] In playing at war, the romanticized "military actions" and similar activities unwittingly brought the Nazi SA by late 1932 to a pattern very close to the Ishutin solution. The Party displayed a dualism within the broader context of the SA-PO dualism, a split between terrorist and non-terrorist wings.

That Hitler himself sometimes thought in these front-life terms was revealed in a conversation he had in 1932: "If the stormtroopers were given a free hand, if it came to twenty to thirty thousand ... lives, the nation would recover.... It would be like fighting in the field."[99] From the top of Nazism to the bottom in 1932, it was assumed that dying on the urban battlefield was not to be avoided, and, as seen in the Heines example, thought in some cases even to be desirable.

There could be explosions of terrorism at any time. As in the Silesian case of young SA man Hannich, attackers and attacked were often neighbors. In this way political and personal differences could often merge as causative factors in individual attacks. The killing of even a neighbor could thus become an expression of the propaganda of the deed. Naturally, SA members so motivated to become involved in violence would need their defenders in the courts. This fact necessitated the building of a corps of lawyers willing to rise to the defense of accused stormtroopers. These were to be found in the "SA Legal Department."

As violence formed an ugly and spreading stain on the surface of German life, the number of SA men awaiting trial increased. The party often provided a kind of Nazi "public defender" for these men. By 1932, a legal department existed in connection with the SA. During April of 1931, Walter Luetgebrune, a lawyer long associated with those encountering legal difficulties on the far Right went to Munich and spoke with Ernst Röhm whom he had known for some time.

Luetgebrune had seen the world of the desperado close at hand when he helped with the defense during the Hitler *Putsch* trial. Luetgebrune, through the distortion of a rightist prism, saw the stormtroopers as a group of "pure and idealistic" militants unhampered by the kind of "presumptuous" *Bonzen* so prominent is the old parties.[100] When the radical terrorist phase of SA activity began after the July elections of 1932 and it became apparent that the seeming victories had not really changed anything, Röhm convinced Hitler to return to Luetgebrune as full-time SA defender. Luetgebrune was made "Gruppenfuhrer SA" and was commonly cited in party correspondence thereafter as *Oberster Rechtsberater der SA Führung* ("Supreme Legal Adviser of the SA").[101]

After his appointment, Luetgebrune organized a staff of lawyers who formed something very nearly like a flying squadron of SA legal representatives to speed from court to court to defend Stormtroopers. Luetgebrune set the pattern of defense they would follow in court; over and over SA lawyers accused Weimar of the "abuse of state power" with respect to stormtroopers and set forth a line holding that SA actions could not be judged by Weimar courts as either legal or illegal because they "superseded legality" in answer to a higher moral calling.[102] Luetgebrune saw Weimar's judicial system as a purposive mechanism devised to limit SA effectiveness by incarcerating as many SA men as possible. It was assumed that this policy was meant to keep trials pending longer than necessary to prohibit targeted SA members' participation in the party effort. It was seen as an attempt to prove that the organization was unlawfully acting violently under military-style orders. And, connected to this last point, it was an attempt to prove Röhm and even Hitler were part of the party chain of command and as legally culpable as was the SA man responsible for a crime.[103]

From the SA chief lawyer's viewpoint, testimony of SA men was secured through harsh treatment like the use of isolation cells and by securing incriminating testimony from young SA men with regard to their fellows in the ranks.[104] Soon enough, SA men began to blame their guilt (in an odd pre-echo of Nuremberg in 1946) on the SA loyalty oath which demanded that they carry out instructions of superiors with unquestioning obedience.[105] During the high tide of arrests, even Edmund Heines (despite the fact that he held a Reichstag seat and owned a degree of parliamentary immunity) was brought in for interrogation.[106] Soon, SA men fled from the law with regularity. They became, in the words of a party official, "itinerant journeymen," on the move from one safe house to yet another.[107]

Despite all the smoke screens produced about defending the rights of abused stormtroopers, it became apparent as proceeding followed proceeding that Luetgebrune was more concerned with protecting higher-ranking party officials than he was ordinary SA men. Whenever the rank and file began to become aware of this, he urged his lawyers not to adopt some form of what would be called the "Nuremberg defense" a decade and a half later. This meant to avoid arguing that the responsibility rested not with some higher official directing an automaton acting under orders. The lawyers were to tell their clients to present under oath contrived alibis, character references, and a considerable amount of other sorts of testimony. Luetgebrune was only partially successful, however, in keeping the charges from reflecting upward in National Socialism. Shortly after SA terrorist activities seemed to reach a new high in August of 1932, the Supreme Court in Leipzig set about implicating Röhm in SA terrorism. Luetgebrune defended the chief of staff in part by questioning the constitutionality of the Terror Ordinance now being used against the SA. In fact, there was actually nothing new here. He had done all this before.[108]

Perhaps Luetgebrune need not have bothered. The minister of justice under both the Papen and Schleicher regimes was Franz Gürtner. Gürtner epitomized the kind of weak chink seen everywhere in Weimar's armor. Gürtner was, according to some, "hypnotized by Hitler's personality" and convinced that the Nazis would eventually triumph in Germany.[109] Luetgebrune was thus able to thwart the attempted implication of Nazi leadership as the benevolent Gürtner eased the judicial pressure on Nazism's leaders.[110]

In contrast to the successful defense of party leaders with respect to terrorism, many ordinary stormtroopers prosecuted under the Terror Ordinance were convicted.[111] Despite the convictions, however, Hitler congratulated Luetgebrune on his "successful" defense of the party on 7 November 1932.[112] In December, Luetgebrune again worked the Gürtner connection in hopes of removing the "terror" courts. Whether the removal of the courts had anything to do with Luetgebrune's efforts is not clear. But Hindenburg did order their use discontinued on 16 December.[113] This was only one day after Chancellor Kurt von Schleicher had made a radio address during which he had extended olive branches to the Nazis.[114]

With Gürtner at work in the Justice Ministry thereafter, further legal moves against SA in the brief time span before Hitler became chancellor became difficult. Gürtner's sympathies for the Nazis were demonstrated again by warnings to Luetgebrune that resuming SA terrorism would at this juncture be counterproductive because Schleicher might take reprisals on the party.[115]

After the consolidation of the Nazi dictatorship, Luetgebrune lost influence quickly. By late 1933, he was no longer very important. He, like the SA he had represented, was a necessity during the *Kampfzeit*, but not later. He was dismissed as chief SA legal counsel in November of 1933 and placed on the SA "Reserve List." Ironically, his eclipse in the world of Nazism may well have saved his life when the SA was purged of its prominent "suspect" leaders in mid–1934. Thereafter, he was periodically questioned by the Gestapo because of his earlier association with Ernst Röhm, but managed to continue the private practice of law.[116]

As the foregoing indicates, the Depression-era SA was multiform in nature, thus resisting easy generalizations. Few of the general evaluations in most of the works on National Socialism come close to describing it. It had within it sizable middle-class and sizeable lower-class elements that fit within the parameters of class definition employed by sociologists and most historians. Moreover, the mix of these elements differed from area to area in Germany, usually depending in large part on the location's extent of urbanization and industrialization and to a lesser extent, but still importantly, on local tradition. The SA of 1931 and 1932 had become nothing more nor less than a vast club of the nation.

As seen, the SA of 1932 incorporated desperadoes at higher leadership ranks. But local units varied greatly in characteristics and quality. Some of these were highly militaristic, even led by former army officers. Some others were little more than street gangs or, in cities like Berlin, criminal bands grouped under a political banner. That current of the participation revolution that ran between

Right-radical, paramilitary banks was almost completely diverted into the Nazi Storm Detachment by 1932, despite the fact that a few skeletons of the old combat leagues had survived.

The SA constituted a continuing and important threat to Weimar until 30 January 1933. In discussions with Hindenburg before Hitler became chancellor, its radicalism became a major consideration. It was Hitler's telling argument that, unless something concrete could be offered to his violent men of the streets, they might turn into Communists. Once within Red ranks, it was argued, SA men could then become a part of a leftist assault on the state. Whether that was realistic or not with only the urban SA having meaningful elements from the proletariat, this argument carried weight with the coterie around Hindenburg.[117]

The Weimar government generally was late in recognizing the threat the SA posed to the state. One indication of the late realization is to be found in the files of the "State Commissioner for the Safeguarding of Public Order." A brief survey of reports from this agency over the years is illustrative of problems the Republic had in dealing with the radical Right. Beginning in 1920, this commission prepared weekly "situation reports." These reports were available to the various government agencies which might take action against radical groups. To review these documents is to gain insight into where Weimar's defense walls were built. In 1920, the overwhelming worry was that the Communist threat, seen originating in Moscow, would spread to Germany to unseat an unsteady government.[118] In 1922, some notice was taken of the Rathenau murder, but it was the "blood flowing" in sixteen German cities because of Red risings that absorbed the information gatherers.[119]

During the 1923 inflation, the radical Left continued to absorb the government department's attention and it was only by the middle of the year that the Bavarian combat leagues drew any interest.[120] Once the Beer Hall *Putsch* had failed, the government spotlight was again fastened on the Left. Hitler's reconstitution of the party was hardly noticed in 1925. The more important problem on the Right for the Berlin regime at that point continued to be found in the *Frontbann*.[121]

Thus it remained until the Depression. The office was then reorganized as the Information Office of the Reichs Interior Ministry and, for the first time, "Right-radical parties" became a matter of concern. For the initial instance, with the hectic election national campaign of 1930, the SA was inspected for the first time. But the threat even then was vastly understated; the SA was still seen as no more than a "larger *Kampfbund*."[122]

This long-term avoidance of seeing the Right and the SA as a threat can be taken as part of a pattern. Within this pattern Gürtner ineffectively dealt with the problem of rightist violence in justice department. Another part of the pattern was the ineffective prohibition of the SA in April of 1932. Then, when Papen repealed the prohibition in the summer, Bavarian Prime Minister Heinrich Held protested directly to Hindenburg. He said that those who voted for the president's reelection had done so in hope of being protected from the SA and the SS. The SA had ought now to outlawed, said Held, to repay those voters and to protect the Weimar Republic. Hindenburg rebuffed Held, holding that the SA was being controlled by the government. He further rationalized SA violence by citing stormtroopers' "strong nationalist feelings."[123]

Perhaps it is unfair to indict Weimar for being casual concerning the violence of the radical Right until it was too late. The Great War, the Free Corps, and the combat leagues had all helped condition the population to violence from the Right, supposedly propelled by patriotism. Even during the somewhat stable years of 1924–29, the level of violence had remained high. The amount of this activity then simply leaped upward with the Depression. And of all the paramilitary groups in the nation, including those of the Left, the SA profited the most from the violent historical atmosphere that had resulted from the paramilitarization of German life being seen as "normal."[124]

By January of 1933, the stormtrooper regarded his organization, not without some justification, as the real victor over Weimar. But the militant and sometimes uncontrollable shape of the SA was to prove anachronistic by 1934. It was of scant use in the Third Reich to have an organization which still had within it the atomistic traditions of the old combat leagues and the terrorist ways of the Organization Consul. The "new man" of the "new order" was not to wear a brown SA shirt. "Clear the streets for the brown battalions!" shouted out to the cadence of drums and the tramp of jackboots, soon became a faint echo. The streets had been cleared and Nazis now moved on to other and more sinister endeavors.

Chapter Nine

Nazism into Power

By December of 1929, the German government was falling into an economic abyss. The dark years of 1930–33 lurked just ahead. The Depression hurried the final crisis of the Republic on two societal levels simultaneously. First, the masses were radicalized through the potential destruction of their future. Second, the Depression signaled the elite classes that the time had come for them to destroy the Republic. Services normally provided by the state were often better supplied by organized groups of the unemployed (SA services, for example). Among these were youth organizations, social clubs, and militias. Men without hope attached themselves to radical political movements. At the governmental level, there was a controversy over unemployment insurance. The government ran out of money in 1929 and Reich Finance Minister Rudolf Hilferding proposed new taxes.[1]

Radical extremism seemed almost normative. However, the initial assault on democracy came from political intrigue.[2] A few schemers, most notably General Kurt von Schleicher, undermined the republican government by persuading Hindenburg that it was unwise to allow the emergency decrees necessary to develop the program of Chancellor Hermann Müller, although the constitution allowed the practice, and by pushing the idea that Heinrich Brüning of the Center Party (*Zentrum*) should become the next chancellor with those executive powers Hindenburg could grant which had been forbidden Müller.

With the prospect that the Müller regime was not in accord with economic schemes supporting the armed forces, the German version of Eisenhower's "military-industrial complex" pressured Hindenburg to make a change. Hindenburg, in accordance with General Schleicher's wish, appointed the leader of the Catholic Center, Heinrich Brüning, to the chancellorship. Brüning was to be responsible to Hindenburg instead of parliamentary coalitions. The procedural problem Brüning faced, however, was that he led a government not supported by the SPD and the Nazis. This made actual coalition rule impossible and rule by legal fiat necessary. Government continued through a series of measures sent to the president's office. Hindenburg then used the emergency powers granted him under the constitution to sign decrees into law. From April 1931 to December 1931, forty decrees issued for the first time since the days of 1919–20 and the radical risings against the state. In 1932 there were 59.[3]

Without a functioning Reichstag, Hindenburg could only hope in vain for a parliamentary majority. Brüning's opening speech to the Reichstag on 1 April 1930 made a reasonable case for the course he meant to pursue. Unusual political bedfellows combined for a brief moment, and Nazis, nationalists, socialists, and Communists all combined to vote negatively on the new course. As the constitution dictated, a new election was scheduled. Brüning might have enjoyed support had he not been so conservative. He believed that each person ought to contribute to state support with notable monetary sacrifice. The budget had to be brought into balance.[4] And at this time the national cupboard was already bare.

Twenty-eight parties representing a fractionated political spectrum had presented candidates for the Reichstag election of September 1930. The Nazis emerged prospering, the center remained about the same, and those supporting the Republic dropped. But almost 19 million people had voted against Weimar. Now the extremes of both Right and Left became key political forces, holding over 30 percent of Reichstag strength. A look at the Nazi vote reveals that their numbers included those voters who had fled the nationalists for something more extreme, farmers (particularly from Schleswig-Holstein where forced sales of land had risen massively since 1925)[5] and young people who had not voted before but were currently suffering economic distress.

The Nazis and Communists had ready explanations for the German catastrophe during those decisive years of 1930–33. For the Reds, the German state had compiled a treasury which had been looted by international capitalists. The Nazis trotted out their usual list of culprits—Bolsheviks, Jews, and the capitalists—who had been "involved" in a new treachery. Hitler had no desire to cooperate with the leadership in the new Reichstag. On the opening day of the new session, bands of stormtroopers beat people who "looked like Jews" in the streets of Berlin.

This poisonous atmosphere surrounded Brüning when he made his opening speech to the Reichstag on 16 October 1930. He walked into the chamber to shouts from the Communists of "Down with the hunger Chancellor!" Brüning said to the assembled that the economy was in dire straits with a gigantic deficit. He defended himself against charges that what he proposed would mean a long-term lowering of wages. Then, in December, Brüning produced more austerity measures. None helped the dismal economic picture to any visible extent.

Along with domestic troubles was the continuing evidence that, despite talk about Versailles being modified, it was still in operation. A positive note for the Germans was rung when the last of the Rhineland bridgeheads was evacuated by the French in June 1930. But the Saar was still separated from the Reich. Poland still occupied what had been German territory in the Polish Corridor. Clearly the only way that the lost lands could be returned to the Reich was by direct negotiations from a position of strength. The issue was highlighted by graphic accounts of terrorism against German minorities in Poland. In May of 1931, the Security Council of the League of Nations admitted that Germany had a case. But little was done. The suffering under Polish overlords continued. Organizations like the *Stahlhelm* were particularly bitter in citing the Polish threat to "Germany's fate."[6]

In January of 1930, General Groener, in his role as minister of defense, wrote a so-called "Pastoral Letter" to the Reichswehr. In it he warned the troops of the danger to the army posed by Communists and Nazis, who threatened civil war. It was the task of the army to require its officers to educate troops in political affairs. A month later, in the so-called "Watch Decree," Groener returned to his theme. He wrote of attempts being made by radical elements to penetrate the Reichswehr. He proposed to reward soldiers who reported extremists with an engraved watch.

The Watch Decree was widely regarded as a comic interlude. But soon enough three lieutenants—Hans Ludin, Richard Scheringer, and Friedrich Wendt—were tried in September 1930 on charges of high treason. They had joined the Nazi Party. Two of them had traveled around Germany to recruit other officers. The trial provided a dramatic setting for Hitler to make a courtroom appearance "on the accused's behalf." He addressed his remarks to the whole nation while ostensibly testifying. Hitler tried to diminish fears about National Socialism. He swore for the benefit of Hindenburg and the electorate that the Nazis meant to come to power constitutionally. He declared that the SA, despite its mass proportions, was a simply a harmless party guard.[7] Hitler did appear, from time to time, to contradict this cultivated image of moderation. He said, for instance, that he would, once in power, establish a state tribunal to take revenge on all responsible for the nation's misfortunes. Possibly, he said, a "few heads would roll." But he was quick to assert that they would roll "legally."

As for the SA, after a few years of self-imposed exile, Ernst Röhm, as mentioned, had returned to succeed Pfeffer as chief of staff, SA. Under "Supreme Leader" Pfeffer, the SA had grown from a small body of men numbering about 5,000 at the end of 1925 to at least 60,000 in time for the 1930 elections. But by 1930, the Berlin SA had revolted against the PO, following Pfeffer's resignation in the summer of 1930. Some months later, there was an even more serious revolt against the PO, led by Pfeffer's deputy leader, Walther Stennes, as demonstrated in the previous chapter. As seen, through concessions and direct intervention, Hitler quelled this rising.[8]

Once Röhm's SA began its work, the new chief of staff took up the reorganization of the stormtroopers. The country was divided into five *Obergruppen* ("Supreme Groups") and some eighteen *Gruppen*. The highest units beneath these were the "Standards" (*Standarten*), meant to compare directly with military regiments. Old auxiliary units were expanded and special units for air, naval, and engineering were announced, but not actually established. The SS was far from the feared instrument it became later. It was built out of what had been a bodyguard unit for Hitler and was still little more than another auxiliary attached to the SA. Its leader since 1929 had been Heinrich Himmler.[9]

Soon enough, the Depression drove thousands into SA ranks. Particularly this was the case after the Storm Detachment of the party moved to establish the national framework of "SA homes." It should be remembered here that a stormtrooper could sleep and eat in these hostels. An organization was established and called the *Hilfswerk* ("Help to Work") and it set about raising donations in money and in kind (food, furniture, etc.) for the SA. Some SA homes were so large they could house up to 250 men. The SA quickly began to refer to them as "SA barracks."[10] These were, as Konrad Heiden observed, places which, dramatically, also could be called "Storm Centers." When Röhm took over the SA in 1931, it had roughly around 100,000 men. It soon was double that. Some had its membership as high as half a million men, perhaps even 600,000, by the end of 1932.[11]

The aim of many SA leaders was to one day graft the *Sturmabteilung* onto the body of the regular army. In the meantime, the SA tried to cultivate friendly relations with the Reichswehr by offering itself as an auxiliary force. However, approaches to the army by this violent organization caused much distrust. In March of 1931, Brüning issued an emergency decree prohibiting political party members from wearing a uniform. The Nazi SA simply put aside brown shirts and replaced them with white ones and swastika armbands. Not too far into the Röhm tenure, a potential schism between the SA and the Political Organization surfaced. Hitler, when informed about the scandalous private lives some of his SA men were leading, made it clear that the stormtroopers were accomplishing too much to make negative judgments about them. His paramilitary unit, he stated, need not be a "moral" institution.[12]

The economic situation of Germany worsened as Nazis argued. An attempt to establish a customs union with Austria to work out beneficial tariffs and thus enhance trade failed. Although the treaty was purely an economic arrangement designed to help both countries which were severely damaged by the Depression, the French regarded it as a steppingstone aimed at helping the annexation by Germany of Austria (*Anschluss*).

Extremists continued to score electoral gains. In May 1931, there were local elections in Schaumberg-Lippe and Oldenburg. Election victories for the Nazis in these little states allowed Hitler to say as part of his torrent of propaganda that the "day of reckoning" was not far away.[13] Then, in the summer of 1931, Hitler went on a fund-raising tour aimed at convincing big business to provide funding for the Nazis.[14] He did not succeed in raising much money, as the business tycoons stayed primarily in support of the nationalists, but at least some contacts were made.[15]

The Nazis also contacted the Stahlhelm and urged the German veterans' organization to bind with Nazism in a new "National Opposition." Shortly afterward, Hitler met with army leaders. The benefits of all this appeared marginal, but it did help make the Nazis more acceptable later to conservatives. All of these attempts to make Nazism more respectable, thus attracting new donors, were suddenly made more difficult by a potentially damaging personal scandal for the party's leader.

Adolf Hitler's niece, Geli Raubel, killed herself in an apartment where she lived with the *Führer* and her mother, Hitler's half-sister. Hitler had been developing an infatuation for this girl. Whether it was platonic or otherwise is argued. One Nazi went so far as to call Geli "an empty-headed slut."[16] She was certainly not that. She was likely an immature girl who resented an uncle who made her feel like a prisoner.[17]

The most important thing about the Geli Raubel affair was the political context in which it transpired and what opponents might make of the incident. It could be held up as an example of Hitler's "aberrant" private life. It is for this reason that Hitler and his entourage immediately moved to quiet talk about it. Friends of the Nazis in the Bavarian justice system succeeded in quieting ugly rumors. Geli Raubel was buried secretly in Vienna without an inquest.

Some three weeks after the Raubel incident, Hitler had his initial meeting with Hindenburg in the company of Göring. He was ill at ease in the presence of a Germanic legend. For his part, Hindenburg clearly resented being lectured by a man called in his circle the "Bohemian corporal." After the meeting, he said that he found the idea of Hitler's becoming chancellor laughable. He held that, at most, the Nazi leader could be "appointed a Postmaster General."[18]

One day after his meeting with "the old gentleman" (11 October 1931) Hitler attended a rally put together by various elements of the Right. Again Hitler was uncomfortable, surrounded by prominent army officers, industrialists, and scions of noble houses. But only a week later, the Nazis were active in what was a more normal setting for them. Hitler presided over a large rally in Brunswick. Some figures had the party membership at 800,000 at that juncture. And this does not count the kind of people around the edges of the Nazis who, in the context of the later Cold War, would have been called "fellow travelers." Then *Landtag* elections in the state of Hesse on 15 November 1931 provided the Nazis with some 37 percent of the votes.

This success in *Land* Hesse brought optimism to Nazi ranks. But a state election outside of Prussia did not actually have great significance. And the road to power, as it turned out, was still a long and hard one. Not long after the mass October rally of the Nazis in Brunswick, the authorities in Hesse discovered a compromising group of documents drafted by the local *Gau* leadership. These were discovered on a rural estate called the Boxheimer Hof. They outlined measures to be taken once the Nazis were in power. Tight totalitarian control, seizure of ministries, and death penalties were to be installed and activated.

Hitler very publicly penalized the Hessian Party district leaders and disavowed all knowledge of the Boxheim papers. A torrent of apologetic propaganda covered over the Boxheim incident and downplayed the number of times in the documents the phrase "will be shot" appeared.[19] Notable here is the fact that, once in power, the Nazis quickly did many of the things which, in late 1931, Hitler so fervently disavowed.

On 8 January 1932, Joseph Goebbels noted in his diary that "the chess game for power has begun."[20] Brüning's aim during the crisis had been to establish proper order in Germany and prepare the way for a restoration of monarchy. As the government's troubles deepened, everything, from Brüning's point of view, depended on Hindenburg continuing in office. This was made difficult because of the decline in Hindenburg's faculties. He appears to have entered the early stages of senile dementia at this juncture. His own son gave testimony that he failed to recognize people that he supposedly knew well.[21] But the old gentleman had to be persuaded to run again or, in accordance with the constitution, two-thirds of the Reichstag had to allow an extension of his term.

Hindenburg's term in office was scheduled to expire on 5 May 1932. It now took pressure from his immediate entourage to persuade him to stand for office again. At the same time, the scheme to extend the president's term by legislative affirmation failed to gain support in the Reichstag. A presidential election was thus scheduled for 13 March 1932. It was only three weeks after the election was scheduled that Hitler joined Hindenburg and other announced candidates in the presidential field. Hitler only recently had become a German citizen (since renunciation of Austrian citizenship he had been stateless) allowing him to run for high office. He had secured this new status by arranging an appointment for himself as a "councilor" in Nazi-run Land Brunswick. As a citizen of Brunswick, he now became a full-fledged citizen of the Reich in time to enter the contest.

The campaign for the presidency was bitter. Hitler toured Germany by air, showing remarkable stamina with numerous speeches.[22] It seemed to many an observer that the country was being drowned in a sea of Nazi posters and banners spread by the SA. However, Hindenburg won. But he fell just short of an absolute majority. There was another run-off election scheduled for April. The Nazis took the campaigning time allowed before the run-off vote (just one week) and used it to their advantage. Hitler chartered a plane and began his "Hitler Over Germany" campaign, visiting twenty-one cities in one week's time.[23]

In the second election, with its candidate withdrawn, the Nationalist Party voted heavily for Hitler. Hindenburg was elected to serve another term with only 53 percent of the vote. This all was a grave disappointment for the aged president. He believed himself to be deserted by his old comrades on the Right. He well knew the center and moderate Left had elected him. Hitler, the "little man," who one observer said looked like a professional "marriage swindler," had put behind him the role of political outsider. He now became something of a "savior," at least to his followers and marginal supporters.[24]

All the political leaders in the national and state governments knew that the Nazi threat

As Hitler flew from city to city as part of his 1932 campaigning, a Nazi propagandist entitled the process "Hitler over Germany." Below, a crowd in a city square looks skyward as Hitler's plane approaches. Above, Hitler approaches the podium at the end of one of his flights.

was very real. In March, police searches in Prussia and Bavaria had unearthed evidence that the Nazis had developed contingency plans. Should Hitler become president, the SA was to be armed from Reichswehr arsenals to take over the government. The ministers of the interior of all the large states—Prussia, Bavaria, Baden, Wurttemberg, Hesse, and Saxony—told Groener the central government had to act to preserve order. If it did not, the state governments would do it. It was up to Groener to make a decision as the minister of defense to which had been added the portfolio of "Home Affairs."

Groener needed little urging to act against the SA. He had a discussion with both army and navy leaders. They agreed on the need for active measures. Groener advised Brüning that Hindenburg should issue an emergency decree banning both the SA and SS. The chancellor was uncertain; he was afraid such a move might increase the Nazi vote in the upcoming election on 24 April. But the Reichswehr leadership thought it essential. The decree went to Hindenburg. Schleicher, acting as liaison to the armed forces, was initially enthusiastic. Then he had second thoughts and advised moving more slowly, if at all. Schleicher did not like Hitler and his entourage. But he did appear to believe that the Nazis had had it too easy in playing the comfortable role of an opposition taking little responsibility for its actions. If brought into the government, they could be "handled." Schleicher began to think of the possibility of Polish intrusions in the East and how the Nazi paramilitary could be essential there.

For some time, the leadership of the army in the East had been trying to prevent an incursion. A collaboration had developed between General Werner von Blomberg and his chief of staff, Walther von Reichenau, on the one hand, and SA standard leaders on the other. They then began to train SA men at illegal sites. Suddenly, however, Hitler forbade the SA from having anything to do with any unit not under his direct command. But if the Nazis came into the government, the SA-army linkage might be reinvigorated. To placate the Nazis, Schleicher urged that they be given the opportunity to dissolve their paramilitary formations while warning that failure to do so would result in dissolution. Schleicher was overruled by Brüning and the cabinet. Hindenburg signed the order after Groener informed him that the *Länder* and the Reichswehr had demanded it. On 23 April 1932, the SA and SS, along with a number of minor auxiliary formations, were banned. The government was immediately placed under pressure to retract the decree.

Some generals, worried about border defense (*Grenschutz*), voiced their opposition. Hindenburg was confused. In his confusion he ignored evidence that the Nazi SA had become dangerous to the state. The stormtroopers were estimated to be 400,000 strong. It was difficult for the Nazi PO to control them. The PO was sworn to observe the party oath to follow the path of legality. Hitler appeared before massed stormtroopers to make the point. He told them to be legal for now, but remember the "day of revenge" was just around the corner.[25]

Hitler needed to follow legality, as he saw it, because the PO had developed a plan to conquer the Reich by winning state governments. Elections made them the leading party in state after state, but never gave them sole control. They participated in coalition governments in Thuringia, Mecklenburg-Streilitz, Brunswick, and Anhalt. The problem with this strategy was Prussia. Three-fifths of the total German population resided there. Nazi gains were considerable in Prussia's election, but again the party fell short of control. This resulted in a *Landtag* majority of Nazis and Communists. These polar opposites could never act together. The SPD-led government in Prussia maintained itself in a caretaker role. Pundits coined the term "Nazi-Communists" to identify obstructionists.[26]

On 10 May 1932 the Reichstag reconvened. General Groener rose to argue the case against an attack that Nazi leader Hermann Göring had made on the SA ban. Groener, not an impressive speaker, performed poorly. Soon after, Schleicher, once "true" to Groener, came forward as "spokesman for the army." Schleicher told the aging chief executive that there was no backing for Groener in the army. Groener was forced to resign as defense minister. The next target was Brüning who fell soon after. He fell because of his unpopular retrenchment policies and the announced *Osthilfe* ("Eastern Help") project. This project had been crafted to strengthen eastern agriculture where economic pressures had caused small holdings to lie fallow. Millions of marks had been supplied for the program since 1930. However, it became widespread knowledge that most of the money had been diverted to greedy landowners. Many wealthy landowners complained about *Osthilfe* to Hindenburg. Their complaints were likely one of a number of reasons that Hindenburg, at the end of May, called in Brüning and asked him to resign.[27]

In picking a successor, Hindenburg relied on Schleicher's advice and again appointed an interim chancellor. Schleicher's choice was Franz von Papen, the scion of a Westphalian family of aristocrats. His career had been unremarkable. But his convivial nature appeared to get him things he did not deserve. In 1914, he received a post as military attaché in Washington, D.C. While there, he was involved in stealing government documents and was expelled. After the war, he resigned his commission and entered politics, joining the conservative extreme of the center in the Prussian *Landtag*. Papen, in the political storm of 1931, served as an empty vessel into which advisers could pour agendas. His unthinking use of the agendas presented was dangerous. The French ambassador at that time, Andre François Poncet, informed Paris that Papen had a reputation as a man who was "blundering, untrue, ambitious, vain, crafty, and an intriguer."[28]

Schleicher's role in installing Papen was not lost on the Nazis. Göring wrote that "General von Schleicher" ought "to have been an admiral, for his military genius lies in shooting under the water at his political enemies."[29] How Schleicher saw Papen was revealed when he answered the objection of a friend that Papen had "no head" for government by saying: "he does not have to have [a head]. He is a hat!"[30] From a practical point of view, the Papen appointment made little sense. Despite momentary toleration by the Nazis, he had far less backing in the Reichstag than had Brüning. He was almost entirely dependent on Hindenburg for his authority. After some behind-the-scenes discussions with the Nazis, he had secured temporary support from them if he agreed to lifting the SA ban. He did so on 15 June 1932. Without thinking, he put the SA into the streets just in time for the July Reichstag election.

The Nazis had believed that Papen would be little more than an interim chancellor. All they wanted from him was the raising of the ban. When they obtained that, they forgot tolerance of the regime. With the ban lifted, the streets of Germany were once more convulsed with violence. The Communists had an old slogan: "If you do not wish to be my brother, I will kick in your head." The Nazis replied: "The SA marches! Clear the streets!" In Berlin alone, one or two men began to die daily.[31]

Soon the press was writing of "Bloody Sunday" (17 July 1932). On that day there were violent incidents all over Germany. Sunday was the day of the week when unemployed paramilitary members of groups like the SA and Stahlhelm (which often marched with stormtroopers in those days) were joined by employed ones. The Hamburg-Altona incident, which was the central feature of media coverage the next day, has been described. An unbiased observer should have seen Bloody Sunday as the direct consequence of unleashing the SA. As for Papen, he drew an opposing conclusion. He carried out the Prussian coup to deal, he maintained, with terroristic threats.

After the Prussian coup of 20 July 1932, the strongest party supporting the Republic had been removed from its center of power. The Nazis were free to campaign as they wished. Just eleven days later, the Republic was given another massive blow. The Nazis had won a stunning victory, receiving 230 seats in the Reichstag, thus replacing the Social Democrats as the largest party. The two other major anti–Republican parties, the Communists and the Nationalists, also gained. The antidemocratic factions now controlled over half the seats.

The German national elections of July provide an excellent example of how the masses flowed into the Nazi ranks. In the July 1932 elections, they had won 37.1 percent of the popular vote. This was an impressive achievement in a highly fractionated multiparty system. From an examination of national voting patterns, the party was least successful among Catholics or organized working classes. Nazi support came from a growing army of white-collar workers whose wages did not differ a great deal from the higher-paid workers in the SPD. These were people who inhabited the dehumanizing offices of the 1920s. Many of the people thus employed were the children of workers. Supposedly having moved upward in status, they resisted the idea that they had come to form an officeworker proletariat. They prized their "educational superiority." This does not mean that any had ever been at a university. Instead, they might have graduated from a secondary school while the average worker might not have gone far beyond elementary school. Normally, they lived in flats located in marginally better areas than the slums of the Communists. By 1932, they made up about one-fifth of the Nazi vote.[32]

There were those in the middle class who believed themselves to be in danger of losing privilege. Heightened anxieties and resentments were seen in nonunion craftsmen and shopkeepers. These people saw themselves caught in a contracting vise; on one side was elitist capitalism and on the other organized labor. Their support for Nazism compared to support of the peasantry. This was another group believing itself threatened by unwelcome change. In this group one can observe another element. These were the civil servants who worked in rural areas (school teachers, forestry officials, etc.), also believing themselves threatened.[33]

By 1932, perpetual Nazi campaigning had become nationwide. In each locale there were constant meetings, posters on every available wall, slide shows, door-to-door solicitation of support, direct mailing, and arranged social occasions. By the July election, Nazi violence generated a sense of dynamism seemingly almost totally lacking in republican parties, thus reassuring conservatives. Here was someone who could defend them against the Reds. The Nazis were also seen by conservatives as respectable because they promised to make no paramilitary assault on the state. They assured change within German traditions and only within normal societal boundaries.[34]

It was at this juncture that the Nazis ability to exploit tendencies in German associational life became apparent. This could be seen in the work of the various Nazi auxiliaries. Through their auxiliaries the Nazis overcame bourgeois "apoliticism," an attitude that was suspicious of mass politics. People who had channeled their energies into the network of German associational life appeared susceptible to being recruited by the Nazis, particularly in smaller towns. There the Nazis spoke the language of apoliticism and penetrated local associations.[35]

The traditional unpolitical Germans were, of course, not so well represented in larger cities.[36] In cities like Berlin, unemployed white-collar workers were drawn into Nazism. A great deal fewer of the unemployed manual workers were lured because the pool was split with the Communists. There were by-products of youth unemployment. Among these were social dislocation, family disruption, and rising criminality. The appearance of youth gangs in turf wars were not just a case of Red versus Brown. Skirmishes also transpired among many unrelated bands or gangs (*Cliquen*). All of this formed a desperate urban subculture.

The more traditionally conservative person, who looked at a culture of lawlessness and was frightened, went to the polls to find control of random violence. Ironically, by 1932, their choice was often one of those agencies sponsoring such violence. Many others who selected Nazism were first-time voters. Mass unemployment had cut purchasing power so that there was a "ripple effect." Peasant food producers and small tradesmen damaged by the failure of their markets often became Nazis. As for workers, they were generally divided in terms of age. Social Democratic workers were older and better housed. Union members were far more likely to have kept their jobs. Most of the Communists were unemployed. And these workers would be forced to report regularly to the welfare offices to receive the dole from a Social Democratic clerk. Often, a Social Democrat and a Communist hated each other passionately although both were ostensibly of the "Left."[37]

One may well ask what was the position of women in all this. How much were they drawn to Nazism? This subject is difficult to quantify. It is apparent that National Socialism was very much a male-dominated movement. Most general works on fascism indicate that the radical Right, almost everywhere in Europe, pushed older ideas to radical extremes. The traditional German family was patriarchal.[38] Traditional attitudes of this kind achieved radical extremes within Nazism.

It was thus argued throughout its history that Nazism was restoring the traditional family. One piece published in 1937 depicted an SA meeting in the early 1930s. At this meeting, an SA man pointed out that "the family" was the "most important cell of the state." And he went on to discuss the proper role of the wife in Nazism. The ideal Nazi wife was one who bore a great burden. She was a comrade, "a fellow combatant." What that meant was that a wife had to feed whatever unmarried stormtrooper appeared. She was to wait at home when, after a night of street fighting, SA men returned. She then allowed these tired stormtroopers to sit around her kitchen table to "unwind."[39]

The Nazi ideal of womanhood provides a good example of the radicalized conservatism pervading National Socialism. The view on the position of women was essentially that held in mid–nineteenth-century society. Man was the master. He determined the course of all public affairs relating to the family. The female sphere was the home, the family, and, for the Nazis, the protection of racial purity through a productive sexual liaison. Arguing from this stance, the Nazis were natural foes of the emancipation of women. Nazis thus opposed women entering workplaces as an "insult to the idea of females" as the "progenitors of the *Volk*."[40] Popular Nazi media urged females to return to proper work at their "natural" labors.[41]

In the first year that Nazism controlled the government, the NSBO (*Nationalsozialistischer Betriebs Obman*) became a part of the Labor Front, meant to replace the trade unions. The NSBO was based on Nazi auxiliaries active in mid-year electioneering. In these auxiliaries and the NSBO females were warned by the party to avoid becoming "painted and powdered women" smoking in public.[42] But the best course, it was advised, was to stay at home to produce many Aryan babies. This was difficult in the disastrous economy prevailing, because so many potential breadwinners could not afford to marry.

Women students at all levels of education were common during the Weimar years. They were advised during the Third Reich: "Intellectual work is harmful to women!"[43] In the same vein, women were to be closely observed because of their love for "Negro music" (indicating western jazz). This all was summed up in the affirmation that "the German resurrection is a male event."[44]

During the Republic, the number of women entering the workplace and remaining there continued to rise. In time, they were close to one-third of the workforce. What became the subject of much debate was the concentration of women in modern sectors of employment. Women became clerk-typists, shop assistants, primary-school teachers, and social workers. In some cases, they even became assembly line workers.[45]

All of these roles had been occupied by men traditionally. Within these employment areas, women were paid far less than men in similar roles.[46] Given the Nazi position on women in an era when they were making even modest gains in the marketplace, it is little wonder that relatively few of them had joined the party by 1932. During that period, they were responsible for no more than just under 8 percent of Nazi membership.[47] The primary contribution of women to Nazism in the July election of 1932 was through party women's formations.[48]

The force of the masses supporting Nazism in 1932 helped interject Hitler, with meaningful negotiating power, into the highest levels of government. After the Papen coup, it was only a matter of time before some kind of authoritarian government was established. It appeared unlikely that this top-down regime would be leftist. In 1932, most Germans still lived in small towns or on farms. These people were too traditionally conservative to be courted by even the moderate Left. Moreover, in all Germany, nationalistic conservatism was the most important sentiment. Testimony came from people like miners, who might be expected in most European societies to be drawn to the Left, that they selected Nazism because socialism appeared tied to internationalism. With Nazism one could have "blood ties" to all "true" Germans.[49]

After the July election, nearly all political observers knew that the Nazis could not be excluded from a share in ruling Germany. From that time forward, most of the leadership cadre began to muse as to how best to accomplish that without giving Nazism too much power. The Nazis rejected all offers. The strength of the party could be seen in the streets where some of the nation's 400,000–500,000 SA men were always marching. This appeared the most powerful political party ever seen in Germany.[50]

The Nazis now had to be courted by the power elite. On 5 August 1932, Hitler met with Schleicher and presented a Nazi list of demands to be conveyed to Hindenburg. The party wanted three cabinet posts (Interior, Agriculture, and Justice). Hitler also desired the government in Prussia to be under Nazi control. Schleicher was noncommittal, but appeared not completely averse. Then, on the thirteenth, Schleicher informed and surprised Hitler by telling him that the ruling elite was not ready to give him what he desired.[51] In an interview with Hindenburg, Hitler was scolded about his lack of respect for the constitution.

Something like political burlesque now transpired in Berlin. On 12 September 1932, the Reichstag reconvened. Before deliberations began, Papen had secured Hindenburg's approval for the body's dissolution to make way for new elections. Not long after the session had commenced, the Communists introduced a motion for a vote of no confidence. Papen, expecting some debate on his program, was caught without the dissolution papers. Then a delay was granted to allow a Nazi Party caucus. Papen sent a messenger to the chancellery to bring back the necessary papers. When the Nazis returned to the chamber, Göring insisted on a vote. As the vote was taken, Papen waived the red dispatch case containing the dissolution decree. He was ignored and was defeated by a staggering 512 to 42. Papen then went directly to Hindenburg who overruled the vote.[52] Another election was at hand.

In this new election, even the Nazis were short of financing. They found it difficult to maintain their fever pitch of electioneering. It was also now clear that Hitler's party had let slip the beast of radicalism. On 10 August, five SA men broke into the home of a Communist worker named Pietrzuch in Potempa (Upper Silesia) and beat him to death in front of his aged mother. The grisly nature of the crime was revealed by the police autopsy report: "The body bore the marks of 29 wounds, the deepest ones at the neck. The carotid artery was completely torn. Death occurred by way of the larynx. Besides these wounds, Pietrzuch's body showed marks caused by severe beatings. He was beaten severely on the head with a blunt axe or a club, and had other wounds probably caused by having the top of a billiard cue thrust in his face."[53]

Caught and sentenced to death in a Beuthen (Silesia) court, the "Potempa Five" instantly joined the pantheon of Nazi heroes. Hitler sent them a telegram, published widely in the press. It indicated: "My Comrades: I am tied to you by loyalty without limit in the face of this most hideous and bloody sentence."[54]

The Nazis' reputation had also been damaged by a politically expedient move. They became strange bedfellows with the Communists in supporting a transport strike in Berlin.

Weary of elections, the Germans once again dragged to the polls on 6 November. Fewer people voted. That appeared to work against the Nazis. When the returns were in, the Nazis had lost two million votes and their national standing had dropped from 37.4 percent to 33.1 percent. However, the new Reichstag was as incapable of producing a working coalition as the old one had been.[55] Papen's minority government was still highly disliked and had virtually no support. It seemed no longer practical to let him continue. Hindenburg ordered the chancellor to secure the confidence of parliament. When he said he could not, Papen had to resign.

Hitler was now approached as the leader of the largest party. But Hitler wanted a presidential cabinet like the one enjoyed by Brüning. Hindenburg told Hitler that he could have the chancellorship only if and when he could put together a working majority in a precisely constitutional manner. To Hitler's request to form a presidential cabinet, Hindenburg replied that he believed the Nazi leader, if given the chance, "would establish a one party dictatorship."[56]

Kurt von Schleicher was motivated in all this by the same sort of calculations as almost every general during the Weimar years who had anything at all to do with civilian authorities. He wished to work for the greater glory of the army. Schleicher differed in that he used the military as a political weapon. He hoped for a new constitution enshrining the idea of army-led government ruling in perpetuity. In the short term, he wished to seduce the SA away from Hitler.[57]

Once Papen had outlived his usefulness, the Schleicher system began to crumble. Hindenburg slipped in and out of the mists of senile dementia as he listened to proposals from both Papen and Schleicher. Papen asked to remain in office to recast the constitution.[58] Schleicher put forth a more moderate idea. He said a high-handed reshaping of the constitution might bring on a civil war. Schleicher called for a new coalition of the moderate Left, bourgeois parties, and even moderate Nazis. In the short term, Hindenburg went with Papen and asked him to form a new government. But Papen could not. Hindenburg told Papen it was time to let Schleicher "try his luck."[59]

Schleicher became chancellor on 2 December 1932. At the same time, he retained the portfolio of Defense. He also inherited Papen's role as Reich commissioner for Prussia. Few German military leaders had ever had that sort of power. Probably the only precedent for it was the so-called "Hindenburg-Ludendorff dictatorship" during World War I. Schleicher believed initially he could sunder the Nazi movement by offering the vice-chancellorship to Gregor Strasser. He also wanted to merge the SA with other paramilitary elements like the Stahlhelm to safeguard the borders. Hitler soon found out about Schleicher's offer and summoned Strasser to Berlin, telling him that no Nazi was to join any government not headed by himself.[60] Strasser decided not to challenge Hitler. He rejected Schleicher's offer and resigned his post in the party leadership. It seemed at this point that Hitler's star was descending. On 1 January 1933 an editorial indicated that the Nazi "assault on the state" had been beaten back.[61]

After the Strasser defection, a momentary gloom hung over the party. Nazi financial coffers were depleted. Hitler, in private, conceded that perhaps his enemies were simply too powerful. In the midst of this downturn for Nazi fortunes, help came from an unexpected source. Papen had been nursing a badly bruised ego since Schleicher had engineered him out of the chancellorship. He was now willing to undermine his former colleague. On 16 December 1932 Papen spoke to a conservative group (the Herrenklub). He criticized Schleicher's tactics in dealing with the Nazis. After the meeting, Papen was approached by Kurt von Schröder, a Cologne banker. He proposed to mediate between Hitler and Papen at his Cologne home.

As President of the Cologne *Herrenklub*, Schröder had constructed a political network involving contacts with Nazis. His network ran into the president's office. Politically, Schröder was a conservative who had just left the DNVP and was thinking of joining the Nazis. Out of this web of backstage contacts came a letter to Hitler. The Nazi leader was informed that Papen was ready to support a Hitler chancellorship and was willing to talk over the details in a secret meeting.[62] Despite elaborate precautions, a photographer near the entrance of Schröder's house took pictures of the visitors arriving for the conference. It turned out that an informant in Hitler's entourage had divulged information about the meeting.[63] This event was then revealed by Schleicher to the president and the public at large. It is not known precisely what was discussed at Schröder's house on 4 January 1933. But it is to be noted that the Schröder meeting marked the opening of lengthy and secretive negotiations between the conservative clique around Hindenburg and Hitler.

Early accounts (in the 1950s) of the rise of Nazism marked the Schröder meeting as the beginning of ties between Nazism and the elite near Hindenburg. Some have claimed that the meeting opened the way to considerable support from big business. More recent research tends to counter that notion. It demonstrates that contributions to the party by big business interest continued to be small, even after this supposedly decisive meeting.[64]

The greatest importance of the January meetings for the Nazis was that the leadership experienced a reinvigoration. The party decided that it would refurbish its image by throwing its resources into the state election in Lippe. The Nazis believed that a landslide there would confirm their reemergence. The party leaders were actually somewhat disappointed with what turned out to be a modest gain in this tiny German state — 4.8 percent. But Nazi propaganda laid fictional claim to success. Hindenburg and the camarilla were impressed.

By mid–January, Schleicher's position was deteriorating. His failure to split the Nazis had been followed by other failed gambits aimed at gaining support. None were successful. Schleicher rejected taking on board DNVP leader Alfred Hugenberg as minister of economics and lost nationalist support. While he made foes of old friends, his former antagonists, the center and the SPD, persisted in opposition to him.

Into the second half of January, meetings between Hitler and the conservative clique continued. Many of them took place in the home of Joachim von Ribbentrop. Ribbentrop arranged meetings at his Berlin suburban house on 10, 18, and 22 January.[65] During the third and decisive meeting, Papen decided to enmesh Oskar von Hindenburg in the deliberations. No one knows what Hitler and the younger Hindenburg discussed at this meeting. The next morning (23 January) the well-informed Schleicher called a person present at the meeting to ask what the president's son had talked about. He did not receive a satisfactory answer. Schleicher then went to Hindenburg and indicated that he did not have enough support to govern under the constitution. He would need emergency-decree powers if he was to lead the nation effectively. The president did not give Schleicher what he had asked. The chancellor was finished.[66]

In talks Hindenburg had with both Papen and Schleicher between 26 and 28 January, the old Prussian general refused to accommodate either one of them. His sentimental side favored somehow reinstalling Papen, a true "comrade" from his own societal level. Schleicher told Hindenburg, in what turned out to be an obvious miscalculation, that even more dangerous than the appointment of Hitler would be a Papen-Hugenberg cabinet. Schleicher had other suggestions, but Hindenburg continued to answer negatively. Schleicher had to return to his cabinet to tell them he had resigned. Papen was called in immediately after Schleicher's departure. Alternatives were examined. But it seemed increasingly that only one was possible; Hitler would have to be put into the chancellorship. Limits on him would be ensured by allowing only two Nazis into the cabinet. Papen then told Hindenburg that he would restrain Hitler as vice-chancellor.

In the last days of January, one of the many rumors floating about had it that the Army High Command, manipulated by Schleicher, planned to determine the choice of chancellor. The rumor of a potential Schleicher *Putsch* was widespread. The story appeared first in the *London Daily Express* and was then picked up by the German papers.[67] Proof that this story was fabricated is seen, among a number of things, in the army's unlikely choice of any kind of action against the esteemed Hindenburg who was "one of their own."

The rumor of a Schleicher-devised plot was used to advantage by Papen. He put forth the notion that Schleicher was playing his last card. If the new government was not installed, there would be a Schleicher-instituted military dictatorship. Oskar von Hindenburg had become certain that Schleicher was guilty of high treason. A new cabinet appeared before Hindenburg during the morning of 30 January. Hitler solemnly swore to uphold the constitution he had actually come to destroy. He was last chancellor of the Weimar Republic.

The crucial period for the emergence of the masses into Nazism was 1929–33. There were various categories of people who came to enter Nazism and support it to some degree in these years. At least three major ones can be observed: those who followed Hitler devotedly from early on, those who were "fellow travelers," and people who voted for the Nazis once the Depression arrived in full force.

The hard-core followers were people who formed the vital core of the Nazi movement. They were overwhelmingly male. Many of them were from the Front Generation.[68] This generation believed that war had formed some sort of spiritual purgative.[69] Most of these men returning from the trenches came from the middle and lower middle classes. The basic sentiment shared by nearly all these men was objectified by Franz Seldte, leader of the *Stahlhelm*. Seldte said: "We must fight to get men into power who will depend on us front soldiers for support."[70]

Over time, many fellow travelers were drawn in by the effective organizational activities of the party. Party membership lists reveal that the Nazis were able to appeal to social groups appearing on the surface to be incompatible with Nazism.[71] In effect, this was the first true umbrella party to arise on German soil. The Nazis were the initial German political organization to establish a mass party of this sort (*Sammelpartei*), drawn from all societal levels. Of course, the SPD had been the first mass party in Germany. But the Nazis drew in more heterogeneous elements.[72] It is easy to get lost in observations about the social composition of the Nazi movement. The more important conclusions to be drawn are rather more narrowly political. The great strength of Nazism was the ability to broaden its base beyond parties tied to narrow interests.

Remember at this point that studies demonstrate that the traditional view that Nazism drew most of its support from the lower middle class, is simplistic. Most recent efforts in scholarship show a mass membership fueled by the lower middle class and by high support in some upper-class and upper-middle-class districts. These studies show also the strength demonstrated by the Nazi Party in rural areas, particularly in North German Protestant towns.[73]

When one speaks of the emergence of the masses into Nazism before 30 January 1933, it is not meant to say that even a majority of the people voted for the Nazis. The highest vote the Nazis received nationally was 37.3 percent. That means about three out of every eight voters cast a ballot for the Nazi list before 1933. But the nature of the Weimar system must be remembered. From the outset of the Republic until 1932, the linchpin of the Reichstag consisted of four parties—the SPD, the German Democratic Party, the Catholic Center, and the German Peoples' Party. They entered a variety of coalitions and over time formed seventeen separate governments.

There were many other splinter groups. Given this polarization of German politics, the large Nazi vote becomes most impressive. The Weimar Republic lacked the committed republicans necessary to save it. By 1932, a widespread discontent among the people made many believe that somewhere there had to be a rapid solution to their problems. The authoritarian answer for all problems appealed unprecedentedly. Perhaps, a number of people held, a non-monarchical version of autocracy was now needed. For only in an autocratic system had Germany ever known security.

During the nineteenth century, the rise of hyper-nationalism and mass democracy were two factors at work in German history which developed an enshrinement of the people, the *Volk*, as a secular religion. The secular and nationalistic faith which became operative accompanied the entrance of the masses into politics.[74] As is often the case, these myths were objectified through concrete forms like public festivals approaching the status of cultic ceremonies and the erection of nationalistic monuments. When the Nazis came along, they adopted and elaborated these cultic ceremonies. In this manner, no matter how much the Nazis changed the content, such basic presuppositions remained intact. There was the longing for a healthy and happy world, and a true national community in which all could join. The men of the Third Reich would soon claim to be installing just that sort of perfected national order.

Epilogue (1933–1934)

Hitler was installed in the chancellorship by Hindenburg in the same manner that he had employed with other chancellors since the breakup of the Great Coalition. It was the fashion in which predecessors Brüning, Papen, and Schleicher had been placed in office. This appointment was made in accordance with article 53 of the Weimar Constitution. It can therefore hardly be denied that the transfer of power to Hitler (power limited by various constitutional checks in place) was a "legal" act. In this manner Hitler's government at first appeared to be yet another regime of yet another presidential chancellor employed by Hindenburg in the absence of a workable parliamentary majority.

With Adolf Hitler's arrival in the chancellorship, a decisive period commenced. It began with the *Führer's* appointment on 30 January 1933 and ended with Hindenburg's death on 1 August 1934. In a shorter part of that time span, between the end of January and the last days of March of 1933, a flood of bills was pushed through by executive decree. To some, this appeared to be a mere continuation of the polices of the three previous "presidential" chancellors. In this case, however, the Nazis were using Article 48 of the constitution. This article allowed laws by executive decree. The Reichstag was circumvented. Germans were deprived of democratic rights under the rules of their own system.

Two days after Hitler moved into the Reich chancellery, Hindenburg dissolved the Reichstag. This meant that yet another round of elections was coming, this time scheduled for 5 March 1933. Hitler's new government then proceeded on 1 February to announce a sweeping program which would act to alter and reestablish the "spiritual unity" of Germany. He said:

> Fourteen years of Marxism have ruined Germany.... The richest and most beautiful cultural center of the world would be turned into chaos and a field of ruins [if Marxism triumphs]. In these hours when worries about the existence of the future of the German nation have become overpowering, the venerable leader of the World War [Hindenburg] called upon us men from the national parties and associations to fight once more at home ... for the salvation of the Reich.... Above status and class, the national government shall return to our people an awareness of this national and political unity and of the duties arising there from.[1]

Hitler's goals were apparent. He wanted to send a clear message that his government would not be swept from office as part of another abrupt change of chancellors. Goebbels had said in mid–1932 that, once the Nazis "have power, we will never surrender it unless we are

Hitler is shown standing up in a Mercedes Kompressor. He was standing in the city square of Nuremberg during the morning of a party day. Left to right, Rudolf Hess, an unidentified SS officer, a "Rider Corps" official, "Thick Herman" Göring in his SA uniform and an SA official.

borne out of our offices as dead men."[2] All of this meant that Hitler could not afford to permit the German people to decide freely on 5 March whether to accept National Socialism or reject it. In the new chancellor's view, it was time to eradicate Marxism before any decision could issue from a ballot box. All the Nazis needed was a pretext.

Hitler had first to neutralize the Reichstag and then rid the new party-state he wanted to build of the nuisance of parliamentarianism altogether. Secondly, he desired very much to control Prussia, the German state within a state. It had been a stronghold of Social Democracy until the Papen coup. As it now turned out, Papen's 1932 action benefitted the Nazis more than the conservative nationalists. The followers of the swastika exploited the opportunity—provided by the action the former chancellor had taken—to pursue their own ends.[3] Göring had been appointed Prussian minister of the interior for the largest and most important *Land*. He confided to another Nazi that "when he was handed the keys to his new office in the Prussian Justice building he held in his hands the keys to power."[4] Once installed in that office he quickly moved to purge the police of any who might oppose Nazism.[5] Göring then took a small department within his ministry and commenced to turn it into the Gestapo.

On the night of 27 February 1933 the Berlin Reichstag building caught fire. The flames spread rapidly and consumed the central hall and dome. A 24-year-old Dutch citizen, Marinus van der Lubbe, was picked up at the scene of the crime. It was established later that the deranged Van der Lubbe, a known arsonist, had once been a KPD member. With great speed and unanimity the press and radio informed the German nation in the early hours of 28 February that the fire had been the signal for a "Red rising." Despite the fact that experts and witnesses could reveal no evidence that the Communists or anyone else save Van der Lubbe acting alone had set the fire, Hitler, with Hindenburg's blessing, promulgated the "Decree of the Reich President for the Protection of the People and the State."[6]

The draft decree suspended most important civil rights "until further notice." Personal liberty, sanctity of the home, privacy of postal communication, freedom of the press, freedom of assembly, and guarantees of private property were also pushed aside. Moreover, death penalties were now ordered for a number of crimes previously punished only through time in prison. In yet another decisive step, the autonomy of the individual states making up the federal system was severely curtailed in favor of centralized authority.[7] In effect, this February night witnessed the demise of the German constitution and the imposition of a lasting state of emergency. When the decree was handed down, it was stated that the strictures would remain in place until otherwise notified. This state of emergency actually lasted until 8 May 1945.

Coming just before the March elections, the decree allowed Hitler and his followers to use the force of law against political opponents. A wave of arrests engulfed the entire country. Communists and any others who had displeased the Nazis in the past were beaten and tortured in secret locations. Censorship of the press was installed, thus keeping the German populace unaware of what was going on in the backrooms of the movement.

Despite all this frenzied activity, the elections of 5 March fell far short of Nazi expectations. It is little short of astonishing that, given the strong-arm methods widely used, the Nazis could not gain an absolute majority. They garnered only 44 percent of the vote. Only with the addition of the 52 seats gained by the Nationalists, who were still represented in Hitler's cabinet, were the Nazis able to remain in control. The Communist Party had lost seats, but this was only natural for they had been effectively shut down and could not campaign.

In the days following the elections, the Nazis capitalized on their "victory" by occupying local and state government offices and subjecting them to the control of Nazi-appointed "Reich Commissioners." In fact, as the National Socialists saw it, there was no further need for state governments. And, of course, in the absence of a federal structure the next logical step was the establishment of the unitary state. With this new form of government starting to appear, the new Reichstag elected on 5 March was to function only on two occasions.

On 21 March 1933 its deliberations were opened ceremoniously in the Potsdam Garrison Church. This location had been picked with the aim of suggesting symbolically that Hitler was the last person to appear in an unbroken line stretching down through time from

Hitler inspects an SA unit. An SS man stands in the foreground.

Frederick the Great, through Bismarck, then Hindenburg, and now to Hitler. Goebbels had been made minister of propaganda on 13 March and now his agency helped stage the spectacle at Potsdam. Hindenburg was intentionally maneuvered to the center of events and princes of the House of Hohenzollern were presented beside him to reinforce the designed imagery.[8]

Some three days later (24 March 1933) the new Reichstag assembled in the Kroll Opera House. It was decorated with swastikas and surrounded by Nazis shouting insults like "Marxist Sows" at the SPD deputies.[9] Once assembled, deputies present were confronted with the so-called "Enabling Act" (*Ermächtigungsgesetz*) which aimed at the total and final removal of Weimar's parliamentary system. The powers and prerogatives of the Reichstag were to be handed over to the Reich executive and legislative powers were to be given to a single body. A two-thirds majority was needed to pass the legislation. The Nazis obtained this with the help of the center party. The leaders of that party decided to vote for it because they believed that Hitler would usurp power with force if they did not. In essence, they calculated that they

Hitler is shown here saluting an adoring crowd in the city square of Nuremberg.

could not block the legislation by any tactic available to them. They therefore acquiesced in hope the Nazis would respect the integrity of the Center Party and Catholic interests in Germany.

Once the Enabling Act had removed the legal foundation of the state, the Nazis had scored a decisive victory over political opponents. They now moved quickly. On 31 March, the government "passed" a law called the "Temporary Law for Co-ordination of the States with the *Reich*." It decreed that the state diets had to issue laws if necessary that contradicted the letter of the law in state constitutions. It was at this point that the term "*Gleichschaltung*" was used for the first time. It was soon proclaimed that the states had been stripped of their powers or "*gleichschaltet*."

"*Gleichschaltung*" turned out to be a constantly used term by the Nazis to describe their policy moves during 1933 and 1934. It was brought into service to describe the multivarious activities the National Socialists used to bring all aspects of German political and associational life under the control of the Nazi Party. The term had originated in physics where it was used to denote a device, a *Gleichrichter*, that caused electrical current to be transformed from one type of transmitted energy into another.

Following the first use of this term, it was used again on 2 May when trade-union facilities were occupied, the unions dissolved, and their properties confiscated by the state. This, from the Nazi point of view, was necessary, because the core of the working class had not moved behind Hitler. It appeared instead to maintain its old loyalties, to the KPD and the SPD. This situation led to the occupation of trade-union offices and the quick imprisonment of most union leaders.[10] German workers and employees thereafter were forced to work through a single, mass trade union. This "union" served the needs of the state and not the workers. This arrangement was called the "*Deutsche Arbeitsfront*" (DAF) and was headed by an alcoholic, Robert Ley, soon to be known widely as *Reichstrunkenbold* ("State Drunkard").

Following this, agriculture was also "coordinated." On 14 July (ironically France's Bastille Day) the government proclaimed that there was only one political party in Germany. The SPD

Hitler reviewing party units.

was suppressed and other parties "voluntarily" disbanded. The 14 July decree also had it that no other political party would be reconstructed so that the Nazis could stand alone. The civil service was purged and German judges agreed to all of this. They maintained that everything had been placed in the hands of Hitler with "complete confidence."[11]

The logical outcome of all this was seen in the "elections" of 12 November. There was only one party on the ballot. Some 92 percent of the vote was cast for the Nazi "unity list." Thereafter, the new Reichstag convened only when Hitler saw a need to give his decrees the aura of legitimacy. Votes were made unanimously as deputies leapt to their feet, in party uniforms, with arms extended.

In one respect, Hitler's power was not yet absolute; the army still took its oath to Hindenburg. Hitler had to wait for the president, in obvious declining health as 1934 began, to expire. Then he could move decisively to control the army. In deciding what would be the role of the armed forces in the new state, Hitler was confronted by Ernst Röhm who was chief of staff, SA. Röhm dreamed of a future Germany in which the SA, now expanded to some four million men, would combine with the Reichswehr to form a true "people's" army. He also led his followers in beginning to make noises to the effect that a "second revolution" was needed in that the first had not gone far enough to bring about a true leveling.

The SA Blood Purge

It is not within the chronological scope of this work to provide a detailed account of the SA purge transpiring on the night of 30 June 1934 and the morning of 1 July 1934. This concise discussion provides a brief outline of the events involved in carrying through the purge, a discussion of the situations leading up to that fateful decision to act on the night of 30 June and the morning of 1 July, and a brief consideration of its importance in the broader history of Nazism.

For the weeks just before the purge there had been continued arguments within the party about the future role of the SA. Röhm was consumed with high ambitions for his stormtroopers. After conversations with Hitler, Ernst Röhm agreed to let things quiet a bit by putting his SA on leave for a period of four weeks. This leave was set to commence in late June of 1934. "Information," likely fabricated by Röhm's enemies within the party, was given to Hitler. It was alleged that, in the manner of immediate postwar Munich, arms caches were being established for possible future insurrectionary activity to promote "a socialist revolution." It should be noted here, however, that "socialism" in this context meant the leveling tendency long seen in the SA. This tendency worked out in 1934 into a call to create places in the ranks of business and government employees for the often poorly educated brownshirts. This would have meant that what many saw as the "rabble" of the SA would pour into established institutions like the Reichswehr. This would have altered the German ground force, making of it a great "people's army" under Röhm's direction.

The decision to carry out the purge resulted in little more than a bloody show of gangsterism. On 30 June and 1 July hundreds of people on a prepared list were executed without formalities. There were no indictments, trials, or sentences. Hitler flew to Munich himself and drove with armed SS men to Bad Wiesee where the SA leadership was vacationing. Some of the leaders were shot in their beds. Others were driven back to Munich to be executed there on the grounds of Stadelheim prison.

Epilogue (1933-1934)

Hitler is shown here reviewing members of the Nazi Rider Corps, a descendant of the SA at the Nuremberg stadium.

In the Munich area, the dragnet was thrown out and many Bavarian SA leaders went to Stadelheim prison under guard. There Sepp Dietrich, leader of Hitler's SS bodyguard, ordered men on a list given him by the *Führer* to be marched into a courtyard, lined up against the wall, and shot without ceremony. Munich SA chief August Schneidhuber could not understand how it was that Dietrich, his old comrade, could be ordering his death. He called out to ask him: "Sepp, Sepp, what on earth is happening?" Dietrich answered simply: "You have been condemned to death by the *Führer*."[12] And then Schneidhuber died.

As this was happened in Munich, Hitler returned to the city from the lakeside hotel where SA men had been initially confronted. Goebbels, traveling with him, phoned Göring in Berlin and gave him the code word "*Kolibri*" (Hummingbird). This message unleashed a wave of terror in the capital and elsewhere.[13] The net result was that murder squads were at work in Munich, Berlin, Lichterfelde, and other places. People were killed, often after torture, as they were checked off fabricated lists prepared by Göring and Himmler.

Those executed in the German capital included former chancellor Kurt von Schleicher and his aide General Kurt von Bredow. Gregor Strasser, having fallen out of favor during 1932 and then abandoned Nazism, was also murdered. Erich Klausener, head of the "Catholic Action," Franz von Papen's aide Edgar Jung (author of a speech the former chancellor made infuriating the Nazis), and others were dispatched in the Berlin area. Back in Bavaria, Gustav von Kahr, long in retirement, had moved far from the political arena in his native state. He lived in Munich, maintaining a low political profile, and was no longer in any position to do any damage to Hitler or his movement. But over a decade earlier he had caused, with help, the failure of the Hitler putsch. Although the Hitlerian coup of 1923 might well have fallen short without Kahr's intervention, he was dragged from his home under arrest by the SS. His body was found later, hacked to pieces, in the hills near Dachau. Father Bernhard Stempfle, who apparently knew too much about Hitler's past and private life, was also discovered with three bullets in him.

Ernst Röhm himself was killed, apparently as a result of continued insistence from Göring and Himmler that he be eliminated. When the execution order came down, SS man Theodor Eicke, later to serve as a demented commander of the Dachau Concentration Camp, was pressed into service. In the early morning hours of 1 July 1934, Eicke went into Röhm's cell. He handed the SA chief of staff a copy of the *Völkischer Beobachter*, just off the press, so that Röhm could read a headline stating that the SA leader had been deposed as part of the "cleansing" of the SA.[14] He then gave Röhm a revolver with a single bullet in it and said that he had been given a "choice" to "do the right thing." Röhm was given ten minutes to shoot himself. When Eicke returned to the cell, he found the ex-captain standing at attention in the middle of it. He then fired two shots into Röhm, killing him almost instantly.[15]

It is hard to know precisely how many died that night and the next morning as part of what was soon being called the "Night of the Long Knives" (a term applied before to an action taken by the SA in Silesia during 1932). The best estimate of those killed is about eighty-five people.[16] What little that Germans knew about what had happened came from media accounts. They were told that the SA chief of staff had been plotting against the state and that General Schleicher had been scheming with him. Röhm was also charged with negotiating, independently of the foreign office, with representatives of foreign powers. The newspapers carried lurid stories about how Hitler had "cleaned up" the homosexual "pig pen" on a lake near Munich. The Nazis claimed that the homosexual tendencies, rampant among SA leaders, had just been revealed to them. This, despite the fact that Hitler and his entire inner circle had known of them for years and had not cared very much about them.

Once the immediate furor over the event had transpired, Hitler gave the purge an after-the-fact justification. On 3 July 1934 the Reich government published a decree indicating that "the measures taken on 30 June and 1 July and 2 July to reveal the treasonous and mutinous attacks are legal and in accordance with the state's right to self-defense." On 13 July a seemingly exhausted Hitler gave an emotional speech before the Reichstag. In it he justified his action and warned that those devising any steps to be taken against the state in the future would receive similar treatment. The *Führer* was the "highest Judge" in Germany. Many of the Reichstag members had long been worried about the SA because of its leader's insistence on a "people's army." Particularly these members were alarmed because the core of that army was to be brown-shirted thugs. Fearful citizens were now placated by a statement that, post-purge, the army was standing alone. It was to be the sole bearer of arms in the state.[17]

The roots for "Operation Hummingbird" grow both from the longer-term history of Nazism and the more immediate post-power situation in 1933–34. Hitler's relationship with Röhm was one of the oldest in the history of the Party. As noted earlier, Röhm belonged to a band of postwar desperadoes whose entire experience was shaped by the war and military adventurism. These people formed a group of men who simply could not adapt to civilian life. As a group, they joined the growing number of right-wing formations and parties, not because of ideological conviction, but because these formations gave them a chance to go on fighting after war's end. Röhm was much like the rest of this group of society's peacetime outsiders. He had been a very good soldier and spent the postwar period with a group of homosexual intimates who also were constantly looking for a fight.

Röhm was sentimentally attached to Hitler. In his mindset, one obviously determined by bluntness and a straightforward attitude, he avoided the brazen dissimilation of practicing politicians. Hitler, for his part, had viewed Röhm from the early days (the captain had joined the DAP in 1919) as a contact crucial for helping develop the SA. Röhm, it should be remembered, arranged for regular subsidies and demobilized officers to be sent to the Storm Detachment to aid in its initial formation and helped define its early duties.

Over time, some of the evidence indicates that Hitler came to believe that he had been led during 1923 into an unwise *Putsch* attempt. The sources of this misdirection seemed to him to be Röhm and others like him, men who had continually resided in the world of the *Putsch*. Hitler over time became aware that it was nearly impossible for the various paramilitary elements represented by Röhm and Hermann Ehrhardt to ever leave the romanticized realm of the *Putsch*-maker. Above all, such men wanted to create a desperado-conformed Germany.

Röhm's establishment of the *Frontbann* while Hitler was still in prison indicated that he continued to dream of an effective roof structure to draw desperadoes together to overthrow Weimar. In fact, the concept behind the development of the *Frontbann* was not far from the 1933–34 dream of a people's army which the chief of staff so emotionally espoused. The major difference between 1924 and 1934 was that, in the earlier year, Röhm still thought of his fledgling army as something to be built from all the paramilitary elements he could find drifting without an anchor. In 1934, he wanted to build the new army from an SA some four million strong, so, many of the other paramilitary forces having been absorbed by the Nazis or dissolved, there were no other sources of manpower rivaling it.

Röhm's 1924 vision was linked to the world of the *Putsch* and Hitler wanted none of it. He gave Röhm a chance and a choice at that juncture; the former army captain could accept Hitler as "Adolf the Legal" (a press term), sworn to avoid the path of insurrection and dedicated to legal electioneering. Faced with options he did not like, Röhm moved on. Eventually, he went to Bolivia as a military adviser. He later returned to Germany and, in the first month of 1931, became SA Chief of Staff and commenced its massive expansion.

It is continually offered by historians, and there is little reason to dispute it, that, by the summer of 1933, Hitler was in full control of Germany except for three major areas he had yet to "coordinate." These were: (1) the power still wielded by an ailing Hindenburg; (2) the revolutionary-minded SA, which was causing profound distress among "respectable" societal elements like business tycoons, generals, what remained socially if not officially of the old

Goebbels appears here in conversation with an SA leader.

noble class, as well as others suspicious of the zealousness and preference for public violence apparent in the Nazi movement; and (3) the traditionalists in the German army.

The stormtroopers had before 1933 been used primarily in electioneering. But with elections no longer contested, the legions of brawlers had taken from them the opportunity to do what had meant so much to them: the constant electioneering Nazi-style, with attendant violence. As this happened, the *Stahlhem* was incorporated into the SA during the second half of 1933, boosting its strength to some four and a half million men. This transpired while the German army was still limited to 100,000 men by Versailles. But the army, although numerically inferior to the SA, remained the far better equipped and more thoroughly trained fighting force. To some, the antagonism between these two forces, both desiring to be the nation's only bearers of arms, raised the threat of a possible Reichswehr-versus-SA civil war.[18]

The Röhm purge transpired at a point when the Nazi regime was losing some ground after an initial period of enthusiasm for the regime had faded. The various grievances held by the populace resulting from Depression-caused anxiety had not gone away. To many, there was an obvious chasm separating the grandiose promises of the NSDAP from the dismal realities of everyday life. For the people of Germany, a continuing Depression did not at all accord with the Nazi propaganda image of a movement "embracing the whole people in national unity and renewal." In power, the Nazi movement had revealed itself at the local level to be anything but a "force for unity, harmony, and integration." It appeared to be just another party which was, as others had been, riven by power struggles, arguments, and rivalries.[19]

Part of the negative attitude about Nazism was due to SA activity nationwide. The SA, immediately after the so-called "seizure of power," had played a dramatic role as an auxiliary police, pursuing Communists and other old foes. But once such elements had been "handled," it quickly became obvious that there was no further need for a private army.[20] The SA, with its continuing calls for a permanent revolutionary army, was anathema to the officers of the regular Reichswehr. The Storm Detachment was now an organization without a purpose.

As for the Reichswehr, its leaders hoped to bargain with Hitler to escape *Gleichschaltung*.[21] One of the things the generals feared most was Röhm's contention that the "Officers' Corps of the SA," as a first step, should be amalgamated with the command staff of the Reichswehr. Hitler was scheming to violate unilaterally the disarmament clause of the Versailles Treaty and arm to an extent well beyond the 100,000-man treaty limitation. The generals believed that the commanders of the SA, men whose private lives had received too much "obscene publicity," were not to be trusted with the vital business of defending Germany. General Walter von Brauchitsch later remarked: "Rearmament was too serious and difficult a business to permit the participation of peculators, drunkards and homosexuals."[22] Because of this attitude displayed by the professionals upon whom Hitler would have to depend if he needed to rearm, the *Führer* knew full well that his Nazi revolution could not, like the Bolsheviks in Russia, produce a revolutionary mass army of the kind Röhm was advocating. In sum, the top military command and even the increasingly feeble Hindenburg openly desired that Hitler take action against Röhm.

On 11 April Hitler joined the top military commanders on the cruiser *Deutschland*. This visit was presented to the public as a normal spring military maneuver where the *Führer* would appear simply to observe. In fact, there was a meeting between Hitler and those commanders who detested Röhm and his SA. It is not known precisely what was said aboard the *Deutschland*, but we do know that some sort of "gentleman's agreement" had been reached at this juncture. By it, Hitler would, in return for the military's support of his regime, suppress Röhm and his loudly proclaimed plans to create a new type of armed force. The traditional nature of the military would be preserved.

Röhm also had dangerous foes within Nazism. Perhaps the two most important of these were Hermann Göring and Heinrich Himmler. Both of these men had much to gain from the SA chief of staff's removal. Göring at this point controlled the Gestapo (an acronym for *Geheime Statspolizei* or "Secret State Police"). He had also received the rank of general from Hindenburg and could thus present himself as a highly decorated hero from World War I and the ideal figure to bring the party and the army closer together.

Göring had appointed Heinrich Himmler (1 April 1934) to head the Prussian Gestapo.

During the first half of the year, Himmler was moving around the chess pieces of power to enlarge his own feudal domain within the Nazi Party. He was already the director of the Bavarian police and chief of the SS. The SS was still officially a sub-section of the SA, but Himmler was gradually moving to detach it from its original moorings. He had the help of his top lieutenant, Reinhard Heydrich, in accomplishing all of his backstage gambits. To begin working toward the superseding of the SA with the SS, Himmler set out to collect complaints and scandals about SA leadership.

As the urgings from these two anti–SA camps intensified, Hitler began to be drawn toward their point of view. The *Führer* tried one last time with Röhm. In a private five-hour talk he apparently tried to convince the SA chief of staff that he must stop antagonizing the Reichswehr officers. Röhm was told that his calls for a central role for the SA in army activities had soured Nazi-army relations. Röhm was not really planning an anti-army revolt. He thus agreed to go on that fatal "sickness leave" to Bad Wiesse.

At this point, Hindenburg intervened. He asked Vice Chancellor Franz von Papen to try to straighten matters out in a Germany troubled by potential inflation, church complaints about new religious policies, and the ruthless suppression of the political parties. Papen agreed to do so.[23] Papen, at this juncture, had been excluded from all matters of importance in Berlin despite the fact that he was still vice-chancellor. Two of his advisers, Edgar Jung and Herbert von Bose, urged him to take at least one decisive anti–Nazi step. Jung wrote a speech for him to be delivered in Marburg on 19 June 1934.

The Marburg speech was given. The text of it denounced the regime for spreading morally reprehensible practices under the guise of a so-called "revolution." Goebbels moved quickly to keep the speech off the radio waves and out of the press. Nevertheless, the address caused a furor. Jung urged Papen to follow it up with a visit to Hindenburg to protest the government's suppression of the Marburg speech.[24] It likely seemed to Papen that he was realizing some success from his Marburg public appearance in that he was greeted at a race-horse meeting in Hamburg (naturally attended only by members of his social class) with shouts of "Hail Marburg!" from the conservative crowd in attendance there.[25]

Papen threatened to resign the vice-chancellorship. As he pointed out, he had been excluded from affairs of state for some time. Hitler, quite anxious that nothing happen which would upset the ailing president, told Papen that in due course the whole matter would be discussed with the "old gentleman" at his estate. Then Hitler, on 21 June, went off alone to see Hindenburg at his estate in Neudeck. When he arrived, the minister of defense, Werner von Blomberg, confronted him. Hitler was told by Blomberg that he had been discussing Papen's Marburg speech with Hindenburg. The army chief pointed out that, if the stormtroopers were not subdued, Hindenburg would declare martial law and turn the country over to the army.[26]

Hitler returned to Berlin knowing that he now had to act. The Gestapo, with Heydrich and Himmler directing it, began to manufacture "evidence" that Röhm and his stormtrooper leadership were planning a rising against the state, a "second revolution." Leading officers in the SS were presented with this "evidence" on 24 June and given instructions on how to deal with the national *Putsch* which "loomed on the horizon." Not long after, lists of "politically unreliable people" were drawn up and local SS leaders were called upon to kill a number of them once the purging operation was set in motion. The army then placed its resources at the disposal of the SS in case there was a serious nationwide conflict with the SA, a conflict involving the mass membership of the organization.[27] As it turned out, the strategy

Hitler is shown inspecting an SS group, with an SA leader directly behind him.

enacted successfully was to "cut off the head of the snake" so that the rest of the body was not involved.

On 27 June, Hitler met with army leaders to secure their cooperation in the anti–SA action. The generals replied by expelling Röhm from the German Officers' League the next day. The army was also placed on full alert. Blomberg then published an article in the Nazi press, declaring the army fully loyal to Hitler.[28] During the same time period, Hitler learned that Hindenburg had agreed to give Papen an audience on 30 June. This fact confirmed Hitler's view that he must strike against the SA. He also believed he had to act against key conservatives who might well work with Hindenburg to install Papen as president when the constantly weakening old man died.[29]

At this point, Hitler nervously went to a wedding reception in Essen where he telephoned Röhm's adjutant at Bad Wiesee. He left orders for Storm Detachment leaders to meet with him on the morning of 30 June. Hitler then organized a hurried conference with Joseph Goebbels and Sepp Dietrich (commander of the *Führer's* personal SS bodyguard) in Bad

Godesberg on 29 June 1934. It was determined that action would be taken against the SA early the next morning. Goebbels, not one of the inner-party plotters against the SA chief of staff, was astonished by this sequence of events, but of course said nothing and moved quickly to play a role in carrying through the purge.[30]

Göring was dispatched to Berlin to take charge of actions to be taken there. Rumors began to be circulated and alarm spread in SA ranks. On the streets of Munich stormtroopers surged back and forth. They shouted that they would crush any army attempts to quiet them. They also openly denounced the *Führer*. Calm was eventually restored in the Bavarian capital by Adolf Wagner, regional SA commander in Munich. But there were similar demonstrations elsewhere in Germany. When Hitler was told of these events on flying into Munich in the early morning hours of 30 June, he decided he could wait no longer. The purge had to be launched at this point.[31]

When one looks at the broader significance of the events of 30 June and 1 July 1934, one issue immediately comes to mind. Is it too much to state, as does Joachim Fest, that 30 June 1934 was the "decisive date after January 30, 1933 in the Nazi seizure of power?"[32] Is it even a greater leap to see a direct connection "between the killings of 30 June and the subsequent practice of mass murder in the concentration camps of the East?"[33] It is perhaps more important for the observer of this period of history to speculate in somewhat more limited ways. One should note that the purge came along at a time in the history of Nazi Germany when the Third Reich seemed to far too many of the people of Germany to be represented by the bullying arrogance of the SA. This situation had thus become offensive to a broad segment of the population.[34]

Popular reactions to the purge must be observed in this context. Of course, to begin, none of the public was aware of the fact that the claims of an existing plot aimed at a coup were fabricated. Perhaps because of this and the widespread disquiet about stormtrooper activities, there was a total absence of criticism. A report from Swabia indicated much popular sympathy on the side of the *Führer*.[35] Similar sentiments came from Upper Bavaria.[36] In sum, far from causing Germans to have any doubts about their national leader, nearly all accounts indicate that this initial mass murder by the Third Reich was not seen as such and, in fact, paid handsome dividends for the new regime.[37] It allowed the Nazis to establish with the German people, with little contradiction, the idea that Hitler had the right to pass sentence on the SA leadership. Moreover, he had the "right" to send other "culprits" to their deaths without a trial.[38]

Once the killings had been accomplished, Hitler withdrew from public view. A press release soon described his "grave conflicts of conscience." There were, of course, many lurid details provided about sexual deviants in the Nazi Party and the fact that many of them had been killed at dawn on 1 July. It was not until 13 July that Hitler emerged from seclusion to deliver that hour-long speech to the Reichstag. In it, he assumed personal responsibility for the purge. He claimed that he had rescued the German people from a threat so deadly that only a drastic action of the kind taken could have eradicated it. He stressed the duty of the National Socialist state "to stamp out and destroy ... every last vestige of this phenomenon which poisons and makes dupes of people." He had destroyed, in his view, nothing but "deserters and mutineers."[39]

When Hitler gave his Reichstag speech, he was wildly applauded. The Reichswehr generals listened to his address with special satisfaction. They particularly liked his statement to the effect that "in the state there is only one bearer of arms, and that is the army."[40] The Reichstag then unanimously approved an after-the-fact law making the murders of 30 June 1934 and 1 July 1934 legal.

The immediate positive feeling of the Germans following the purge developed into a lasting belief that the end of SA terrorism meant a return to a nation typified by law and order. A positive feeling about Hitler spread from the officers down throughout the German army.[41] Hindenburg apparently expressed some regrets that generals Schleicher and Bredow had been killed along with the SA leaders. But he too sent a congratulatory telegram to the Nazi leader, giving him credit for "saving the nation from serious danger."[42]

The long-expected death of Paul von Hindenburg transpired on 2 August 1934. It took Hitler only an hour after the old field marshal's death to announce that he had merged the presidential office with the chancellorship. This made him head of state and supreme commander of the armed forces. It was also on 2 August that the army's supreme command required all German soldiers to swear a "sacred oath" of "unconditional obedience to the head of state."[43] The unlimited nature of the Hitlerian dictatorship was now fully established.

It is generally agreed that 30 June dealt a decisive blow to the SA. But the *Sturmabteilung* of the Nazi Party did not disappear. The Nazi bureaucracy was rather like a Christmas tree to which one adds ornaments constantly while never removing any. The SA remained an ornament on the Third Reich's bureaucratic tree until the end of the Third Reich. But it did not shine brightly again. Its brass knuckles and blackjacks were replaced by collection boxes for the "Winter Relief," a Nazi charity drive. Soon enough, as the Third Reich began to rearm, the best of the organization's membership was siphoned off into the army. The only major use of the SA before World War II which in any way resembled its pre–1934 activities was during the infamous Kristallnacht in 1938.

During this anti–Jewish pogrom, fires were ignited all over Germany and the streets of the nation were littered with shattered glass from synagogues and Jewish businesses. The causation and details of the course of this deplorable event deserve considerably more space than it can receive in this epilogue. And it does get considerable attention in works covering Nazism during 1938. Suffice it to state here that this so-called "spontaneous reaction of the German people" was designed by Goebbels. The term "spontaneous reaction" was used to describe an event which, supposedly, rose from the people to meet a "world Jewish conspiracy." But in actuality it needed to be launched in several areas by calling in SA squads from outside the area where the "rising" was desired and spontaneity was obviously nearly completely lacking in these locations.[44]

The years of SA struggle in the streets of Germany could not simply be erased from the minds of radical and violent stormtroopers after 1933, or even after 1934. Yet, after 1934, the energy of the stormtrooper was truly aimless in character. But it could still be used, and was used, against Germany's Jews between 1935 and 1938. The programmed anti–Semitism provided party paramilitary segments with an outlet for violent tendencies. Perhaps the greatest significance of the purge was that the romantic revolutionaries found in the old SA were replaced with passionless men. These "new men" could be counted on for violence on behalf of the state, but this violence was highly controlled and channeled. Most of these "new men" were to be found in the SS.

One of the great ironies in the history of National Socialism was the fact that the SS, under Himmler, replaced the SA as a new party army and became a direct competitor with the traditional Germany army in the form of the *Waffen SS* ("SS in Arms"). By this juncture, the history of the paramilitary in the party was completely transformed. The "freebooters" of the postwar "war after the war" and the street gangs of the SA had disappeared from the scene. As has happened in other historical instances, the revolutionary, important in the seeking for power, quickly became anachronistic once his movement was in power.

Chapter Notes

Chapter One

1. F. Meinecke, *The German Catastrophe*, trans. S. B. Fay (Boston: Beacon Press, 1950), p. 10.
2. J. W. Wheeler-Bennett, *The Nemisis of Power: The German Army in Politics, 1918–1945* (London: Macmillan, 1969), p. 9.
3. R. Dahrendorf, *Society and Democracy in Germany* (New York: Doubleday, 1969), pp. 33, 37.
4. F. Stern, *The Failure of Illiberalism: Essays on the Political Culture of Modern Germany* (New York: : A. A. Knopf, 1972), p. xxiii.
5. F. Fischer, *Germany's Aims in the First World War* (New York: W. W. Norton, 1967), Introduction.
6. K. Hildebrand, *The Foreign Policy of the Third Reich* (Berkeley, CA: University of California Press, 1973), pp. 2, 7, 136.
7. E. Kahler, *The Jews Among the Nations* (New York: F. Ungar, 1967), p. 99.
8. Quoted in H. von Maltitz, *The Evolution of Hitler's Germany: The Ideology, the Personality, the Movement* (New York: McGraw-Hill, 1973), p. 85.
9. Ibid., p. 115.
10. H. Arendt, *The Origins of Totalitarianism* (New York: Meridian Books, 1958), p. 37.
11. F. Stern, *Gold and Iron: Bismarck Bleihschröder, and the Building of the German Empire* (New York: A. A. Knopf, 1977), especially chapter 18.
12. P. Massing, *Rehearsal for Destruction* (New York: Harper, 1949), p. 12.
13. See P. Pulzer, *The Rise of Political Anti-Semitism in Germany and Austria* (New York: Wiley, 1964).
14. W. Daim, *Der Mann der Hitler die Ideen gab* (Munich: Isar Verlag, 1958), pp. 20–21.
15. L. Poliakov, *The Aryan Myth: A History of Racist and Nationalist Ideas in Europe* (New York: Basic Books, 1974), p. 269.
16. O. Büsch, *Militärsystem und sozialleben im alten Preussen, 1713–1807* (Berlin: DeGreyter, 1962).
17. H. U. Wehler, *Deutsche Gesellschaftgeschichte*, Vol. III (Munich: C. H. Beck, 1987), pp. 873–887.
18. H. Bley, *Namibia under German Rule* (London: Transaction Publishers, 1998).
19. G. Schmidt, "Innen politische Blockbildungen am Vorabend des ersten Weltkrieges," in *Aus Politik und Zeitgeschichte*, May 13, 1972.
20. K. Saul, "Der deutsche Kriegerbund: zur innenpolitischen Funktion eines 'national' Verbändes in kaiserlichen Deutschlands" in *Militärgeschichte Mitteilungen*, 1969/1972.
21. A. Westphal, *Die Kriegervereine in Deutschland als Weltmacht: Vierzig Jahre Deutsches Reich* (Berlin: Verlag Walter de Gruyter, 1911), p. 768.
22. K. Rohe, *Das Reichsbanner Schwarz Rot Gold: Ein Beitrag zur Geschichte der politischen Kampfverbände zur Zeit der Weimar Republik* (Dusseldorf: Droste, 1966), pp. 163–166.
23. H.U. Wehler, *Das Deutsche Kaiserreich 1871–1918* (Göttingen: Vandenhoeck & Ruprecht, 1973), pp. 158–165.
24. R. Nissen, *Helle Blätter, Dunkle Blätter* (Stuttgart: Deutsche Verlags-Anstalt, 1969), p. 42.
25. B. Smith, *Heinrich Himmler: A Nazi in the Making, 1900–1926* (Stanford, CA: Hoover Institution Press, 1971), pp. 35–76.
26. G. Almond and S. Verba, *The Civic Culture* (Princeton, NJ: Princeton University Press, 1963), p. 4.

Chapter Two

1. A. Palmer, *The Kaiser: Warlord of the Second Reich* (New York: Scribner, 1978), p. 175.
2. G. Craig, *War, Politics, and Diplomacy* (New York: Praeger, 1966), pp. 45–57.
3. For origins of the myth see: J. W. Wheeler-Bennett, *Wooden Titan: Hindenburg* (New York: W. Morrow, 1936), p. 238.
4. R. Rupp, "Problems of the German Revolution, 1918–19," *Journal of Central European History* 3 (1968), pp. 109–135.
5. See K. D. Bracher, *Die Auflösung der Weimarer Republik* (Villingen-Schwarzwald: Ring-Verl, 1960).
6. K. W. Meyer, *Karl Liebknecht: Man Without a Country* (Washington, D.C.: Public Affairs Press, 1957), pp. 120–148.
7. G. Mann, *The History of Germany Since 1789* (New York: Praeger, 1968).
8. P. Scheidemann, *The Making of a New Germany*, Vol. II (New York: D. Appleton, 1929), pp. 262–264.
9. A. Brecht, *The Political Education of Arnold Brecht: an Autobiography, 1884–1970* (Princeton University Press, 1970), pp. 110–111.
10. H. U. Wehler, *The German Empire, 1871–1918*. (Providence: Berg Publishers, 1993), p. 229.
11. See R. Waite, *Vanguard of Nazism: The Free Corps Movement in Germany 1918–1923* (Cambridge, MA: Harvard University Press, 1952).
12. E. Waldman, *The Spartacist Rising of 1919 and the*

Crisis of the German Socialist Movement (Milwaukee: Marquette University Press, 1958).
13. *New York Times,* December 15, 1918.
14. R. Leviné-Meyer, *Leviné, the Spartacist.* (London: Gordon & Cremonesi, 1972), p.6.
15. J. M. Keynes, *Economic Consequences of the Peace* (New York: Harcourt, Brace and Howe, 1920), p. 78.
16. A. Sharpe, *The Versailles Settlement: Peacemaking in Paris, 1919* (New York: St. Martin's Press, 1991), p.79.
17. Ibid., p. 87.
18. D. Lloyd George, *The Truth About Peace Treaties,* Vol. I (London: V. Gollancz, 1938), p. 312.
19. H. Holborn, *Germany and Europe* (Garden City, New York: Doubleday, 1971), p. 170.
20. A. M. van den Bruck, *Das Dritte Reich* (Munich: Der Ring, 1923).
21. J. Erger, *Der Kapp Lüttwitz Putsch* (Dusseldorf: Droste, 1967).
22. G. Craig, *Politics of the Prussian Army, 1640–1945* (New York: Oxford University Press, 1955) pp. 375–381.
23. A. Mitchell. *Revolution in Bavaria 1918–1919* (Princeton, NJ: Princeton University Press, 1965), and G. Franz-Willing, *Ursprung der Hitlerbewegung 1919–1922* (Preussich Olendorf: Schütz, 1975). Also see: W. Maser, *Der Sturm auf die Republik: Frühgeschichte der NSDAP* (Stuttgart: DVA, 1973), and K. Schwend, *Bayern zwischen Monarchie und Diktatur* (Munich: R. Pflaum, 1954).
24. Quoted in P. Gay, *Weimar Culture, The Outsider as Insider* (New York: Harper & Row, 1968), p. 153.
25. F. Ringer, *The German Inflation of 1923* (New York: Oxford University Press, 1969).
26. On the Ruhr, see P. Wentzschke, *Ruhrkampf: Einbruch und Abwehr im Rheinish Westfalischen Industriegebeit* (Berlin: R. Flobbing, 1930).
27. W. Sauer, "National Socialism: Totalitarianism or Fascism?," *American Historical Review* 73, no.2 (December 1967), pp. 404–424.
28. On the role of the desperado outside Germany, see: O. Mitchell, "Enter the Desperado: Paramilitary Life in Postwar Europe," *Midwest Quarterly* 26, no. 1 (Autumn 1989), pp. 9–24.
29. Ibid., pp. 16–19.
30. Ibid.
31. On the Black and Tans, see: R. Bennett, *The Black and Tans: The British Special Police in Ireland* (New York: Barnes and Noble Books, 1995).
32. H. H. Hofmann, *Der Hitlerputsch: Krisenjahre deutsche Geschichte 1920–1924* (Munich: Nymphenburger Verlagshandlung, 1961).

Chapter Three

1. H. Frank, *Im Angesicht des Galgens* (Munich: F.A. Beck, 1953).
2. W. Maser, *Hitler* (London: Allen Lane, 1973), p. 19.
3. A. Hitler, *Mein Kampf* (New York: Reynal & Hitchcock, 1941), p. 6.
4. B. Hitler, "My Brother-in-Law Adolf," Unpublished manuscript, New York Public Library.
5. Stories about Alois beating his children, his wife, and his dog probably originate with Bridget Hitler who was obviously not present at the time.
6. See, for example, R. G. L. Waite, *The Psychopathic God: Adolf Hitler* (New York: Basic Books, 1970), pp. 168–170.

7. L. Bezymenski, *The Death of Adolf Hitler* (New York: Pyramid, 1969), pp. 44–45.
8. F. Redlich, *Hitler: Diagnosis of a Destructive Prophet* (New York: Oxford University Press, 1999), pp. 44–45.
9. Maser, *Hitler*, p. 25.
10. *Mein Kampf*, pp. 10–15.
11. A. Kubizek, *The Young Hitler I Knew* (Boston: Houghton Mifflin, 1955), p. 85.
12. *Mein Kampf*, p. 27.
13. E. Bloch, "Erinnerungen an den Führer und dessen verewigte Muter," NSDAP Central Archives, NS 25/26.
14. Maser, *Hitler*, p. 43.
15. J. S. Jones, *Hitler in Vienna, 1907–1913* (London: Blond & Briggs, 1983), p. 133.
16. J. Fest, *Hitler* (New York: Harcourt Brace Jovanovich, 1973), p. 46.
17. *Mein Kampf*, p. 392.
18. Ibid., p. 52.
19. Jones, *Hitler in Vienna*, pp. 146, 163.
20. Fest, *Hitler*, p. 37.
21. W. A. Jenks. *Vienna and the Young Hitler* (New York: Columbia University Press, 1960), pp. 118–120.
22. *Mein Kampf*, p. 75.
23. Waite, *Psychopathic God*, 412–425.
24. See *Diagnostic and Statistiscal Manual of Mental Disorders*. 3rd ed. (Washington, D.C.: American Psychiatric Association, 1987), pp. 342–347.
25. See K. Bäthe, *Wer Whonte in Schwabing*. (Munich: Süddeutscher Verlag, 1967) and L. Hummer, *Bayern von Kaiserreich zur Diktatur* (Pfaffenhohen: Verlag W. Ludwig, 1979).
26. F. Schuadle, *Kurt Eisner und die bayerische Sozialdemokratie* (Hannover: Verlag für Literatur und Zeitgeschehen, 1961).
27. Fest, *Hitler*, pp. 61–62.
28. Ibid., p. 68.
29. *Mein Kampf*, p. 210.
30. R. Hanser, *Putsch! How Hitler Made a Revolution* (New York: Pyramid Publications, 1971), p. 81.
30. P. von Hindenburg, *Aus meinem Leben* (Leipzig: S. Hirzel, 1920), pp. 80, 96.
31. W. Maser, *Hitlers Briefe und Notizen*. (Vienna: Econ Verlag, 1973), p. 63.
32. Quoted in Hanser, *Putsch*, p. 89.
33. Quoted in Fest, *Hitler*, p. 69.
34. Ibid., p. 68.
35. Ibid., p. 104.
36. Quoted In Hanser, *Putsch*, p. 85.
37. Fest, *Hitler*, pp.65–70.
38. J. Toland, *Adolf Hitler*, vol. I (New York: Doubleday, 1976), p. 89.

Interpolation I

1. T. Mann, "At the Prophets" in *Stories of Three Decades* (New York: A. A. Knopf, 1966), p. 288.
2. L. Hollweck, *Unser München* (Munich: Süddeutscher Verlag, 1967), p. 125.
3. W. Rudolff, "Notjahre Statpolitik in Krieg Inflation und Weltwirtschaftskrise 1914 bis 1933" in R. Bauer, ed., *Geschichte der Stat München* (Munich: C.H. Beck, 1922), pp. 337–339.
4. Ibid., 339.
5. E. Toller, *I Was a German: The Autobiography of Ernst Toller* (New York: Paragon House, 1991), pp. 130–131.

6. E. Müsham. *Tagebucher 1910–1924* (Munich: Olzog, 1994), pp. 174–177.
7. S. Fishman, "Prophets, Poets, and Priests: A Study of the Men and Ideas that made the Munich Revolution of 1918/1919" (PhD diss., University of Wisconsin, 1960), pp. 15–16.
8. This account is based on newspapers for the period, among them the *Münchner Post* and the *Münchner-Augsberger Abendzeitung*.
9. R. Grunberger, *Red Rising in Bavaria* (London: Barker, 1973), pp. 83–93.
10. Ibid., p. 90.
11. Ibid., 110–111.
12. Ibid., pp. 111–114.
13. Ibid., pp. 114–145.
14. M. Halbe, *Jahrhundertwende* (Danzig: 1935), pp. 32–35.
15. It must be remembered that these "aliens" were often identified in the popular mind as anyone from outside Bavaria who had moved there to work in the armament and munitions factories during World War I.
16. R. S. Garnett, *Lion, Eagle, and Swastika: Bavarian Monarchism in Weimar Germany, 1918–1933* (New York: Garland, 1991), pp.40–43.
17. Ibid.
18. R. Kanzler, *Bayerns Kampf gegen den Bolchewismus: Geschichte der bayerischen Einwohnerwehren* (Munich: Verlag Parcus & Co., 1931).

Chapter Four

1. Grunberger, *Red Rising in Bavaria* (London: Barker, 1973), p. 68.
2. J.M. Bridgman, *The Revolt of the Hereros* (Berkeley: University of California Press, 1981).
3. R.H. Phelps, "Before Hitler Came: Thule Society and Germanic Orden," *Journal of Modern History*, 35 (1963), pp. 245–261.
4. K.D. Bracher, *The German Dictatorship* (New York: Praeger, 1970), p. 81.
5. See the discussion of the DAP in Franz-Willing, *Ursprung*.
6. D. Orlow, *The History of the Nazi Party, 1919–1933* (Pittsburgh: University of Pittsburgh Press, 1969), p. 11.
7. Maser, *Sturm auf die Republik*, p. 145.
8. R. Parkinson, *Tormented Warrior: Ludendorff and the Supreme Command* (New York: Stein & Day, 1978), p. 8.
9. K. Heiden, *Der Fuehrer* (Boston: Houghton Mifflin, 1944), pp. 253–254.
10. B. Mazlish, *The Revolutionary Ascetic: Evolution of a Political Type.* (New York: Basic Books, 1976).
11. Orlow, *Nazi Party*, I, p. 15.
12. *Mein Kampf*, pp. 511–514.
13. Orlow, *Nazi Party*, I, p.23.
14. *Münchner Neutste Nachrichten*, 3–4 January, 28 January 1920.
15. *Berliner Tageblatt*, 6 May 1920.
16. E. Deuerlein. "Hitlers Eintrit in die Politik und die Reichswehr," in *Vierteljahrshefte für Zeitgeschichte* (April 1959), p. 206. Hereafter cited as *VfZ*.
17. R.H. Phelps, "Hitler als Parteiredner im Jahre 1920," in *Vfz* (July 1963), pp. 314–316.
18. Ibid., p. 297.
19. Fest, *Hitler*, pp. 128–129.
20. Orlow, *History of the Nazi Party*, I, p.23.
21. Fest, *Hitler*, p. 161.
22. *Völkischer Beobachter*, 9 September 1920. Hereafter cited as *VB*.
23. Ibid., 22 August 1928.
24. Franz-Willing, *Ursprung*, p. 180.
25. P. Hoffman, *Hitler's Personal Security: Protecting the Führer, 1921–1945* (New York: Da Capo Press: 2000), p. 5.
26. See, for example, the fairly recent general work, D. Welch, *The Hilter Conspiracy* (Washington, D.C.: Public Affairs Press, 2001), p. 19.
27. Ibid., p.287.
28. A.Werner, *SA und NSDAP: Wehrbund, Parteitruppe, oder "Revolutionsarmee?,"* PhD Dissertation, Erlanger: 1964, p. 20.
29. J. Erdmann, *Coburg Bayern und Das Reich 1918–1923* (Coburg: Rossteutscher, 1969), p. 75.
30. Major E. Schmidt, *Argonnen Schlachten des Weltkrieges.* (Berlin: Gehard Stalling, 1927), p.45. B.I. Gudmundsson, *Stormtroop Tactics: Innovation in the German Army, 1914–1918* (New York: Praeger, 1989).
31. Ibid.
32. W. Sauer, "Die Mobilmachung der Gewalt," in K.D. Bracher (et.al.). *Die Nationalsozialistische Machtergreifung: Studien zur Erichtung des totalitaren Herrschaftssystems in Deutschland, 1932–34* (Cologne: Westdeutscher Verlag, 1960), pp. 832–833.
33. *VB*, 3 August 1921.
34. Ibid., 11 August 1921.
35. See Z. Sternhall, "Fascist Ideology" in W. Laquer (ed.). *Fascism: A Reader's Guide- Analysis, Interpretation, Bibliography.* (Berkeley: University of California Press, 1976), p. 338.
36. G. Valois. *La Révolution Nationale.* Paris: Nouvelle Libraire Nationale, 1924, p. 151.
37. *VB*, 22 November 1922.
38. Sauer, *"Mobilmachung der Gewalt,"* p. 832.
39. On the subject of cover formations for outlawed Free Corps, see L. Freiwald, *Der Weg der brauenen Kampfer: Ein Frontbuch von 1918–1933.* (Munich: J.F. Lehmann, 1934), pp. 170–172.
40. *Münchener Post*, 27 December 1922.
41. Files of Dr. W. Lutgebrune, Statement of Alfred Hoffman, 31 October 1921. Captured German Documents, National Archives, Washington, D.C., Microfilm roll numbers T253-15, 65313–65314, and T253-16, 6702. Hereafter cited as NA, followed by roll and frame numbers.
42. L. Hertzman, *DNVP: Right Wing Opposition in the Weimar Republic.* (Lincoln: University of Nebraska Press, 1963), p. 141.
43. E. von Salomon. *Der Fragebogen* (Hamburg: Rowohlt, 1951), p. 398.
44. Hauptarchiv of the Nazi Party, 651/1481. Hereafter cited as HA.
45. Werner, "SA," p. 22.
46. *Mein Kampf*, p. 748.
47. Fest, *Hitler*, p. 162.
48. H. Bennecke, *Hitler und die SA* (Munich: G. Olzog, 1962), pp. 28–29.
49. *Bayerisches Hauptstatsarchiv*, 6803, SA. Hererafter cited as BHSA.
50. Ibid.
51. P. Longerich, *Die braunen Bataillone: Geschichte der SA* (Munich: Beck, 1989), pp. 9–32.
52. H. Höhne, *The Order of the Death's Head* (New York: Ballantine, 1971), p. 21.
53. H. Kallenbuch, *Mit Hitler auf Festung Landsberg* (Munich: Kress & Hornung, 1939), pp. 13–15.

54. H. Volz, *Daten der Geschichte der NSDAP* (Munich: Ploetz, 1934), p. 8.
55. See Maser, *Fruhgeschichte* pp. 314, 315, and U. Lohalm, *Völkischer Radicalismus: Die Geschichte der Deutsche Völkischen Schutz und Truzbundes* (Hamburg: Leibniz-Verlag, 1970), p. 312.
56. E. Reiche, *The Development of the SA in Nurnberg, 1922–1939* (Cambridge, MA: Cambridge University Press, 2002, 1986), pp. 20 ff.
57. J.H. Grill. *The Nazi Movement in Baden, 1920–1945.* (Chapel Hill: University of North Carolina Press, 1983), pp. 39 ff.
58. A. Bullock. *Hitler: A Study in Tyranny.* (London: Hamlyn, 1973), p. 94.

Interpolation II

1. Quoted in G. Noske, *Zehn Jahre deutsche Geschichte, 1918–1928* (Berlin: Verlag für Politik und Wirtschaft, 1928), pp. 30–31.
2. W. Pabst, "Spartakus" in C. Hotzel, ed., *Deutsche Aufstand: die Revolution des Nachkrieg* (Stuttgart: W. Kohlhammer, 1934), pp. 30–31.
3. F. von Lüttwitz, "Einmarsch der Gardkavalertie Schutzen Division in Berlin" in *Deutsche Soldaten* (Leipzig: F.K. Koehler, 1937), p. 52.
4. H. Brauweiler, *Generäle in der deutschen Republik: Groener, Schleicher, Seeckt* (Berlin: Tell-Verl., 1932), p. 36.
5. G. Noske, *Von Kiel bis Kapp: zur Geschichte der deutsche Revolution* (Berlin: Verlag für Politik und Wirtschaft, 1920), p. 54.
6. L. von Maercker, *Vom Kasierheer zur Reichswehr: Geschichte des freiwilligen Landesjäger*, 3rd ed. (Leipzig: Koehler, 1922), pp. 63–64.
7. E. J. Gumbel, *Vier jahre Politische Mord*, 5th ed. (Berlin: Verlag der Neuen Gesellschaft, 1922), pp. 12–14.
8. Noske, *Von Kiel bis Kapp*, p. 74.
9. P. Scheidemann, *Memoiren eine sozialdemokraten*, Vol. II (Dresden: Reissner, 1928), p. 345.
10. Maercker, *Vom Kaiserheer zur Reichswehr*, pp. 89–92.
11. C. Zetkin, *Les Batailles Révolutionnaires de L'Allemagne*, pub. No 47, (Petrograd: Editions de l'Internationale Communiste, 1920), pp. 8–10.
12. E. von Schmidt-Pauli, *Geschichte der Freikorps 1918–1924* (Stuttgart: R. Lutz, 1936), pp. 191–195.
13. *Times* (London), May 15, 1919.
14. E. Toller, *Eine Jugend in Deutschland* (Amsterdam: Querido Verlag, 1936), pp. 231–233.
15. E. O. Volkmann, *Revolution über Deutschland* (Amsterdam: Brill, 1936), pp. 92–93.
16. A. Loessner, *Der Abfall Posens: 1918–1919 im polischen Schriftum* (Danzig: Kommissionsverlag der Danziger Verlags-Gesellschaft, 1933), pp. 27–28.
17. For this attitude, see B. von Hülsen, "Freikorps im Osten" in H. Roden, *Deutsche Soldaten, vom Frontheer und Freikorps* (Leipzig: Breitkopf & Härtel, 1935).
18. G. R. von der Goltz, *Mein Sendung in Finnland und im Baltikum* (Leipzig: F.K. Koehler, 1920), p. 127.
19. Quoted in Ibid., p. 135.
20. F. W. von Oertzen, *Die deutschen Freikorps, 1918–1923* (Munich: F. Bruckmann, 1939), pp. 35–172.
21. F.W. Heinz, *Die Narion greift an: Geschichte und Kritik des sodatischen Nationalismus* (Berlin: Verlag Das Reich, 1932), p. 57.
22. J. Benoist-Méchin, *Historie de L'Armee Allemande 1919–1936*, Vol II (Paris: Albin Michel, 1938), p. 28.
23. Ibid., p. 36.
24. F. Awaloff, *Im Kampf gegen den Bolschewismus* (Glückstadt and Hamburg: Verlag J.J. Augustin, 1925), p. 217.
25. Von Oertzen, *Die deutschen Freikorps*, pp. 114–115.
26. Noske, *Von Kiel bis Kapp*, p. 116.
27. Von Salomon, *Die Geächten*, p. 267.
28. Waite, *Vanguard*, pp. 56–57.
29. Waite, *Hitler: The Psychopathic God*, pp. 303–304.
30. Dahrendorf, *Society and Democracy*, p. 331.
31. M. Tatar, *The Hard Facts of the Grimm's Fairy Tales* (Princeton, NJ: Princeton University Press, 2003), p. 60.
32. *Washington Post*, October 24, 1945.
33. C. Severing, *1919–1920 im Wetter und Watterwinkel* (Bielefeld: Buchhandlung Volkswacht, 1927), pp. 216–217.
34. E. J. Gumbel, "*Verrater verfallen der Feme,*" in *Opfer, Morder, Richter 1919–1920* (Berlin: Malik-Verlag, 1919), pp. 98–99.
35. H. von Seeckt, *Die Reichswehr* (Leipzig: R. Kittler, 1933), pp. 14–15.
36. E.J. Gumbel, "Le Capitaine Ehrhardt et L'Organization C," in *L'Europe Neuville* VI (August 25, 1923), p. 1073.
37. E. Röhm, *Geschichte eines Hochverräter*. 7th ed. (Munich: Eher, 1934), p. 131.
38. *Reichsgesetzblatt* (Jahrgang, 1920).
39. O. Landsberg, "Die Münchener Feme" in J. Wirth, ed., *Deutsche Republik*, Vol. III (*Erster Jahrgang*, 1926).
42. BSHA II, MA-10376.
43. Röhm, *Geschichte*, p. 1.
44. C. Fischer, "Ernst Julius Röhm: Chief of Staff of the SA and Indispensable Outsider" in R. Smelser and R. Zietelmann, eds., *The Nazi Elite* (New York: NYU Press, 1993), pp. 173–82.
45. Deurlein, "Hitler's Eintritt," pp. 203–205.
46. Röhm, *Geschichte*, pp. 104–151.
47. Ibid., p. 171
48. Ibid., p. 190–193.
49. Werner, "SA und NSDAP," pp. 84–90.

Chapter Five

1. A. E. Cornbise, *The Weimar in Crisis: Cuno's Germany and the Ruhr Occupation* (Washington, D.C.: University Press of America, 1977), pp. 41–42.
2. F. von Rabenau, *Seeckt: Aus seinem Lebern 1918–1936*, Vol. II (Leipzig: Hase und Koehler, 1934), p. 328, and E. von Schmidt-Pauli, *General von Seeckt* (Berlin: Hobbing, 1937), p. 116.
3. P. von Heydebreck, *Wir Wehrwölfe:Einnerungen eines Freikorpsführer* (Leipzig: F.K. Koehler, 1931), p. 154.
4. G. E. R. Gedye, *The Revolver Republic: France's Bid for the Rhine* (London: Arrowsmith, 1930), p. 138.
5. E.V. D'Abernon, *An Ambassador of Peace*, (London: Hodder and Stoughton, 1929–1930), p. 24.
6. *Münchener Neueste Nachrichten*, December 5, 1923.
7. See "Regimental Order No. 86 of SA Regiment Munich," N.A., T81–90, 102831 and Regimental Orders in *Ibid.*, 102828–02958.

8. See "From the SA High Command to all SA," N.A., T81-90, l02857- 102859.
9. Ibid., 102874.
10. *Münchener Neueste Nachricten*, December 5, 1923.
11. O. Gessler, *Reichswehrpolitik in der Weimarer Zeit* (Stuttgart: Deutsche Verlags-Anstalt, 1958), p. 248.
12. *Augsburger Postzeitung*, April 17, 1923.
13. Gessler, *Reichswehr Politik*, pp. 246–247.
14. *Augsburger Zeitung*, May 1, 1923.
15. F. von Rabenau, *Seecket: Aus Seinem Leben* (Leipzig: Hase und Koehler, 1940), p. 341.
16. Gessler, *Reichswehr Politik*, pp. 254–255.
17. H. Michaelis and E. Schraepler, ed., *Ursachen un Folgen*, vol. 5, (Berlin: n.d.), pp. 402–404.
18. Ibid., pp. 404–407.
19. T. Vogelsang, "Die Reichswehr in Bayern und der Munchener Putsch 1923," *VfZ*, 1957, pp. 100–101.
20. Michaelis and Schraepler, *Ursachen*, vol. 5, p. 432.
21. Ibid., p. 434.
22. J. Dornberg, *Munich 1923: The Story of Hitler's First Grab for Power* (New York: Harper and Row, 1982), p. 174.
23. Cited in Hanser, *Putsch*, pp. 335–336.
24. Ibid., p. 337.
25. Maser, *Sturm auf die Republik*, p. 435.
26. Hanser, *Putsch*, p. 351.
27. Dornberg, *Munich 1923,* p. 293.
28. H. J. Gordon, *Hitler and the Beer Hall Putsch* (Princeton, NJ: Princeton University Press, 1972), pp. 475–485.
29. Ibid., pp. 144–145.
30. *The Hitler Trial Before the Peoples' Court in Munich*, vol. I, (Arlington, Virginia: University Publications of America, 1976), pp. 144–145.
31. Ibid.
32. Ibid., p. 445.
33. Ibid., vol. III, p. 366.
34. Fest, *Hitler*, p. 193.
35. E. Hanfstaengl, *Unheard Witness* (Philadelphia: Lippincott, 1957), p. 119.
36. W. Maser, *Hitler's Mein Kampf: Entstehung, Aufbau, Stil Änderungen, Quellen, Quellenwert, Kommentierte Aufzuge* (Munich: Bechtle Verlag, 1966), p. 13.
37. Hanfstaengl, *Witness*, p. 145.
38. Bullock, *Hitler*, pp. 121–122.
39. E. Jäckel, *Hitler's Weltanschauung. Entwurf einer Herrschaft.* Stuttgart: Deutsche Verlags-Anstalt, 1983), p. 129.
40. Waite, *Psychopathic God*, p. 72.
41. *Mein Kampf*, p. 580.
42. Ibid., pp. 669–670.
43. Ibid., p. 116.
44. Ibid., p. 234.
45. Ibid., pp. 642–645.
46. D. Jablonsky, *The Nazi Party in Dissolution: Hitler and the Verbotzeit, 1922–1925* (London: F. Cass, 1989), p. 53.
47. Quoted in H. Vogt, *The Burden of Guilt* (New York: Oxford University Press, 1964), p. 81.

Chapter Six

1. MA, 100424, BHSA.
2. C. B. Flood, *Hitler, the Path to Power* (Boston: Houghton Mifflin, 1989), p. 600.
3. Institute für Zeitgeschichte (ed.), *Hitler: Reden, Schriften, Anordnungen: Februar1925 bis Januar 1933*, I (Munich: Selbstverlag des Institut für Zeitgeschichte, 1993), pp. 14–16.
4. Ibid., pp. 96, 115–116.
5. G. Pridham, *Hitler's Rise to Power: The Nazi Movement in Bavaria 1923–1933* (London: Hart-Davis MacGibbon, 1973.)
6. "Ernst von Salomon," *Berliner Zeitung,* April 17, 1994.
7. F. A. Krummacher and A. Wucher, eds., *Die Weimarer Republik* (Munich: R. Pflaum, 1961), pp. 271–272.
8. Werner, "SA und NSDAP," pp. 187–189.
9. Ibid., p. 196–198.
10. Ibid., 178–185.
11. H. J. Kuron, *Freikorps und Bund Oberland*, PhD diss., Friedrich Alexander Universität zu Erlangen, 1960.
12. Werner, "SA und NSDAP," pp. 196–198.
13. "Reichskommisar für Ueberwachung der Öffentlichen Ordnung" ("Reichskommisar for Oversight of the Offical Order"), 107, October 11, 1924. Hereafter cited as RKO.
14. Röhm, Geschichte, p. 322.
15. Ibid.
16. RKO 111, April 25, 1925.
17. Ibid., 112, July 25, 1925 and J. Noakes, *The Nazi Party in Lower Saxony* (London: Oxford University Press, 1971), Chapters 3 and 4.
18. Röhm, *Geschichte*, p. 322.
19. *VB*, February 26, 1925.
20. *Der Angriff, Aufsatze aus der Kampfzeit* (Munich: Eher Verlag, 1940), p. 71.
21. *Axis History Forum*, October 2007.
22. J. Noakes, "Conflict and Development in the NSDAP 1924–1927," *Journal of Contemporary History* 1, no. 4 (1966), p. 17.
23. Orlow, *Nazi Party*, p. 67.
24. C. Riess, *Joseph Goebbels* (New York: 1948), p. 25.
25. Orlow, *Nazi Party*, p. 72.
26. HA, Munich Collection, 52.
27. G. Stresemann, *Vermächtnis*, Vol. 3, (Berlin: Ullstein, 1932), pp. 556 ff.
28. Bracher, *Auflösung*, pp. 137ff.
29. Orlow, *Nazi Party*, p. 80.
30. Heiber, Goebbels, p. 55.
31. Ibid.
32. Goebbels, *Angriff*, p. 71.
33. The thesis that the Nazi Party was lower-middle-class in structure and thus a party of teachers, farmers, craftsmen, etc. began with Harold Laswell in 1933. See H. Laswell, "The Psychology of Hitlerism," *Political Science Quarterly* 4 (1933), pp. 373–384. This notion held until the studies appearing that revealed Nazi voting paterrns during the elections leading to the demise of Weimar. These studies called for a revision of the lower-middle-class thesis. See R. Hamilton, *Who Voted for Hitler?* (Princeton, NJ: Princeton University Press, 1987), and T. Childers, *The Nazi Voter: The Social Foundation of Fascism in Germany 1919–1933* (Chapel Hill: University of North Carolina Press, 1983).
34. On the *Gauleiter*, see P. Hüttenberger, *Die Gauleiter* (Stuttgart: Deutsche Verlags-Anstalt, 1970), and K. Höffkes, *Hitler's politische Generale: Die Gauleiter des Dritten Reiches* (Tübingen: Grabert-Verlag, 1986).
35. Bennecke, *Hitler und die SA*, pp. 131–132.
36. H. Höhne, *Die Machtergreifung: Deutschlands Weg in die Hitler Diktatur* (Hamburg: Rowohlt, 1983), p. 120.
37. Bennecke, *Hitler und die SA*, p. 139.

38. For more on the auxiliaries of the Nazi Party see K. P. Fischer, *Nazi Germany: A New History* (New York: Continuum, 1995), pp. 207–208.
39. For an exhaustive breakdown of the SA class and age structure see C. F. Fischer, *Stormtroopers: A Social, Economic and Ideological Analysis 1929–35* (London: Allen & Unwin, 1983), pp. 25–81.
40. Fest, *Hitler*, p. 261.
41. H. A. Turner, *German Big Business and the Rise of Hitler* (New York: Oxford University Press, 1985), pp. 90–91.

Chapter Seven

1. Maser, *Frugeschichte*, pp. 416–417 and Orlow, *Nazi Party*, pp. 11–45.
2. N.A., T-580, 85, 403.
3. See, for example, *VB*, June 2, 1927 and HA/16/303.
4. M. Brozat, "Die Anfange der Berlin NSDAP 1926/1927," *VJHZ*, 8 (1960), pp. 93, 104–108, 114–115.
5. HA, 5/136.
6. N.A., T-580, 19, 199a.
7. *VB*, August 10, 1927, p. 3, and A. Hellweg, *Vom Kampf und Sieg des Nationalsozialismus in Kreise Lübbecke* (Lübbecke: NSDAP, Kreisleitg, 1933) p. 20.
8. HA, 3, 81/82.Walter Stennes, East.
9. Ibid., 70, 510.
10. *Berliner Tageblatt*, December 9, 1930.
11. *NS Jahrbuch (1931)*, pp. 141–142. On the eve of the 1930 election
these were: Walter Stennes (East); Viktor Lutze (North); Werner von Fichte (West), Manfred von Killinger (Middle); and August Scheidhuber (South).
12. *Reichsarbeitsblatt*, No. 14, Table 250, pp. 9–10, Part II, No. 25.
13. *Vorwärts*, September 4, 1930 and *Die Post*, xvii (January 1931).
14. W. Oehme and K. Karo, *Kommt "Das Drite Reich?"* (Munich: Eher Verlag, 1935), 31.
15. HA, 77/1563, 1566.
16. O. Hale, *The Captive Press in the Third Reich* (Princeton, NJ: Princeton University Press, 1964), p. 40.
17. HA, 10/ 203.
18. *VB*, July 20–21, 1930.
19. U. Schelen-Spanenberg, *Die Deutsche Volkspartei im Lande Braunschweig* (Braunschweig: Waisenhaus-Buchdruckerei und Verlag, 1969), p. 114.
20. T. Childers, ed., *The Formation of the Nazi Constituency 1919–1933* (London: Croom Helm, 1986), pp. 25–32.
21. Turner, *German Big Business and the Rise of Hitler*, pp. 114–124.
22. Bracher, *Auflösung*, p. 339.
23. *Badische Presse*, June 17, 1930.
24. A. Schweitzer, *Big Business in the Third Reich* (London: Eyre & Spottiswoode, 1964), p. 35.
25. C. Bloch, *Die SA und die Krise des NS-Regimes 1934* (Frankfurt-am-Main: Suhrkamp, 1970), p. 46.
26. R. Bessel, "Militarismus in innenpolitischen Leben der Weimarer Republik: von den Freikorps zur SA" in K.-J. Muller and E. Opitz, eds., *Militar und Mitlitarismus in der Weimarer Republik* (Dusseldorf: Droste, 1978), pp. 193–222.
27. E. Rosenhaft, "Working-class Life and Working-class Politics: Communists, Nazis, and the State in the Battle for the Streets," in R. Bessel and E. J. Feuchtwanger, eds., *Social Change and Political Development in Weimar Germany* (London: Croom Helm, 1981), pp. 207–240.
28. Ibid., p. 220.
29. Ibid.
30. *Weissbuch uber die Erschiessungen des 30 Juni 1934* (Paris: Editions du Carrefour, 1935).
31. K. Bredow, *Hitlerrast* (Saarbrücken: Saarbrücker Druckerei und Verlag, 1935), p. 27.
32. International Military Tribunal, Trial of the Major War Criminals Before the International Tribunal: Proceedings and Documents, Vol. xxi, p. 135. Hereafter cited as *TMWC*.
33. P. Merkl, *The Making of a Stormtrooper* (Princeton, NJ: Princeton University Press, 1980), pp. 7–8.
34. Abel Collection, Autobiography No. 381, Stanford University, Hoover Library, Stanford, California.
35. Fischer, *Stormtroopers*, p. *149.*
36. Cited in Ibid.
37. M. Kater, *The Nazi Party: A Social Profile of Members and Leaders*, 1919–1945 (Cambridge, MA: Harvard University Press, 1983), p. 52.
38. K. Klotzbach, *Gegen den Nationalsozialismus: Widerstand und Verfolgung in Dortmund 1930–1945: eine historisch-Politische studie* (Hanover: Verl. Für Literatur und Zeitgeschehen, 1969), p. 40.
39. M. Kele, *Nazis and Workers: National Socialist Appeals to German Labor 1919–1933* (Chapel Hill: University of North Carolina Press, 1972), pp. 204–208.
40. Fischer, *Stormtroopers*, p. 154.
41. Ibid., Fischer's term.
42. O. Dietrich, *Mit Hitler in die Macht* (Munich: F. Eher Nachf., 1934), pp. 9–11.
43. For this technique as it was exercised in 1932 see: *VB*, July 19, 1932.
44. J. Goebbels, *Kampf um Berlin* (Munich: F. Eher Nachf., 1936), p. 30.
45. R. Bessel, *Political Violence and the Rise of Nazism: The Stormtroopers in Eastern Germany* (New Haven: Yale University Press, 1984), p. 75.
46. H. Volz, *Die Geschichte der SA* (Berlin: Verlag der Reimar Hobbing, 1934), p. 163.
47. D. Peukert, *The Weimar Republic: The Crisis of Classical Modernity* (New York: Hill and Wang, 1992), p. 95.
48. Heiden, *Der Fuehrer*, pp. 393–396.
49. Ibid., pp. 402–403.

Interpolation III

1. W. Berges, "Das Reich ohne Hauptstadt," in *Das Hauptstadt Problem in Geschichte* (Tübingen: Nieneyer, 1952), pp. 1–2, and L. Mumford, *The City in History* (New York: Harcourt Brace Jovanovich, 1961).
2. B. Schultze, "Berlins Grundung und erster Aufsteig," in *Berlin Neuen Kapital: Seiner Geschichte* (Berlin: Ullstein, 1960).
3. Ibid., pp. 65.
4. H. Rothfels, ed., *Berlin in Vergangenheit und Gegenwart* (Tübingen: Mohr,1961), p. 2.
5. D. Clausewitz, *Die Stätdeordnung von 1808 und die Stadt Berlin* (Berlin: E. Ehering, 1908), p. 42.
6. R. Dietrich, "Berlins Weg Zur Industrie und Handelsstadt," in *Berlin: Neuen Kapital seiner Geschichte* (Berlin: Duncken & Humboldt, 1960).
7. F. Sass, *Berlin in Seiner neuesten Zeit und Entwicklung* (Leipzig: Koffka, 1846), p. 46.

8. L. von Rochau, *Grundsätze der Realpolitik* (Stuttgart: K. Göpel, 1853).
9. K. von Raumer, "Deutschland um 1800," in *Handbuch d.Deutsche Geschichte*, Vol. 2 (Potsdam: Hoffman, Gmbh., 1935), p. 214.
10. E. Spanger, "Gedenkrede zur 150. Jahrefeier der Friedrich-Wilhelms Universität," in H. Rothefels, ed., *Berlin in Vergangenheit und Gegenwart* (Tübingen: Ullstein, 1961), p. 62.
11. *Verhandlungen der durch die allerhöchste Verordung vom 1 Februar 1872 einberufenen Hauser des Landtages*, Session of February 3, 1873, p. 934.
12. R. Glatzer, ed., *Berliner Leben, 1870–1918.* (Berlin: Rütter & Loening, 1963), pp. 371 ff.
13. See the coverage of Lagarde and others in F. Stern, *The Politics of Cultural Despair* (Berkeley: University of California Press, 1961).
14. G. Stein, ed., *Berlin* (Oldenburg: 1914), p. 182.
15. W. Polz, *Sozialistenfrage und Revolutionsfurcht* (Lubeck: Matthiesen, 1960).
16. There is a wealth of literature on this. See, for instance, C. Schorske, *German Social Democracy, 1905–1917* (Cambridge, MA: Harvard University Press, 1955).
17. F. Lederer, *Berlin um Umgebung* (Berlin: Neue Verlagsanstalt, 1929), pp. 15–17.
18. A. B. Grzesinski, *Inside Germany* (New York: E. P. Dutton, 1939), pp. 117, 124.
19. J. K. von Engelbrechten and Hans Volz, eds., *Wir Wandren durch das Nationalsozialistische Berlin*, (Munich: Zentralverlag der NSDAP, Franz Eher nachf., 1937), pp. 185–189.
20. H. Ullmann, *Flucht aus Berlin* (Jena: E Diederichs, 1932), pp. 22–23.
21. I. Petersen. *Our Street: A Chronicle Written in the Heart of Fascist Germany* (London: V. Gollancz, 1938), and R. Italiaander and W. Hass, *Berliner Cocktail* (Hamburg and Vienna: P. Zsolnay, 1959), 453–456.
22. Goebbels, *Kampf*, p. 23.
23. Ibid., pp.24–26.
24. Ibid.
25. B. von Borresholm, ed., *Dr. Goebbels. Nach Aufzeichnungen um seiner Umgebung* (Berlin: Journal, 1949), p. 50.
26. Goebbels, *Kampf*, p. 70.
27. E. Ebermayer and H. Roos. *Gefährtin des Teufels: Leben und Tod den Magda Goebbels* (Hamburg: Hoffmann und Campe, 1952), p. 97.
28. Goebbels, *Kampf*, pp. 102ff.
29. Quoted in *Vossiche Zeitung*, May 6, 1927.
30. Goebbels, *Kampf.* p. 146.
31. *Deutsche Allgemeine Zeitung*, May 6, 1927.
32. *B.Z. am Mittag*, May 30, 1927.
33. There are many accounts of the Wessel story. As highly detailed as any is H. B. Gisevius, *To the Bitter End* (Boston: Houghton Mifflin, 1947).
34. Cited in O. Friedrich, *Before the Deluge: A Portrait of Berlin in the 1920s* (New York: Harper & Row, 1972), pp. 340–341.
35. HA, 47, 968/ (for Berlin).
36. HA, *Befehl* I, No. 637/32. and HA, 89, 849.
37. HA, 89, 1846.
38. Grzesinski, *Inside Germany*, pp. 152 ff., and C. Severing, *Mein Lebensweg*, Vol. II (Cologne: Greven Verlag, 1950), pp. 340–341.
39. *Vossiche Zeitung*, June 29, 1932.
40. J. Goebbels, *Vom Kaiserhof zur Reichskanzlei* (Munich: Zentralverlag der NSDAP, Franz Eher nachf., 1934), p. 117.
41. *Vossiche Zeitung*, August 9, 1932.
42. Ibid., September 6, 1932.
43. On this phenomenon, see D. Fleming and B. Bailyn, eds., *The Intellectual Migration, Europe and America, 1930–1960* (Cambridge, MA: Belknap Press of Harvard University Press, 1969) and L. Fermi, *Illustrious Immigrants: The Intellectual Migration From Europe, 1930–1941* (Chicago: University of Chicago Press, 1960).

Chapter Eight

1. Erger, *Der Kapp-Lüttwitz-Putsch*, p. 51.
2. T. Nipperdey, "Verein als soziale Struktur im Spaten 18. Und Frühen 19. Jahrhundert" in H. Brockman, ed., *Geschichtswissenschaft und Verein-wesen in 19. Jahrhundert* (Göttingen: Wallstein Verlag, 1972), p. 4.
3. R. Gellately, *The Politics of Economic Despair: Shopkeepers and German Politics, 1890–1914* (Beverly Hills, CA: Sage Publications, 1974).
4. See the evidence for Marburg in R. J. Koshar, *Social Life, Local Politics and Nazism: Marburg, 1880–1935* (Chapel Hill: University of North Carolina Press, 1986), Chapter 3.
5. M. Jamin, *Zwischen den Klassen, zur Sozialstruktur der SA-Führerschaft* (Wuppertal: P. Hammer, 1984).
6. On the topic of SA as "roof" formation, see O. C. Mitchell, "The Nazi SA Club of the Nation," *Halcyon/1987: A Journal of the Humanities* 9, pp. 111–113.
7. "To the Regime's President in Arnsberg from the Hagen City Attorney," September 24, 1931, NA T81–90, 103179.
8. Report of the Hagen Police for October 30, 1932. Ibid., 103192 and 103201.
9. Reports of 13 and 18 November from the Hagen Police. Ibid., 103188–89.
10. Reports of Hagen Police of 21 March 1932. Ibid., 103204–103218.
11. Ibid., 103220.
12. Ibid., 103236–37.
13. *VB*, November 10, 1932.
14. [Hagen] *Volksstimme*, December 2, 1932.
15. *Westfälischen Tageblatt*, January 27, 1933.
16. On the Magdeburg situation, see Abel Collection of 581 autobiographical statements, Essay No.2. Hoover Institution, Stanford, California.
17. R. H. Bainton, *The Reformation of the Sixteenth Century* (Boston: Beacon Press, 1952), p. 228.
18. HA/531/1280.
19. Heiber, *Goebbels*, p. 82.
20. W. Bade, *Joseph Goebbels* (Lübeck: C. Coleman, 1933), pp. 52–55.
21. Gisevius, *To the Bitter End*, p. 60.
22. Goebbels, *Kampf um Berlin*, p. 71.
23. J. Goebbels, *Wetterleuchten: Aufsätze aus der Kampfzeit* (Munich: Zentralverlag der NSDAP, Franz Eher nachf., 1939), p. 30.
24. J. Baird, "Goebbels, Horst Wessel, and the Myth of Resurrection and Return," *Journal of Contemporary History* 1, no. 17 (1982), p. 633.
25. See the idealization of "SA Leader Schirmer" in B. Roth, *Kampf: Lebensdokumente deutscher Jugend von 1914–1934* (Leipzig: P. Reclam,1934), pp. 228–232.
26. G. L. Mosse, *The Crisis of German Ideology: Intellectual Origins of the Third Reich.* (New York: Grosset & Dunlap, 1964).
27. Ibid., p. 25

28. Hermann Löns, *Der Wehrwolf* (Jena: Diederichs, 1917).
29. Roth, *Kampf*, p. 228.
30. Dieter Fricke, et al., *Der Bürgerlichen Parteien in Deutschland: Handbuch der Geschichte der bürgerlichen Interresen Organization von Vormärz bis zum Jahre 1945*, Vol II (Leipzig: Bibliographisches Institut, 1970), p. 403.
31. K. Heiden, *History of National Socialism* (New York: A. A. Knopf, 1935), pp. 18 and 28.
32. Schweitzer, *Big Business in the Third Reich*, pp. 117–119.
33. Kater, *The Nazi Party: A Social Profile of Members and Leaders, 1919–1945*, pp. 155–165.
34. Bloch, *Die SA*, p.146.
35. Brozat, "Die Anfänge," pp. 85–91.
36. Stennes to Röhm, HA/17/322.
37. K. D. Bracher, et. al. *Die Nationalsozialistische Machtergreifung: Studien zur Errichtung des totalitären Herrschaftssystem in Deutschland, 1933/1934*, 3 vols. (Berlin: Ullstein, 1983), p. 47.
38. Cited in C. Fischer, "The Occupational Background of the SA Rank and File During the Depression Years, 1929 to mid-1934," in P. D. Stachura, ed., *The Shaping of the Nazi State* (London: Croom Helm, 1978), p. 134.
39. Ibid., pp. 137–144.
40. C. Fischer, *Stormtroopers: A Social, Economic and Ideological Analysis* (London: Allen & Unwin, 1983), pp. 114–119.
41. M. Kater, "Ansätze su einer Soziologie der SA bis zur Röhm Krise," in U. Engelhardt, V. Stellin, and H. Stucke, eds., *Soziale Bewegung und politische Verfussung* (Stuttgart: Klett, 1970).
42. On the SA in East Germany, see R. J. Bessel, *Political Violence*.
43. On Eutin, see L. P. Stokes, "The Social Composition of the Party in Eutin, 1925–32," *International Review of Social History* 23 (1978), p. 27.
44. See tables on occupational categories in Reiche, *The Development of the SA in Nuremberg*.
45. H. Bennecke, "Die SA in Sachsen von der Macht Übernahme" in *Bundesarchiv Koblenz. Kleine Erwerbungen/569*.
46. *Statistisches Jahrbuch* (Berlin: 1932).
47. K. Rohe, *Das Reichsbanner Schwarz Rot Gold: Ein Beitrag zur Geschichte und Struktur der politischen Kampfverbäbande zur Zeit der Weimarer Republik* (Düsseldorf: Droste, 1966), p. 272.
48. International Military Tribunal, *Trial of the Major War Criminals*, Vol. 21 (Washington, DC: 1946), p. 124.
49. Ibid., p. 135.
50. See O. C. Mitchell, "Terror as a Neo-Marxian Revolutionary Mechanism in the Nazi SA (1932)," *Wichita State University Bulletin* 41, no. 2 (May 1965).
51. On this tendency, see O.-E. Schüddekopf, *Linke Leute von Rechts: Die National revolutionären Minderheiten under der Kommunismus in der Weimarer Republik* (Stuttgart: Kohlhammer, 1960), p. 335.
52. J. Goebbels, *Signale die Neuen Zeit* (Munich: F. Eher Nachf., 1934), pp. 88–89.
53. Röhm, *Geschichte*, pp. 365–366.
54. *Statistische Jahrbuch* for the years cited.
55. See Kater, *Verhältnis*, pp. 361–362.
56. NA, T81-91, 105050-105246.
57. Fischer, *Stormtroopers*, pp. 48–50.
58. Merkel, *Stormtrooper*, p. 191.
59. Ibid., p. viii.
60. T. D. Grant, *Stormtroopers and Crisis in the Nazi Movement: Activism, Ideology, and Dissolution* (New York: Routledge, 2004).
61. H. A. Winkler. "German Society, Hitler and the Illusion of Restoration 1930–1933," *Journal of Contemporary History* 2, no.4.
62. J. Nyomarkay, *Charisma and Factionalism in the Nazi Party* (Minneapolis: University of Minnesota Press, 1967), p. 3.
63. Ibid., p. 4.
64. M. Weber (A. M. Henderson and T. Parsons, trans.), *The Theory of Social and Economic Organization* (New York: Free Press, 1947), p. 130.
65. Z. Barbu, *Democracy and Dictatorship: Their Psychology and Patterns of Life* (New York: Grove Press, 1956).
66. P. Lowenberg, "Psycohistorical Origins of the Nazi Youth Cohort," *American Historical Review* 76, no. 5 (December 1971), p. 1458.
67. Ibid., p. 1465.
68. Ibid., 1499.
69. Jochmann, *Nationalsozialismus*, 340.
70. Luedecke, *I Knew Hitler*, p. 320.
71. Nyomarkay, *Charisma*, pp. 135–136.
73. M. Weber (trans. S. N. Eisenstadt), *On Charisma and Institution Building* (Chicago: University of Chicago Press, 1968), pp. 51–52.
74. Mitchell, *Hitler Over Germany*, p. 191.
75. Katscher Police Records in NA T253-22, 422816.
76. O. Mitchell, *Hitler Over Germany: The Establishment of the Nazi Dictatorship, 1918–1934* (Philadelphia: Institute for the Study of Human Issues, 1983), pp. 192–193.
77. See E. Rosenhaft, *Beating the Fascists? The German Communists and Political Violence* (Cambridge: Cambridge University Press, 1983).
78. B. Jenkins, *International Terrorism: A New Mode of Conflict* (Los Angeles: Crescent Publications, 1975), p. 1.
79. Inter-American Committee of the Organization of American States, *Statement of Reasons for Draft Convention on Terrorism and Kidnapping*, Document CP/doc. 54/70, October 5, 1970.
80. C. Leiden and K. Schmidt, *The Politics of Violence: Revolution in the Modern World* (Englewood Cliffs, NJ: Prentice-Hall, 1968).
81. See, for example, S. Aronson, "Nazi Terrorism: The Complete Trap and the Final Solution," in D. C. Rapaport and Y. Alexander (eds.), *The Morality of Terrorism: Religious and Secular Justification*, 2nd ed. (New York: Columbia University Press, 1989), pp. 169–186.
82. See the explanation of the "revolutionary tradition" in J. H. Billington, *Fire in the Minds of Men: Origins of the Revolutionary Faith* (New York: Basic Books, 1980).
83. W. Laqueur, *Terrorism* (Boston: Little, Brown, 1977), pp. 14–17.
84. E. Weber, "Romania" in H. Rogger and E. Weber (eds.), *The European Right: A Historical Profile* (Berkeley: University of California Press, 1966), p. 541.
85. Miklós Lackó, *Arrow-Cross Men: National Socialists, 1935–1944* (Budapest: Akadémiai Kiadó, 1969), p. 43.
86. Laqueur, *Terrorism*, p. 75.
87. "Document on Terror" in *News From the Iron Curtain* I (March 3, 1952).
88. W. Bley, *SA Marschiert: Leben und Kampf der Brauen Batallione* (Stuttgart: Union Deutsche Verlagsgesellschaft, 1934), p. 74. Also see H. Okrass, "*Hamburg

bleibt rot": *Das Ende einer Parole* (Hamburg: Hanseatische Verlagsanstalt, 1934), p. 198.
89. Bennecke, *SA*, pp. 194–195.
90. *Reichsgesetzblatt* (1932), p. 389.
91. Ibid., 403–407.
92. H. M. Jones, *Revolution and Romanticism* (Cambridge, MA: Belknap Press of Harvard University Press, 1974), p. 432.
93. "On Dying for the Movement," Heines to Röhm, February 9, 1931, HA/77,1565.
94. C. Sterling, *The Terror Network: The Secret War of International Terrorism* (New York: Holt, Rinehart and Winston, 1981), pp. 203–204.
95. *Görlitzer Nachrichten*, August 11, 1932.
96. Records of the City Attorney, Görlitz, November 19, 1932, NA T-253–23, 474379.
97. *"Die Kampzeit war die beste Zeit,"* a paper presented to the annual conference of the American Historical Association (1964).
98. Noakes, *Party in Lower Saxony*, p. 98.
99. H. Rauschning, *Germany's Revolution of Destruction* (London: William Heinemann, 1939), p. 11.
100. Salomon, *Fragebogen*, p. 437.
101. For the use of this title, see Ernst Röhm's regulations for the legal protection of SA and SS men, October 7, 1932 in NAT253–23, 47451.
102. NA T253–22, 472890–472891.
103. Ibid., 472900 ff.
104. Ibid., 472975.
105. Ibid., 472980.
106. Ibid., 473632.
107. Ibid., 472978.
108. NAT253–22 and 23 contain numerous *Prozessnotizen* in which Luetgebrune made such points.
109. F. von Papen, *Memoirs* (London: A. Deutsch, 1952), p. 291.
110. NAT253–23, 474527–474528.
111. See the verdicts in Ibid., 473984 ff.
112. Ibid., 474220.
113. Ibid., 474552.
114. A. Dorpalen, *Hindenburg and the Weimar Republic* (Princeton, NJ: Princeton University Press, 1964) pp. 403–404.
115. NAT253–23, 474552.
116. Salomon, *Fragebogen*, pp. 436–437, 439.
117. Meissner, *Staatssekretär*, pp. 253–254.
118. *Reichskommisar für überwachung der offenlichen Ordnung.* L.1, M.1, for August 3 and L.20, M.8.
119. Ibid., L.65, M.66, August 4, 1922.
120. Ibid., L. 83, M. 70 for January 16, 1923 and L. 91 for June 15, 1923.
121. Ibid., L.112, M.99, July 22, 1925.
122. *Nachrichtensammelstelle im Reichsministerium des Innern*, September of 1930, Vol. I, pp. 33–36, M. 369.
123. T. Vogelsang, *Reichswehr Staat und NSDAP, Beitrage zur deutschen Geschichte 1930–1932* (Stuttgart: 1962), pp. 466–470.
124. Werner, "SA," pp. 544–542.

Chapter Nine

1. Höhne, *Machtergreifung*, pp. 63–65.
2. See W. Görlitz, *History of the German General Staff, 1657–1945* (New York: Praeger, 1953) and Vogelsang, *Reichswehr Staat und NSDAP*, Stuttgart: Deutsche Verlags-Anstalt, 1962).
3. Meissner, *Staatssekretar unter Ebert, Hindenburg, Hitler*, p. 210.
4. Krummacher and Wacher, *Die Weimarer Republik*, p. 299.
5. W. Görlitz, *Hindenburg: Ein Lebensbild* (Bonn: Athenäum, 1953), p. 334.
6. E. Eyck, *Geschichte der Weimarer Republik* (Stuttgart: Rentsch Verlag, 1956), p. 379.
7. Deuerlein, *Der Aufsteig*, p. 337.
8. Mitchell, *Hitler Over Germany*, p. 178.
9. W. Sauer, *Die Nationalsozialistische Machtergreifung*, Vol. III (Berlin: Westdeutscher Verl., 1962), p. 23.
10. Ibid. p. 222.
11. E. Calic, *Unmasked: Two Confidential Interviews with Hitler in 1931* (London: Chatto & Windus, 1971), pp. 17–46.
12. O. Dietrich, *Zwolf Jahre mit Hitler* (Munich: 1955), p. 185.
13. Hanfstaengl, *Unheard Witness*, p. 169.
14. Dietrich, *Mit Hitler in die Macht.*
15. H .O. Meissner and H. Wilde, *Die Matchergreifung: Eine Bericht uber die Technik des nationalsozialistischen Statsreiche* (Stuttgart: J.G. Cotta, 1958), p. 49.
16. Bracher, *Auflösung*, pp. 431–432.
17. J. Goebbels, *Vom Kaiserhof zur Reichskanzlei* (Munich: Zentralverlag der NSDAP, Franz Eher nachf., 1934).
18. H. Bruning, *Memoiren 1918–1934* (Stuttgart: Deutsche Verlags-Anstalt, 1970), p. 183.
19. O. Braun, *Von Weimar zur Hitler* (Hamburg: Hammonia Nordeutsche Verlag, 1949), pp. 218–242.
20. Fest, *Hitler*, p. 320.
21. A. Wucher, *Die Fahne Hoch* (Munich: Süddeutsher Verlag, 1963), p. 16.
22. M. Hauner, *Hitler, A Chronicle of His Life and Times* (New York: St. Martin's Press, 1983).
23. Fest, *Hitler*, p. 329.
24. Bracher, *Auflösung*, p. 490.
25. Ibid.
26. Ibid., pp. 503–509.
27. Brüning, *Memoiren 1918–1934* , p. 599.
28. A. François Poncet, *Souvenirs d'une ambassade a' Berlin, Septembre 1931-Octobre 1938* (Paris: Flamirion, 1946), pp. 42–43.
29. Quoted in Wheeler-Bennett, *Nemesis of Power*, p. 250.
30. G. R. Treviranus, *Das Ende von Weimar: Heinrich Brüning und zeine Zeit* (Dusseldorf: Econ-Verlag, 1968), p. 334.
31. Crossman, R. H. S., ed., *The God that Failed* (New York: Harper, 1949), pp. 46–47.
32. H. Speier, *German White Collar Workers and the Rise of Hitler* (New Haven, CT: Yale University Press, 1987).
33. T. Childers, ed., *The Formation of the Nazi Constituency 1919–1933* (London: Croom Helm, 1986).
34. Ibid.
35. See, for example, the story of a small town in Koshar, *Social Life, Local Politics, and Nazism.*
36. Ibid.
37. R. J. Evans and D. Geary, eds., *The German Unemployed: Experiences and Consequences of Mass Unemployment from the Weimar Republic to the Third: Reich* (London: Croom Helm, 1987).
38. J. Weiss, *The Fascist Tradition* (New York: Harper & Row, 1967), pp. 9–11, 20.
39. H. Anderlahn, *Gegner erkannt! Kampferlebenkrise der SA* (Munich: F. Eher Nachf., 1937), pp. 60–63.

40. A. Rosenberg, *Der Mythus des XX Jahrhunderts* (Munich: Hoheneichen-verlag, 1930), p. 512.
41. *VB*, February 2, 1936.
42. *Frankfurter Zeitung*, June 1, 1937.
43. *VB*, August 30, 1932 and December 11, 1935.
44. E. Huber, *Das ist Nationalsozialismus* (Stuttgart: Union Deutsche Verlagsgesellschaft, 1933), p. 122.
45. G. Wellner, "Industriarbeiten in der Weimar Republik," in *Geschichte und Gesellschaft*, 7, 148, pp. 534–554.
46. L. Hausen, "Unemployment Also Hits Women: The New and the Old Women in the Dark Side of the Golden Twenties in Germany" in P. Stachura, ed., *Unemployment and the Great Depression in Weimar Germany* (London: Macmillan, 1986), pp. 78–120.
47. Kater, *The Nazi Party,* pp.150–151.
48. *VB*, October 3, 1931.
49. T. Abel, *Why Hitler Came to Power* (Cambridge, MA: Harvard University Press, 1986), p. 139.
50. Bullock, *Hitler: A Study in Tyranny,* p. 218.
51. Ibid., 221–223.
52. Meissner and Wilde, *Machtergreifung*, pp. 100–101.
53. Cited in Vogt, *The Burden of Guilt,* p. 114.
54. Ibid.
55. Eyck, *Weimar Republic,* pp. 387–388.
56. Bracher, *Auflösung,* p. 666.
57. Affadavit of H. O. Meissner, November 28, 1945, TMWC Document No. 3309.
58. Bracher, *Auflösung,* p. 672.
59. Papen, *Memoirs,* p. 223.
60. P. Stachura, *Gregor Strasser and the Rise of Nazism* (London: Allen & Unwin, 1983), p. 108.
61. *Frankfurter Zeitung*, January 1, 1933.
62. Höhne, *Machtergreifung,* p. 239.
63. E. B. Wheaton, *The Nazi Revolution 1933–1935* (New York: Doubleday, 1969), p. 150.
64. Turner, *German Big Business and the Rise of Hitler,* pp. 313–319.
65. Hohne, *Machtergreifung,* pp. 161–163.
66. Meissner, *Machtergreifung,* pp. 166–167.
67. *London Daily Express*, January 29, 1936.
68. Able, *Why Hitler Came to Power,* p. 142.
69. R. Wohl, *The Generation of 1914* (Cambridge, MA: Harvard University Press, 1979), p. 53.
70. Quoted in Waite, *Vanguard of Nazism,* p. 267.
71. Childers, *The Nazi Voter,* pp. 13–14.
72. P. Ayçoberry, *The Nazi Question: An Essay on the Interpretations of National Socialism 1922–1975* (New York: Pantheon Books, 1981), p. 15.
73. Hamilton, *Who Voted for Hitler?,* pp. 72, 110–112, 364.
74. G. Mosse, *The Nationalization of the Masses* (New York: H. Fertig, 1975), pp. 4–7.

Epilogue

1. Domarus, *Hitler,* Vol. I, pp. 197–198.
2. Goebbels, *Vom Kaiserhof zur Reichskanzlei,* p. 139.
3. Brozat, *Hitler State,* p. 63.
4. L. Mosley, *Reich Marshal: A Biography of Hermann Göring* (New York: Doubleday, 1974), p. 69.
5. H. Höhne, *Order of the Death's Head* (New York: Ballantine, 1971).
6. F. Tobias, *Der Reichstagbrand: Legende und Wirklichkeit* (Darmstadt, Baden: Grote, 1962).
7. Noakes and Pridham, *Nazism,* Vol. I, p. 142.
8. Wheaton, *Nazi Revolution.*
9. Noakes and Pridham, *Nazism,* Vol. I, pp. 161–162.
10. Wheaton, *Nazi Revolution,* p. 236.
11. I. Müller, *Hitler's Justice: The Courts of the Third Reich,* trans. D. L. Schneider (Cambridge, MA: Harvard University Press, 1991), p. 37.
12. Quoted in D. C. Large, *Where Ghosts Walked: Munich's Road to the Third Reich* (New York: W. W. Norton, 1992), p. 253.
13. H. Mau, "Die Zweite Revolution—Der 30 Juni 1934," *Vierteljahrshefte für Zeitgeschichte,* 2 (1953), p. 270.
14. *VB*, July 1, 1934.
15. Mau, "Zweite Revolution," p. 294.
16. H. Höhne, *Mordsache Röhm: Hitler's Durchbruch zur Alleinherrschaft 1933–1934* (Hamburg: Rowohlt, 1989), pp. 3–9–321.
17. Domarus, *Hitler,* Vol. I, p. 409.
18. Longerich, *Braunen Bataillone,* p. 184.
19. I. Kershaw, *The "Hitler Myth": Image and Reality in the Third Reich* (New York: Oxford University Press, 1987), pp. 84–85.
20. S. Aronson, *Reinhard Heydrich und die Frühgeschichte von Gestapo und SA* (Stuttgart: Deutsche Verlags-Anstalt, 1971), p. 191.
21. Ibid., p. 192.
22. Cited in Wheeler-Bennett, *The Nemesis of Power,* p. 310.
23. Fest, *Hitler,* p. 457.
24. Ibid.
25. Papen, *Memoirs,* pp. 307–311.
26. Wheeler-Bennett, *Nemesis,* pp. 319–320.
27. Longerich, *Braunen Bataillone,* pp. 215–216.
28. *VB*, June 29, 1934.
29. R. J. O'Neill, *The German Army and the Nazi Party 1933–1939* (London: Cassell, 1968), p.46.
30. R. G. Reuth, *Goebbels: Eine Biographie* (Munich: Piper, 1990), p. 313.
31. Domarus, *Hitler,* Vol. I, pp. 468–469.
32. Fest, *Hitler,* p. 468.
33. *Ibid.*
34. *Hitler Myth,* p. 85.
35. BSHA, MA 106682, July 3, 1939.
36. Ibid., 106670.
37. Longerich, *Braunen Bataillone,* pp. 227–228.
38. R. Gellately, *Backing Hitler: Consent and Coercion in Nazi Germany* (Oxford: Oxford University Press, 2001), p. 38.
39. Domarus, *Hitler,* Vol. I, p. 432.
40. Ibid., p. 417.
41. Höhne, Mordsache, Röhm, p. 303.
42. Bullock, *Hitler,* p. 304.
43. Noakes and Pridham, *Nazism,* Vol. I, p. 186.
44. H. Graml, *Der 9 November 1938. "Reichskristallnacht."* (Bonn: Bundeszentrale für Heimat dienst, 1953), p. 16

Bibliography

Unpubished Documents

Bayerisches Hauptstaatsarchiv: 6803, SA; MA-10276; MA-10024.
Captured German Documents, National Archives, Washington, D.C. Microfilm roll numbers: T-81–90; T-253–15; T-253–16, T253–22, T-253–23.
Hitler, B. "My Brother-in-Law Adolf." Unpublished manuscript, New York Public Library.
NSDAP (Nationalsozialistische Deutsche Arbeiterpartei) Hauptarchiv, Hoover Institution on War Revolution and Peace, Stanford University.

Published Documents

Abel Collection of Nazi Party Member Biographies. Hoover Library, Stanford University.
Der Angriff: Aufsätze aus der Kampfzeit. Munich: Eher Verlag, 1940.
"Document on Terror." *News From the Iron Curtain*, I, 3 March 1952.
The Hitler Trial Before the People's Court in Munich. Vol. I. Arlington, Virginia: University Publications of America, 1976.
Institut für Zeitgeschichte (ed.). *Hitler: Reden, Schriften, Anordungen: Februar 1925 bis Januar 1933*. Munich: Selbstverlag des Institut für Zeitgeschichte, 1933. Vol. I.
Inter-American Committee of the Organization of American States. *Statement of Reasons for the Draft Convention on Terrorism and Kidnapping*. Document CP/doc. 54/70, 5 October 1970.
International Military Tribunal: *Trial of the Major War Criminals Before the International Military Tribunal.* Proceedings and Documents. 42 vols. Washington D.C. 1947–1949.
Maser, W. *Hitlers Briefe und Notizen*. Vienna: Econ Verlag, 1973.
Michaelis, H. and Schraepler (eds.), *Ursachen und Folgen*. Vol. 5. Berlin: n.d. *Nacrichtensammelstelle im Reichsministerium des Innern,* September of 1930, Vol. I.
NS Jahrbuch (1931).
Partei-Statistik. Munich: Eher Verlag, 1935.
Reichsarbeitsblatt, No. 14, Table 250.
Reichsgesetzblatt (Jahrgang, 1926, 1932).
Reichskommisar für Ueberwachung der Öffentlichen Ordnung (RKO).
Statistisches Jahrbuch. Berlin: published annually by the German government, 1932.
Verhandlungen der durch die alterhöchste Verordnung vom 1 Februar 1872 einberufenen Häuser des Landtages, Session of 3 February 1873.

Newspapers

Augsburger Postzeitung, 17 April 1923.
Badische Presse, 17 June 1930.
Berliner Tageblatt, 6 May 1920, 9 December 1930.
B.Z. am Mittag. 30 May 1927.
Deutsche Allgemeine Zeitung. 6 May 1927.
Frankfurter Zeitung, 1 January 1933, 1 June 1937.
Görlitzer Nachrichten, 11 August 1932.
London Daily Express, 29 January 1936.
Münchner-Augsberger Abendzeitung, 1918–1919.
Münchner Neutste Nachrichten, 3–4 January, 28 January 1920, 5 December 1923.
Münchner Post, 1918–1919, 1922.
New York Times, 15 December 1918.
Times (London), 15 May 1919.
Vökischer Beobachter, 1919–1933.
Volkstimme [Hagen], 2 December 1932.
Vorwärts, 4 September 1930.
Vossiche Zeitung. 9 August 1932, 6 September 1932.
Washington Post, 24 October 1945.
Westfälishen Tageblatt, 27 January 1933.

Books — Autobiographies, Memoirs, and Speeches

Braun, O. *Von Weimar zur Hitler*. Hamburg: Hammonia Nordeutsche Verlag, 1949.
Brecht, Arnold. *The Political Education of Arnold Brecht: An Autobiography, 1884–1970*. Princeton: Princeton University Press, 1970.
Brüning, H. *Memoiren 1918–1934*. Stuttgart: Deutsche Verlags-Anstalt, 1970.
D'Abernon, E.V. *An Ambassador of Peace*. London: Hodder and Stoughton, 1929–1930.

François Poncet, A. *Souveniers d"une ambassade a' Berlin, Septembre 1931 Octobre 1938*. Paris: Flam-irion, 1946.
Frank, H. *Im Angesicht des Galgens*. Munich: F.A. Beck, 1953.
Golz, G.R. von. *Mein Sendung in Finnland und in Baltikum*. Leipzig: F.K. Koehler, 1920.
Grzesinski, Albert C. *Inside Germany*. New York: E. P. Dutton, 1939.
Hanfstaengl, Ernst. *Unheard Witness*. Philadelphia: Lippincott, 1957.
Heydebreck, P. von. *Wir Wehrwölfe: Einnerungen eines Freikorpführer*. Leipzig: F.K. Koehler, 1931.
Hindenburg, Paul von. *Aus meinem Leben*. Leipzig: S. Hirzel, 1920.
Hitler, Adolf. *Mein Kampf*. New York: Reynal & Hitchcock, 1941.
Kallenbach, H. *Mit Hitler auf Festung Landsberg*. Munich: Kress & Hornung, 1939.
Meissner, O. *Staatssekretär unter Ebert, Hindenburg, Hitler: deutschen Volkes vom 1918–1945, wie ich ihm erlebte*. Hamburg: Hoffmann und Campe, 1950.
Müsham, E. *Tagebucher 1920–1924*. Munich: Olzog, 1994.
Noske, G. *Zehn Jahre Deutsche Geschichte, 1918–1928*. Berlin: O. Stollberg, 1928.
Papen, Franz von. *Memoirs*. London: A. Deutsch, 1952.
Röhm, E. *Die Geschichte eines Hochverräters*, 7th ed. Munich: Eher, 1934.
Scheidemann, Philipp. *The Making of a New Germany*. New York: D. Appleton, 1929.
_____. *Memoiren eine sozialdemokraten*. Dresden: Reissner, 1928.
Severing, C. *Mein Lebensweg*, Vol. II. Cologne: Greven Verlag, 1950.
Stresemann, G. *Vermächtnis*, Vol. 3, Berlin: Ullstein, 1932.
Toller, Ernst. *Eine Jugend in Deutschland*. Amsterdam: Querido Verlag, 1936.
_____. *I Was a German: the Autobiography of a Revolutionary*. New York: Paragon House, 1991. First published 1934 by William Morrow.

Books — Secondary Sources

Abel, Theodore Fred. *Why Hitler Came to Power*. Cambridge, MA: Harvard University Press, 1986, 1938.
Almond, Gabriel A. and Sidney Verba. *The Civic Culture: Political Attitudes and Democracy in Five Nations*. Princeton, NJ: Princeton University Press, 1963.
Anderlahn, H. *Gegner erkannt! Kampferlebenkrise der SA*. Munich: F. Eher Nachf., 1937.
Arendt, Hannah. *The Origins of Totalitarianism*. New York: Meridian Books, 1958.
Aronson, S. *Reinhard Heydrich und die Frühgeschichte von Gestapo und SA*. Stuttgart: Deutsche Verlags-Anstalt, 1971.
Awaloff, F. *Im Kampf gegen den Bolschewismus*. Glückstadt and Hamburg: Verlag J.J. Augustin, 1925.
Ayçoberry, Pierre. *The Nazi Question: An Essay on the Interpretations of National Socialism, 1922–1975*. New York: Pantheon Books, 1981.
Bade, Wilfred. *Joseph Goebbels*. Lübeck: C. Coleman, 1933.
Bainton, Roland Herbert. *The Reformation of the Sixteenth Century*. Boston: Beacon Press, 1952.

Barbu, Zevedei. *Democracy and Dictatorship: Their Psychology and Patterns of Life*. New York: Grove Press, 1956.
Bäthe, K. *Wer Whonte in Schwabing*. Munich: Süddeutscher Verlag, 1967.
Bennecke, H. *Hitler und die SA*. Munich: G. Olzog, 1962.
Bennett, Richard. *The Black and Tans: The British Special Police in Ireland*. New York: Barnes and Noble Books, 1995. First published 1959.
Benoist-Méchin, J. *Historie de L'Armee Allemande 1919–1936*. Vol II. Paris: Albin Michel, 1938.
Bessel, Richard. *Political Violence and the Rise of Nazism: The Stormtroopers in Eastern Germany, 1925–1934*. New Haven: Yale University Press, 1984.
Bezymenski, L. *The Death of Adolf Hitler: Unknown Documents from Soviet Archives*. New York: Pyramid, 1969.
Billington, James H. *Fire in the Minds of Men: Origins of the Revolutionary Faith*. New York: Basic Books, 1980.
Bley, H. *Namibia under German Rule*. London: Transaction Publishers, 1998.
Bley, W. *SA Marschiert: Leben und Kampf der Braunen Bataillone*. Stuttgart: Union Deutsche Verlagsgesellschaft, 1934.
Bloch, C. *Die SA und die Krise des NS-Regimes 1934*. Frankfurt-am-Main: Suhrkamp, 1970.
Borresholm, B. von (ed.). *Dr. Goebbels: Nach Aufzeichnungen aus seiner Umgebung*. Berlin: Journal, 1949.
Bracher, K.D. *Die Auflösung der Weimarer Republik*. Villingen-Schwarzwald: Ring-Verl, 1960.
_____. *Die Nationalsozialistische Machtergreifung: Studien zur Errichtung des totalitären Herschaftssystem in Deutschland, 1933/1934*. 3 vols. Berlin: Ullstein, 1983.
_____. *The German Dictatorship*. New York: Praeger, 1970.
Brauweiler, H. *Generäle in der deutschen Republik: Groener, Schleicher, Seeckt*. Berlin: Tell-Verl., 1932.
Bredow, K. *Hitlerrast*. Saarbrücken: Saarbrücker Druckerei und Verlag, 1935.
Bridgman, Jon. *The Revolt of the Hereros*. Berkeley: University of California Press, 1981.
Bruck, A.M. van den. *Das Dritte Reich*. Munich: Der Ring, 1923.
Bukeris, A. *Politik des. 20 Jahrhundert*. Munich: C.H. Beck, 1983.
Bullock, Alan. *Hitler: A Study in Tyranny*. London: Hamlyn, 1973.
Büsch, O. *Militärsystem und sozialleben im alten Preussen, 1713–1807*. Berlin: DeGreyter, 1962.
Calic, Édouard, editor. *Unmasked: Two Confidential Interviews with Hitler in 1931*. London: Chatto & Windus, 1971.
Childers, Thomas. *The Formation of the Nazi Constituency*. London: Croom Helm, 1986.
_____. *The Nazi Voter: The Social Foundation of Fascism in Germany 1919–1933*. Chapel Hill: University of North Carolina Press, 1983.
Clausewitz, D. *Die Städte-ordnung von 1808 und die Stadt Berlin*. Berlin: E. Ehering, 1908.
Cornebise, Alfred E. *The Weimar in Crisis: Cuno's Germany and the Ruhr Occupation*. Washington, DC: University Press of America, 1977.
Craig, Gordon Alexander. *The Politics of the Prussian Army, 1640–1945*. New York: Oxford University Press, 1955.
_____. *War, Politics and Diplomacy*. New York: Praeger, 1966.

Crossman, R. H. S., ed. *The God that Failed.* New York: Harper, 1949.
Dahrendorf, Ralf. *Society and Democracy in Germany.* New York: Doubleday, 1969.
Daim, W. *Der Mann der Hitler die Ideen gab.* Munich: Isar Verlag, 1958.
Diagnostic and Statistical Manual of Mental Disorders: DSM-III-R. Washington D.C.: American Psychiatric Association, 1987.
Dietrich, O. *Mit Hitler in die Macht.* Munich: F. Eher Nachf., 1934.
_____. *Zwolf Jahre mit Hitler.* Munich: Isar Verlag, 1955.
Dornberg, John. *Munich 1923: The Story of Hitler's First Grab for Power.* New York: Harper and Row, 1982.
Dorpalen, Andreas. *Hindenburg and the Weimar Republic.* Princeton, NJ: Princeton University Press, 1964.
Ebermayer, E. and Roos, H. *Gefährtin des Teufels. Leben und Tod den Magda Goebbels.* Hamburg: Hoffmann und Campe, 1952.
Engelbrechten, J.K. von. And Volz, H. (eds.). *Wir Wandren durch das Nationalsozialistische Berlin.* Munich: Zentralverlag der NSDAP, Franz Eher nachf., 1937.
Erdmann, J. *Coburg Bayern und Das Reich 1918–1923.* Coburg: Rossteutscher, 1969.
Erger, J. *Der Kapp Lüttwitz Putsch.* Dusseldorf: Droste, 1967.
Evans, Richard J., and Dick Geary, eds. *The German Unemployed: Experiences and Consequences of Mass Unemployment from the Weimar Republic to the Third Reich.* London: Croom Helm, 1987.
Eyck, E. *Geschichte der Weimarer Republik.* Stutt-gart: Rentsch Verlag, 1956.
Fermi, Laura. *Illustrious Immigrants: The Intellectual Migration From Europe, 1930–1941.* Chi-cago: University of Chicago Press, 1960.
Fest, Joachim C. *Hitler.* New York: Harcourt Brace Jovanovich, 1974.
Fischer, Conan. *Stormtroopers: A Social, Economic and Ideological Analysis 1919–35.* London: Allen & Unwin, 1983.
Fischer, Fritz. *Germany's Aims in the First World War.* New York: W. W. Norton, 1967.
Fischer, K. P. *Nazi Germany: A New History.* New York: Continuum, 1995.
Fishman, S. "Prophets, Poets: A Study of the Men and Ideas that Made the Munich Revolution of 1918/1919." PhD diss., University of Wisconsin, 1960.
Fleming, Donald and Bernard Bailyn, eds. *The Intellectual Migration: Europe and America, 1930–1960.* Cambridge, MA: Belknap Press of Harvard University Press, 1969.
Flood, Charles Bracelen. *Hitler, the Path to Power.* Boston: Houghton Mifflin, 1989.
Franz-Willing, G. *Ursprung der Hitlerbewegung 1919–1922.* Preussich Oldendorf: Schütz, 1975.
Freiwald, L. *Der Weg der braunen Kämpfer: Ein Frontbuch von 1918–1933.* Munich: J.F. Lehmann, 1934.
Fricke, Dieter, et. al. *Der Bügerlichen Parteien in Deutschland: Handbuch der Geschichte der bürgerlichen Interresen Organization von Vormärz bis zum Jahre 1945.* Leipzig: Bibliographisches Institut, 1970.
Friedrich, Otto. *Before the Deluge: A Portrtait of Berlin in the 1920's.* New York: Harper & Row, 1972.
Garnett, Robert S. *Lion, Eagle, and Swastika: Bavarian Monarchism in Weimar Germany, 1918–1933.* New York: Garland, 1991.
Gay, Peter. *Weimar Culture: The Outsider as Insider.* New York: Harper & Row, 1968.

Gedye, G. E. R. b. *The Revolver Republic: France's Bid for the Rhine.* London: Arrowsmith, 1930.
Gellately, Robert. *Backing Hitler: Consent and Coercion in Nazi Germany.* Oxford: Oxford University Press, 2001.
_____. *The Politics of Economic Despair: Shopkeepers and German Politics, 1890–1914.* Beverly Hills, CA: Sage Publications, 1974.
Gessler, O. *Reichswehrpolitik in der Weimarer Zeit.* Stuttgart: Deutsche Verlags-Anstalt, 1958.
Gisevius, Hans Bernd. *To the Bitter End.* Boston: Houghton Mifflin, 1947.
Glatzer, R. (ed.) *Berliner Leben, 1870–1918.* Berlin: Rütter & Loening, 1963.
Goebbels, J. *Kampf um Berlin.* Munich: F. Eher Nachf., 1936.
_____. *Signale die Neuen Zeit.* Munich: Zentralverlag der NSDAP, Franz Eher nachf., 1934.
_____. *Vom Kaiserhof zur Reichskanzlei.* Munich: Zentralverlag der NSDAP, Franz Eher nachf., 1934.
_____. *Wetterleuchten: Aufsätze aus der Kampfzeit.* Munich: Zentralverlag der NSDAP, Franz Eher nachf., 1939.
Gordon, Harold J. *Hitler and the Beer Hall Putsch.* Princeton, NJ: Princeton University Press, 1972.
_____. *The Reichswehr and the German Republic 1919–1926.* Princeton, NJ: Princeton University Press, 1957.
Görlitz, Walter. *Hindenburg: Ein Lebensbild.* Bonn: Athenäum, 1953.
_____. *History of the German General Staff, 1657–1945.* New York: Praeger, 1953.
Graml. D. *Der 9 November 1938. "Reichskristallnacht."* Bonn: Bundeszentrale für Heimat dienst, 1953.
Grant, Thomas D. *Stormtroopers and Crisis in the Nazi Movement: Activism, Ideology, and Dissolution.* New York: Routledge, 2004.
Grill, Johnpeter Horst. *The Nazi Movement in Baden, 1920–1945.* Chapel Hill: University of North Carolina Press, 1983.
Grunberger, Richard. *Red Rising in Bavaria.* London: Barker, 1973.
Gudmundsson, Bruce. *Stormtroop Tactics: Innovation in the German Army, 1914–1918.* New York: Praeger, 1989.
Gumbel, E.J. *Vier Jahre Politischer Mord.* (5th ed). Berlin: Verlag der Neuen Gesellschaft, 1922.
Halbe, M. *Jahrhundertwende.* Danzig: 1935.
Hale, Oron J. *The Captive Press in the Third Reich.* Princeton, NJ: Princeton University Press, 1964.
Hamilton, Richard F. *Who Voted for Hitler?* Princeton, NJ: Princeton University Press, 1987.
Hanser, Richard. *Putsch! How Hitler Made a Revolution.* New York: Pyramid Publications, 1971.
Hauner, Milan. *Hitler, A Chronology of His Life and Times.* New York: St. Martin's Press, 1983.
Heiber, Helmut. *Goebbels.* New York: Hawthorn Books, 1972.
Heiden, Konrad. *Der Fuehrer: Hitler's Rise to Power.* Boston: Houghton Mifflin, 1944.
_____. *A History of National Socialism.* New York: A. A. Knopf, 1935.
Heinz, F.W. *Die Nation greift an: Geschichte und Kritik des soldatischen Nationalismus.* Berlin: Verlag Das Reich, 1932.
Hellweg, A. *Vom Kampf und Sieg des Nationalsozialismus in Kreise Lübbecke.* Lübbecke: NSDAP, Kreisleitg, 1933.

Hertzman, Lewis. *DNVP: Right-wing Opposition in the Weimar Republic, 1918–1924*. Lincoln: University of Nebraska Press, 1963.

Hildebrand, Klaus. *The Foreign Policy of the Third Reich*. Berkeley, CA: University of California Press, 1973.

Höffkes, K. *Hitlers politische Generale: Die Gauleiter des Dritten Reiches*. Tübingen: Grabert-Verlag, 1986.

Hoffmann, Peter. *Hitler's Personal Security: Protecting the Führer, 1921–1945*. New York: Da Capo Press: 2000.

Hofmann, H. H. *Der Hitlerputsch: Krisenjahre deutsche Geschichte 1920–1924*. Munich: Nymphenburger Verlagshandlung, 1961.

Höhne, Heinz Zollin. *Die Machtergreifung: Deutschlands Weg in die Hitler Diktatur* Hamburg: Rowohlt, 1983.

———. *Mordsache Röhm: Hitlers Durchbruch zure Alleinherrschaft 1933–1934*. Hamburg: Rowohlt, 1989.

———. *The Order of the Death's Head: The Story of Hitler's S.S.* New York: Ballantine, 1971.

Holborn, Hajo. *Germany and Europe*. Garden City, New York: Doubleday, 1971.

Hollweck, L. *Unser München*. Munich: Süddeutscher Verlag, 1967.

Huber, E. *Das ist Nationalsozialismus*. Stuttgart: Union Deutsche Verlagsgesellschaft, 1933.

Hummer, L. *Bayern von Kaiserreich zur Diktatur*. Pfaffenhohen: Verlag W. Ludwig, 1979.

Hüttenberger, P. *Die Gauleiter*. Stuttgart: Deutsche Verlags-Anstalt, 1969.

Italiaander, R. and Hass, W. *Berliner Cocktail*. Hamburg and Vienna: P. Zsolnay, 1959.

Jablonsky, David. *The Nazi Party in Dissolution: Hitler and the Verbotzeit, 1922–1925*. London: F. Cass, 1989.

Jäckel, E. *Hitlers Weltanschauung. Entwurf einer Herrschaft*. Stuttgart: Deutsche Verlags-Anstalt, 1983.

Jamin, M. *Zwischen den Klassen:, zur Sozialstruktur der SA-Führerschaft*. Wuppertal: P. Hammer, 1984.

Jenkins, Brian Michael. *International Terrorism: A New Mode of Conflict*. Los Angeles: Crescent Publications, 1975.

Jenks, William A. *Vienna and the Young Hitler*. New York: Columbia University Press, 1960.

Jones, Howard Mumford. *Revolution and Romanticism*. Cambridge, MA: Belknap Press of Harvard University Press, 1974.

Jones, J. Sydney. *Hitler in Vienna, 1907–13*. London: Blond & Briggs, 1983.

Kanzler, R. *Bayerns Kampf gegen den Bolcshewismus: Geschichte der bayerischen Einwohnerwehren*. Munich: Verlag Parcus & Co., 1931.

Kahler, Erich. *The Jews Among the Nations*. New York: F. Ungar, 1967.

Kater, Michael H. *The Nazi Party: A Social Profile of Members and Leaders, 1919–1945*. Cambridge, MA: Harvard University Press, 1983.

Kele, Max H. *Nazis and Workers: National Socialist Appeals to German Labor 1919–1933*. Chapel Hill: University of North Carolina Press, 1972.

Kershaw, Ian. *The "Hitler Myth": Image and Reality in the Third Reich*. New York: Oxford University Press, 1987.

Keynes, John Maynard. *The Economic Consequences of the Peace*. New York: Harcourt, Brace and Howe, 1920.

Klotzbach, K. *Gegen den Nationalsozialismus: Widerstand und Verfolgung in Dortmund 1930–1945*. Hanover: Verl. Für Literatur und Zietgeschehen, 1969.

Koshar, Rudy. *Social Life, Local Politics and Nazism: Marburg, 1880–1935*. Chapel Hill: University of North Carolina Press, 1986.

Krummacher, F.A. and Wucher, A. (eds). *Die Weimarer Republik*. Munich: R. Pflaum, 1961.

Kubizek, August. *The Young Hitler I Knew*. Boston: Houghton Mifflin, 1955.

Kuron, H.J. *Freikorps und Bund Oberland*. Doctoral Dissertation. Friedrich Alexander Uinversität zu Erlangen, 1960.

Lackó, Miklós. *Arrow-Cross Men: National Socialists, 1935–1944*. Budapest: Akadémiai Kiadó, 1969.

Laqueur, Walter. *Terrorism*. Boston: Little, Brown, 1977.

Large, David Clay. *Where Ghosts Walked: Munich's Road to the Third Reich*. New York: W. W. Norton, 1997.

Lederer, F. *Berlin und Umgebung*. Berlin: Neue Verlagsanstalt, 1929.

Leiden, Carl and Karl Michael Schmidt. *The Politics of Violence: Revolution in the Modern World*. Englewood Cliffs, NJ: Prentice-Hall, 1968.

Leviné-Meyer, Rosa. *Leviné, the Spartacist*. London: Gordon & Cremonesi, 1973.

Lloyd George, David. *The Truth about the Peace Treaties*. London: V. Gollancz, 1938.

Loessner, A. *Der Abfall Posens: 1918–1919 im politischen Schriftum*. Danzig: Kommissionsverlag der Danziger Verlags-Gesellschaft, 1933.

Lohalm, U. *Völkischer Radicalismus: Die Geschichte der Deutsche Völkschen Schutz und Trutzbundes*. Hamburg: Leibniz-Verlag, 1970.

Longerich, P. *Die braunen Bataillone: Geschichte der SA*. Munich: Beck, 1989.

Löns, Hermann. *Der Wehrwolf*. Jena: Diederichs, 1917.

Maltitz, Horst von. *The Evolution of Hitler's Germany: The Ideology, the Personality, the Movement*. New York: McGraw-Hill, 1973.

Mann, Golo. *The History of Germany Since 1789*. New York: Praeger, 1968.

Mann, Thomas. *Stories of Three Decades*. New York: A. A. Knopf, 1936.

Maercker, L. von. *Vom Kaiserheer zur Reichswehr* (3rd ed). Leipzig: Koehler, 1922.

Maser, Werner. *Der Sturm auf die Republik: Frügeschichte der NSDAP*. Stuttgart: DVA, 1973.

———. *Hitler*. London: Allen Lane, 1973.

———. *Hitlers Mein Kampf: Entstehung, Aufbau, Stil Änderungen, Quellen, Ouellenwert, Kommentierte Aufzüge*. Munich: Bechtle Verlag, 1966.

Massing, Paul W. *Rehearsal for Destruction: A Study of Political Anti-Semitism in Imperial Germany*. New York: Harper, 1949.

Mazlish, Bruce. *The Revolutionary Ascetic: Evolution of a Political Type*. New York: Basic Books, 1976.

Meinecke, Friedrich. *The German Catastrophe: Reflections and Recollections*. Transl. S.B. Fay. Boston: Beacon Press, 1950.

Meissner, H.O. and Wilde, H. *Die Machtergreifung: Eine Bericht über die Technik des nationalsozialistischen Staatsreiche*. Stuttgart: J.G. Cotta, 1958.

Merkl, P. *The Making of a Stormtrooper*. Princeton, NJ: Princeton University Press, 1980.

Meyer, Karl W. *Karl Liebknecht: Man Without a Country*. Washington, DC: Public Affairs Press, 1957.

Mitchell, Allan. *Revolution in Bavaria 1918–1919: the Eisner Regime and the Soviet Republic*. Princeton, NJ: Princeton University Press, 1965.

Mitchell, Otis C. *Hitler Over Germany: The Establishment of the Nazi Dictatorship (1918–1934)*. Phil-

adelphia: Institute for the Study of Human Issues, 1983.
Mosley, Leonard. *Reich Marshal: A Biography of Hermann Göring*. New York: Doubleday, 1974.
Mosse, George L.. *The Crisis of German Ideology: Intellectual Origins of the Third Reich*. New York: Grosset & Dunlap, 1964.
_____. *The Nationalization of the Masses: Political Symbolism and Mass Movements in Germany from the Napoleonic Wars through the Third Reich*. New York: H. Fertig, 1975.
Müller, Ingo. *Hitler's Justice: The Courts of the Third Reich*. Cambridge, MA: Harvard University Press, 1991.
Mumford, L. *The City in History*. New York: Harcourt Brace Jovanovich, 1961.
Noakes, J. *The Nazi Party in Lower Saxony*. London: Oxford University Press, 1971.
Noske, G. *Von Kiel bis Kapp: zur Geschichte der deutsche Revolution*. Berlin: Verlag für Politik und Wirtschaft, 1928.
Nissen, R. *Helle Blätter, Dunkle Blätter*. Stuttgart: Deutsche Verlags-Anstalt, 1969.
Nyomarkay, Joseph. *Charisma and Factionalism in the Nazi Party*. Minneapolis: University of Minnesota Press, 1967.
Oehme, W. and Karo, K. *Kommt "Das Dritte Reich?"* Munich: Eher Verlag, 1935.
Oertzen, F.W. von. *Die deutschen Freikorps, 1918–1923*. Munich: F. Bruckmann, 1939.
Okrass, H. *"Hamburg bleibt rot": Das Ende einer Parole*. Hamburg: Hanseatische Verlagsanstalt, 1934.
O'Neill, Robert John. *The German Army and the Nazi Party 1933–1939*. London: Cassell, 1968.
Orlow, Dietrich. *The History of the Nazi Party, 1919–1933*. Pittsburgh: University of Pittsburgh Press, 1969.
Palmer, Alan Warwick. *The Kaiser: Warlord of the Second Reich*. New York: Scribner, 1978.
Parkinson, Roger. *Tormented Warrior: Ludendorff and the Supreme Command*. New York: Stein & Day, 1978.
Petersen, Jan. *Our Street: A Chronicle Written in the Heart of Fascist Germany*. London: V. Gollancz, 1938.
Peukert, Detlev. *The Weimar Republic: The Crisis of Classical Modernity*. New York: Hill and Wang, 1992.
Poliakov, Léon. *The Aryan Myth: A History of Racist and Nationalist Ideas in Europe*. New York: Basic Books, 1974.
Polz, W. *Sozialistenfrage und Revolutionsfurcht*. Lubeck: Matthiesen, 1960.
Pridham, Geoffrey. *Hitler's Rise to Power: The Nazi Movement in Bavaria 1923–1933*. London: Hart-Davis MacGibbon, 1973.
Pulzer, Peter G. J. *The Rise of Political Anti-Semitism in Germany and Austria*. New York: Wiley, 1964.
Rabenau, F. von. *Seeckt: Aus seinem Leben 1918–1936*. Vol II. Leipzig: Hase und Koehler, 1934.
Rauschning, Hermann. *Germany's Revolution of Destruction*. London: William Heinemann, 1939.
Redlich, Fredrick C. *Hitler: Diagnosis of a Destructive Prophet*. New York: Oxford University Press, 1999.
Reiche, Eric G. *The Development of the SA in Nurnberg, 1922–1939*. Cambridge: Cambridge University Press, 2002, 1986.
Reuth, R. *Goebbels: Eine Biographie*. Munich: Piper, 1990.
Riess, Curt. *Joseph Goebbels*. New York: Doubleday, 1948.
Ringer, Fritz K. *The German Inflation of 1923*. New York: Oxford University Press, 1969.
Rochau, L. von. *Grundsätze der Realpolitik*. Stuttgart: K. Göpel, 1853.
Rohe, K. *Das Reichsbanner Schwarz Rot Gold: Ein Beitrag zur Geschichte und Struktur der politischen Kampfverbände zur Zeit der Weimarer Republik*. Dusseldorf: Droste, 1966.
Rosenberg, A. *Der Mythus des XX Jahrhunderts*. Munich: Hoheneichen-verlag, 1930.
Rosenhaft, Eve. *Beating the Fascists? The German Communists and Political Violence, 1929–1933*. Cambridge: Cambridge University Press, 1983.
Roth, B. *Kampf: Lebensdokumente deutscher Jugend von 1914–1934*. Leipzig: P. Reclam, 1934.
Rothfels, H. (ed). *Berlin in Vergangenheit und Gegenwart*. Tübingen: Mohr, 1961.
Salomon, E. von. *Der Fragebogen*. Hamburg: Rowohlt, 1951.
Sass, F. *Berlin in seiner Neuesten Zeit und Entwicklung*. Leipzig: Koffka, 1846.
Sauer, W. *Die Nationalsozialistische Machtergrefung*. Berlin: Westdeutscher Verl., 1962.
Schade, F. *Kurt Eisner und die bayerische Sozialdemokratie*. Hannover: Verlag für Literatur und Zeitgeschehen, 1961.
Schelen-Spanenberg, U. *Die Deutsche Volkspartei im Lande Braunschweig*. Braunschweig: Waisenhaus-Buchdruckerie und Verlag, 1969.
Schmidt, E. *Argonnen Schlachten des Weltkrieges*. Berlin: Gehard Stalling, 1927.
Schmidt-Pauli, E. von. *General von Seeckt*. Berlin: Hobbing, 1937.
_____. *Geschichte der Freikorps 1918–1924*. Stuttgart: R. Lutz, 1936.
Schorske, Carl E. *German Social Democracy, 1905–1917: The Development of the Great Schism*. Cambridge, MA: Harvard University Press, 1955.
Schüddekopf, O.E. *Linke Leute von Rechts: Die Nationalrevolutionären Minderheiten unter dem Kommunismus in der Weimarer Republik*. Stuttgart: Kohlhammer, 1960.
Schweitzer, Arthur. *Big Business in the Third Reich*. London: Eyre & Spottiswoode, 1964.
Schwend, K. *Bayern zwischen Monarchie und Diktatur*. Munich: R. Pflaum, 1954.
Seeckt, H. von. *Die Reichswehr*. Leipzig: R. Kittler, 1933.
Severing, C. *1919–1920 im Wetter und Wattenwinkel*. Bielefeld: Buchhandlung Volkswacht, 1927.
Sharpe, Alan. *The Versailles Settlement: Peacemaking in Paris, 1919*. New York: St. Martin's Press, 1991.
Smith, Bradley F. *Heinrich Himmler: A Nazi in the Making, 1900–1926*. Stanford, CA: Hoover Institution Press, 1971.
Speier, Hans. *German White Collar Workers and the Rise of Hitler*. New Haven, CT: Yale University Press, 1986.
Stachura, Peter D. *Gregor Strasser and the Rise of Nazism*. London: Allen & Unwin, 1983.
Stein, Erwin Otto. *Berlin*. Oldenburg: G. Stalling, 1914.
Sterling, Claire. *The Terror Network: The Secret War of International Terrorism*. New York: Holt, Rinehart and Winston, 1981.
Stern, Fritz Richard. *The Failure of Illiberalism: Essays on the Political Culture of Modern Germany*. New York: A. A. Knopf, 1972. 1977.
_____. *Gold and Iron: Bismarck, Bleichröder, and the Building of the German Empire*. New York: A. A. Knopf, 1977.

_____. *The Politics of Cultural Despair: A Study in the Rise of Germanic Ideology.* Berkeley: University of California Press, 1961.
Tatar, Maria. *The Hard Facts of the Grimm's Fairy Tales.* Princeton, NJ: Princeton University Press, 2003. First published 1987.
Tobias, F. *Der Reichstagbrand: Legende und Wirlichkeit.* Darmstadt, Baden: Grote, 1962.
Toland, John. *Adolf Hitler.* Vol. I. New York: Doubleday, 1976.
Trevanius, G.R. *Das Ende von Weimar: Heinrich Brüning und zeine Zeit.* Dusseldorf: Econ-Verlag, 1968.
Turner, Henry Ashby. *German Big Business and the Rise of Hitler.* New York: Oxford University Press, 1985.
Ullman, H. *Flucht aus Berlin.* Jena: E Diederichs, 1932.
Valois, G. *La Révolution Nationale.* Paris: Nouvelle Libraire Nationale, 1924.
Vogelsang, T. *Reichswehr, Staat und NSDAP, Beitrage zur deutschen Geschichte 1930–32.* Stuttgart: Deutsche Verlags-Anstalt, 1962.
Vogt, Hannah. *The Burden of Guilt: A Short History of Germany, 1914–1945.* New York: Oxford University Press, 1964.
Volkmann, E.O. *Revolution über Deutschland.* Amsterdam: Brill, 1936.
Volz, H. *Daten der Geschichte der NSDAP.* Berlin: Ploetz, 1934.
_____. *Die Geschichte der SA.* Berlin: Verlag der Reimar Hobbing, 1934.
Waite, Robert G. *The Psychopathic God: Adolf Hitler.* New York: Basic Books, 1977.
_____. *Vanguard of Nazism: The Free Corps Movement in Post-War Germany, 1918–1923.* Cambridge, MA: Harvard University Press, 1952.
Waldman, Eric. *The Spartacist Upising of 1919 and the Crisis of the German Socialist Movement: A Study of the Relation of Political Theory and Party Practice.* Milwaukee: Marquette University Press, 1958.
Weber, Max. *On Charisma and Institution Building: Selected Papers.* Chicago: University of Chicago Press, 1968.
_____. *The Theory of Social and Economic Organization.* New York: Free Press, 1947.
Wehler, Hans Ulrich. *Das Deutsche Kaiserreich 1871–1918.* Gottingen: Vandenhoeck & Ruprecht, 1973.
_____. *Deutsche Gesellschaftgeschichte.* Vol. 2. Munich: C. H. Beck, 1987.
_____. *The German Empire, 1871–1918.* Providence: Berg Publishers, 1993.
Weiss, John. *The Fascist Tradition: Radical Right-wing Extremism in Modern Europe.* New York: Harper & Row, 1967.
Weissbuch uber die Erschiessungen des 30 June 1934. Paris: Editions du Carrefour, 1935.
Welch, D. *The Hitler Conspiracy.* Washington, D.C.: Public Affairs Press, 2001.
Wentzschke, P. *Ruhrkampf: Einbruch und Abwehr im Rhenisch Westfalischen Industriegebiet.* Berlin: R. Flobbing, 1930.
Werner, *SA und NSDAP: Wehrbund, Parteitruppe, oder "Revolutionsarmee?."* Phd Dissertation, Erlanger: 1964.
Westphal, A. *Die Kriegvereine in Deutschland als Weltmacht: Vierzig Jahre Deutsches Reich.* Berlin: Verlag Walter de Gruyter, 1911.
Wheaton, Eliot Barculo. *The Nazi Revolution 1933–1935: Prelude to Calamity.* New York: Doubleday, 1968.

Wheeler-Bennett, John Wheeler. *The Nemesis of Power: The German Army in Politics, 1918–1945.* New York: St. Martin's Press, 1954.
_____. *Wooden Titan: Hindenburg in Twenty Years of German History, 1914–1934.* New York: W. Morrow, 1936.
Wohl, Robert. *The Generation of 1914.* Cambridge, MA: Harvard University Press, 1979.
Wucher, A. *Die Fahne Hoch.* Munich: Süddeutsher Verlag, 1963.
Zetkin, C. *Les Batailles Révolutionnaires de L'Allemagne,* pub. 47. Petrograd: Editions de l'Internationale Communiste, 1920.

Articles and Book Chapters

Aronson, S. "Nazi Terrorism: The Complete Trap and the Final Solution." In Rapaport, D. C. and Alexander, Y. (eds.). *The Morality of Terrorism: Religious and Secular Justification,* (2nd ed.). New York: Columbia University Press, 1989.
Axis History Forum, October 2007.
Baird, J. "Goebbels, Horst Wessel, and the Myth of Ressurection and Return." *Journal of Contemporary History,* Vol. I 17 (1982).
Berges, W. "Das Reich ohne Hauptstadt." In *Das Hauptstadt Problem in Geschichte.* Tübingen: Nieneyer, 1952.
Bessel, R. "Militarismus in innenpolitischen Leben der Weimarer Republik: von den Freikorps zur SA." In Muller, K.-J. and Opitz, E. (eds.). *Militar und Militarismus in der Weimarer Republik.* Dusseldorf: Droste, 1978.
Bloch, E. "Errinerungen an den Führer und dessen verewigte Muter." NSDAP Central Archives, NS 25/26.
Brozat, M. "Die Anfange der Berlin NSDAP 1916/1927." In *Vierteljahrshefte für Zeitgeschichte,* 8 (1960).
Deuerlein, E. "Hitlers Eintrit in die Politik und die Reichswehr." In *Vierteljahrshefte für Zeitgeschichte,* April 1959.
Dietrich, R. "Berlins Weg zur Industrie und Handelstadt." In *Berlin Neuen Kapital seiner Geschichte.* Berlin: Duncken & Humboldt, 1960.
"Ernst von Salomon." *Berliner Zeitung* (17 April 1994).
Fischer, C. "Ernst Julius Röhm: Chief of Staff of the SA and Indispensable Outsider." In Smelser, R. and Zitelmann, R. (eds). *The Nazi Elite.* New York: NYU Press, 1993.
_____. "The Occupational Background of the SA Rank and File During the Depression Years, 1929 to mid-1934." In P.D. Stachura (ed.). *The Shaping of the Nazi State.* London: Croom Helm, 1978.
Gumbel, E.J. "Le Capitaine Erhardt et L'Organization C." In *L'Europe Neuville* VI (25 August 1923).
_____. "Verrater verfallen der Feme." In *Opfer, Morder, Richter 1919–1920.* Berlin: Malik-Verlag, 1920.
Hausen, L. "Unemployment also Hits Women: The New and the Old Women in the Dark Side of the Golden Twenties In Germany." In Stachura, P. (ed.). *Unemployment and the Great Depression in Weimar Germany.* London: Macmillan, 1986.
Hülsen, B. von. "Freikorps im Osten." In Roden, H. *Deutsche Soldaten, vom Frontheer und Freikorps.* Leipzig: Breitkopf & Härtel, 1935.
Kater, M. "Ansätze su einer Soziologie der SA bis zur

Röhm Krise." In Engelhardt, U., Stellin, V. and Stucke H. (eds.), *Soziale Bewegung und politische Verfassung.* Stuttgart: Klett, 1970.

Laswell, H. "The Psychology of Hitlerism." In *Political Science Quarterly* (1993).

Lowenberg, P. "Psychohistorical Origins of the Nazi Youth Cohort." *The American Historical Review*, Vol. 76. No. 5 (December 1971).

Lüttwitz, F.von. "Einmarsch der Gardkavalertie Schutzen Division in Berlin." In *Deutsche Soldaten.* Leipzig: F.K. Koehler, 1934.

Mau, H. "Die Zweite Revolution — Der 30 Junit 1934." *Vierteljahrshefte für Zeitgeschichte* (1953).

Mitchell, O. "Enter the Desperado: Paramilitary Life in Postwar Europe." *The Midwest Quarterly*, Vol XVIII, No. 1, Autumn 1989.

_____. "Terror as a Neo-Marxian Mechanism in the Nazi SA (1932)." In *Wichita State University Bulletin*, University Studies No 63, Vol. XLT (May 1965), No. 2.

_____. "The Nazi SA Club of the Nation." *Halcyon/1987: A Journal of the Humanities*, Vol. 9.

Nipperdey, T. "Verein als soziale Struktur im Spaten 18. Und frühen Jahrhundert." In H. Brockmann (ed.). *Geschichtswissenschaft und Verein-wesen in 19. Jahrhundert.* Göttingen: Wallstein Verlag, 1972.

Noakes, L. "Conflict and Development in the NSDAP 1924–1927." In *Journal of Contemporary History*, 1, No.4 (1966).

Pabst, W. "Spartakus." In C. Hotzel (ed.). *Deutscher Aufstand: die Revolution des Nachkrieg.* Stuttgart: W. Kohlhammer, 1934.

Phelps, R.H. "Before Hitler Came: Thule Society and Germanic Orden." *Journal of Modern History*, 35 (1963).

_____. "Hitler als Parteiredner im Jahre 1920." In *Vierteljahrsheft für Zeitgeschichte,* July 1963.

Raumer, K. von. "Deutschland um 1800." In *Handbuch d. Deutsche Geschichte.* Potsdam: Hoffman, Gmbh., 1935.

Rosenhaft, E. "Working-class Life and Working-class Politics: Communists, Nazis, and the State in the Battle for the Streets." In Bessel, R. and Feuchtwanger, J. (eds.). *Social Change and Political Development in Weimar Germany.* London: Croom Helm, 1981.

Rudolff, W. "Notjahre Statpolitik in Krieg Inflation und Weltwirtschaftskrise 1914 bis 1933." In R. Bauer (ed.). *Geschichte der Stat München.* Munich: C.H. Beck, 1922.

Rupp, R. "Problems of the German Revolution, 1918–19." *Journal of Central European History*, 3 (1968).

Sauer, W. "Die Mobilmachung der Gewalt." In K.D. Bracher (et.al.). *Die Nationalsozialistische Machtergreifung: Studien zur Erichtung des totalitaren Herrschaftssystems in Deutschland, 1932–34.* Cologne: Westdeutscher Verlag, 1960.

_____. "National Socialism: Totalitarianism or Fascism?." *American Historical Review*, Vol. LXXIII, No. 2, December 1967.

Saul, K. "Der deutsche Kreigerbund: zur innenpolitischen Funktion eines 'national' Verbändes in kaiserlichen Deutschlands." In *Militärgeschichte Mitteilungen,* 1969/1972.

Schmidt, G. "Innen politische Blockbildungen am Vorabend des ersten Weltkreiges." In *Aus Politk und Zeitgeschichte.* 13 May 1972.

Schultze, B. "Berlins Grundung und erster Aufsteig." In *Berlin Neuen Kapital: Seiner Geschichte.* Berlin: Ullstein, 1960.

Spanger, E. "Gedenkrede zur 150. Jahrefeier der Friedrich-Wilhelms Universitat." In H. Rothefels (ed.). *Berlin in Vergangenheit und Gegenwart.* Tübingen: Universität Tübingen, 1961.

Stokes, L.P. "The Social Composition of the Party in Eutin, 1925–1932." In *International Review of Social History,*" xxiii (1978).

Sternhall, Z. "Fascist Ideology." In W. Laquer (ed.). *Fascism: A Reader's Guide-Analysis, Interpretation, Bibliography.* Berkeley: University of California Press, 1976.

Weber, E. "Romania." In Rogger, H. and Weber, E. (eds.). *The European Right: A Historical Profile.* Berkeley: University of California Press, 1966.

Wellner, G. "Industrialarbeiten in der Weimar Republik." In *Geschichte und Gesellschaft,* 7, 148.

Winkler, H.A. "German Society, Hitler and the Illusion of Restoration 1930–1933." In *Journal of Contemporary* History, Vol. II.

Index

Der Angriff 90, 111
Anschluss 33
Anti-Semitism 12, 33–35, 44–48, 49
Arbeitsgemeinschaft 71
Arco-Valley, Count Anton 41
"*Arditi*" (Italian World War I shock troops) 27
Armistice of 1918 14
"Arrow Cross" (Hungarian) 133
Article 231 of the Versailles Treaty (War Guilt Clause) *see* Versailles Treaty
Article 48 of the Weimar Constitution *see* Weimar Constitution
Article 53 of the Weimar Constitution *see* Weimar Constitution
"At the Prophets" (1904) by Thomas Mann 39
Auer, Erhard 76
"Automatic Procedure" 88

Baden, Max of 14
Bainton, Roland H. 120
Baird, Jay W. 2, 121
Baltische Landwehr 62
Bamberg party meeting (1926) 88
Barbu, Zevedei 128
Bastille Day 159
Bauhaus 116
Bavarian Life Guard 46
Bavarian Red Army 42
Bavarian Soviet Republic (1919) 42–43, 46
Berlin 106, 107, 108–109
Berlin-Coelln 106
Berthold, Rudolf 65
Bennecke, Heinrich 124
Bismarck, Otto von 4, 6, 8, 13, 107
Black and Tans 27
Black Reichswehr 72, 74–75
Bleischroder, Gerson 6
Blomberg, Werner von 145, 166–167
Blücher Bund 69
Bolshevik Revolution of 1917 125
Boxer Rebellion (China) 3

Boxheim Papers 143
Bredow, General Kurt von 162, 169
Brest-Litovsk, Treaty of 61
Bruck, Arthur Moeller van den 22
Brüning, Heinrich 97, 139–140, 141, 145- 146, 157
Bund Frankenland 69
Bund Oberland 60
Bund Unterland 69
Burgerbräukeller 76–77
Burgfrieden (1914) moratorium on politics 13

Catholic Center Party (*Zentrum*) 135, 139 157–158
Christian Social Party of Adolf Stöcker 8
The Civil Guards 44, 70
Clemenceau, George 22
Coburg "march-out" (1922) 54
Colonial Society 5
Comintern (Communist International) 42
Communist Party of Germany (KPD) 41, 75, 93, 96, 111, 102; Karl Liebknecht House Defense 133; May Day uprising of 1929 109
Confiscation bill for property of nobility 87
Congress of Vienna 107
Cuno, Wilhelm 73
Cyfka, Johann 130–131

Daluege, Kurt 123
DAP (German Worker's Party) 47–48, 51
Darré, Walter 91
Dawes, Charles 83
Dawes Plan 83, 94
The Decline of the West 34
Deutsche Arbeiter Partei (DAP) 37, 47, 48
Deutsche Kampfbund (German Fighting League) 56
Deutscher Schütz und Wanderbund 6
Deutscher Studentenbund (German Student League) 91, 94

Dickel, Otto 50
Dietrich, Otto 91
Dietrich, Sepp 158–159,161, 165, 167
Doelle, Werner 86
Drang nach Osten 13
Drexler, Anton 47, 51

Eastern Jews ("*Ostjuden*") 5, 33–34, 49
Ebert, Friedrich 16, 18, 23, 25
Eichorn, Emil 58
Eichorn's security police 58
Eicke, Theodor 162
Einstein, Albert 109
Eiserne Schar 65
Eisner, Kurt 15, 17, 34, 36, 41
"Enabling Act" 157
Engmann, Helmut 134
Ehrhardt, Hermann 23, 69, 84, 163
Ehrhardt Brigade 23, 53, 69, 60; marching song 53
Epp, Colonel Ritter von 46, 60, 64
Erzberger, Matthias 14, 25, 68
Escherich, Georg 44
Esser, Hermann 47

Feckenbach, Felix 80, 137
Fest, Joachim 101
Fischer, Conan 102
Fischer, Eugen 8
Fourteen Points, Wilsonian Doctrine 22
Frank, Hans 29
Frederick the Great of Prussia 4, 107, 157
Frederick William I of Prussia 106
Frederick William of Prussia (the "Great Elector") 107
Free Corps (Freikorps) 17–18, 52, 57–71, 72, 99, 117
Freebooters 60–62
Frick, Wilhelm 91
Fritsch, Theodor 7
"Front Ring" 85
Frontbann ("Front Band") 84–86

Gau structure of Nazi Party 90–91
German National People's Party (DNVP) 96–97, 143
German Officers League 167
German People's Party 96–97
German Reform Party 7
German Social Union 39
German Socialist Party (*völkisch*) 50
German Supreme Court (Leipzig) 136
Germanic Confederation 107
Gessler, Otto 73
Gestapo 156, 165
Gleichschaltung 158–159, 165
Godin, Michael von 78
Goebbels, Joseph 50, 85, 86, 104, 109–110, 112, 114, 125, 128, 143, 154–155, 167–168
Goltz, General Graf Rudiger von der 62–63
Graf, Ulrich 78
The Grand Coalition 89, 97
Greater German People's Community 87
The Green Police 78
Grenschutz ("border defense") 145
Grimm, the Brothers 66
Groener, Wilhelm 58, 140, 144, 145
Gropius, Walter 116
Grzesinski, Police Chief Albert 114

Hagen, the Abbot 31
Hamburg-Altona march-out 114
Hammer Publishing Company 7
Hanisch, Reinhard 32–33
Hannich, Ernst 130
Hanseatic League 106
Hansel and Gretel 66
Hanser, Richard 35
Harrar, Karl 47
Heiden, Konrad 104–105, 122, 125, 141
Heidler, Johann Georg 29
Heidler, Johann Nepomuk 29
Heines, Edmund 133–134, 136
Held, Heinrich 83–84
Hereros 9, 46
Hess, Rudolf 80, 93
Hessian election 142
Heydebreck, Peter von 65
Hierl, Konstantin 91
Hilferding, Rudolf 139
Hilfswerk ("Help to Work") 141
Himmler, Heinrich 11, 141, 161, 165
Hindenburg, Paul von 14, 97, 139, 142, 143, 149, 150–151, 159–160, 160
Hitler, Adolf 7, 31–35, 46, 73, 81, 83, 91, 99, 103–104, 114, 127–128, 140–141; ancestry 29–30; personality 30–31; presidential campaign (1931) 112–114; Reichstag speech after Röhm purge 168–169; World War I experience 36
Hitler, Alois 29
Hitler, Alois, Jr. 31
Hitler (Raubal), Angela 30
Hitler, Patrick 30
Hitler, Paula 30–32
Hitler Youth 10, 91
Hoffmann, Alfred 53
Hoffmann, Heinrich 35
Hoffmann, Johannes 42–44
Home Guard (*Einwohnerwehr* in Bavaria) 69
Horthy, Admiral Nicholas 26
Hotel *Vierjahrzeiten* (Munich) 47
Hugenberg, Alfred 94, 95–96, 152

Independent Socialist Party (USPD) 15, 41–42, 58, 108
Information Office of the Reich Interior Ministry 137
Iron Brigades (two) 59–60, 62, 63

Jazi, Oscar 26
Jews 5; *see also* anti-Semitism
Julich-Cleves, Duchy of 106
Jung, Edgar 162
Jünger, Ernst 36
Jüttner, Max 102, 124

Kahr, Gustav von 23, 56, 67, 68, 83, 162
Kampfbund 56, 69, 73–74, 76, 84
Kapp, Wolfgang 33
Kapp *Putsch* 63, 66–67
Keynes, John Maynard 21
Kiel naval revolt (1919) 58
Killinger, Manfred von 53
Klintsch, Johann Ulrich 53
Knilling, Eugen von 83
Koestler, Arthur 116
Kreuzzeitung, German newspaper 6
Kriebel, Hermann 56
Krupp, Alfred 7–8
Kubizek, August 31–32
Kun, Bela 42
Kyffhäuser Bund 9

Lagarde, Paul de 108
Landsberg prison 80
Landsknechte ("freebooters") 64
League of Anti-Semites 6–7
Lebensraum ("living room") 13
Lenin, V.I. 14–15, 34
Levien, Max 41–42
Leviné, Eugen 43
Ley, Robert 159
Liebenfels, Georg Lanz von (Adolf Lang) 7, 33
Liebknecht, Karl 15
Liebknecht, Wilhelm 15
"Little Wedding" (Berlin-Charlottenburg) 109
Lloyd George, David 22
Lossow, General Otto von 56, 68, 75, 79
Ludendorff, Erich 13–14, 55, 73, 76, 85
Ludin, Hans 140
Ludwig III of Bavaria 40–41
Lueger, Karl 7
Luitpold School executions 43
Lutze, Viktor 102
Luxemburg, Rosa 15–16

Magyar Defense League 26
Mann, Thomas 39–40
Marburg Speech (Papen in 1934) 166
Marx, Karl 7, 23, 107
Masurian Lakes, battle of (1914) 14
Maurice, Emil 54
Mayr, Karl 37
Mazlish, Bruce 47
Mein Kampf 30, 32, 48, 53, 80–82, 87
Memoirs of a High Traitor by E. Röhm 64
Metternich, Clemens von 22;
Meyer, Rudolf 108
Mosse, George 2
Mueslum, Dr. Margaret 112
Münchener Post 34, 77
Musham, Eric 34
Mussolini, Benito 27, 79

National Socialist Freedom Movement 87
Naval League 5, 9
Nazi Party (NSDAP) 48, 75, 76, 80, 90, 91, 96, 98, 100, 140, 143, 149, 147, 152; beer hall *Putzch* 75–79; *Gleichschaltung* 158–159
Neithardt, Gregory 79
Neumann, Josef 33
"Night of the Long Knives" 162
North German Confederation 108
Noske, Gustav 18, 59–60
"November Criminals" 46
Nuremberg Party Congress (first annual) 91

"Operation Hummingbird" 161–163
"Order of the Temple" 7
"Orderly Compartment of Bavaria" 23
Organization Consul 25, 33, 132
Orgesch 67
Orka 44
Ostara 7, 33
Osthilfe ("Eastern Help") 146
Oven, General Ernst von 60

Pan-German League 5, 39
Papen, Franz von 114, 133, 144, 149, 150, 155, 162, 166
"People's Naval Division" (1918) 58
Pfeffer, Franz von 98, 129, 141
Pietrzuch (Communist Worker) 150
PO (political organization of the Nazi Party) 97, 141, 144–145

Pöhner, Ernst 54, 67–68, 76
Pölzl, Klara 30
Popp, Josef 34
Potempa Five 150
Potempa Murder 150
Potsdam Garrison Church meeting of Reichstag 156–157
"Protocols of the Elders of Zion" 81
Prussia, Duchy of 106

Rapallo, Treaty of 24–25
Rathenau, Walther 5–6, 23–24
Raubal, Geli 142
Raubal, Leo 30
Realpolitik 107
Red Front Fighters (KPD) 98, 101
Red Swastika (Nazi women's medical auxiliary) 93
Reichenau, Walter von 145
Reichsflagge ("Reich Flag") 69, 71
Reichskreigflagge ("Reich War Banner") 69
Reichstag fire (27 February 1933) 156
Rentenmark 83
Revision of lower-middle class thesis (Nazism) 175 f.n.
Revolutionary ascetic 47–48
Rhenische Zeitung 107
Ribbentrop, Joachim von 152
Riga, Free Corps attacks on 62–63
Röhm, Ernst 26, 28, 46–47, 53–54, 64, 70–71, 84–86, 122–123, 141, 160–163, 166
Rosenberg, Alfred 87
Rote Fahne ("Red Flag," the KPD newspaper) 110
Royal Irish Constabulary 27
Ruhr Occupation (1923) 25, 72–74

SA (*Sturmabteilung* or "Storm Detachment") 88–89, 97, 98, 100, 117, 122, 124, 139; arrests in Berlin 111 ff.; ban on in Berlin 111; Beer Hall *Putsch* 73, 84, 86, 88; criminal element in 123; early development 52–56; electioneering 99; gangsterism 112; Hagen (Westphalia) SA 119–120; "Homes" 119–120; ideal SA family 148; ideological profile (1930) 103; Legal Department 135; machismo in 130, 149; mythology 121; Pharus Hall battle (1927) 110; prohibition of (1932) 145; purge of 160–170; Reichstag members 112; Röhm reorganization 141; squad formations 119; Tetlow "march-out" 110–111
Sauer, Wolfgang 25
Schar (smallest SA unit) 92
Scharnagl, Karl 83
Scheidemann, Philip 16, 18
Scheringer, Richard 140
Schickelgruber, Maria Anna 29
Schirach, Baldur von 91
Schlageter, Albert Leo 73
Schleicher, General Kurt von 59, 97, 136, 139, 149, 150, 152, 162, 169
Schönerer, Georg Ritter von 7
Schreck, Julius 55
Schwartz, Franz Xaver 91
Sebattendorf, Rudolf von (Adam Glauer) 47
Seeckt, Hans von 75
Seisser, Hans Ritter von 76
Shaw, George Bernard 27
Sidman, Charles F. 2
Social Darwinism 81
Social Democratic Party (SPD) 16, 17, 108, 114, 115, 117–118, 147, 153
Social Reich Party 7
Soviet Republic of Bavaria (first) 42
Soviet Republic of Bavaria (second) 42
Spartacist revolt 15–18, 61
Spartacists 15–18, 61, 108
Spengler, Oswald 34
SS (*Schutzstaffel* or "protection formations") 55
Stab-in-the-back legend (*Dolchstosslegende*) 14
Stabswache 55
Strasser, Gregor 86–88, 90
Stein, Baron vom 107
Stemple, Father Bernhard 47
Stöcker, Adolf 6

"Storm Centers" for the SA 105–119
Stosstrupp Hitler 55, 76
Streck, Hans 73
Streicher, Julius 50
Stresemann, Gustav 25, 88, 94, 95
Stucke, Lutheran vicar 111

Tannenburg, Battle of 1914, 14
Teutonic Knights 106
"The Three Penny Opera" 116
Thule Society 47
Tirpitz, Alfred von 4–5, 16
Toller, Ernst 42
Trianon, Treaty of 26
Trupp (an SA "troop") 92

"Unknown SA Man" 110
Urban Pand 90, 98

Valois, George 52
Versailles Treaty 20–22, 44, 105, 140; War Guilt Clause 21–22
Völkisch ideology 44
Völkischer Beobachter (the "Racist Observer") 49, 75, 99
Von Epp Free Corps 67

Waite, Robert G.L. 65–66
Wallenstein, Count Albrecht von 64
War Food Office 40
Weber, Friedrich 73
Der Wehrwolf 121
Wehrwölfe 65
Weil, Kurt 116
Weimar Constitution 154
Weiss, Bernhard 114
Wendt, Friedrich 140
Wessel, Horst 112
Westarp, Countess von 47
White Terror (Munich) 44
Wiedemann, Fritz 36
Wiking Bund (the "Vikings") 53, 69
William II of Hohenzollern, German emperor 3, 4, 13, 14
Wilson, Woodrow 14, 22
Wolfram, Ludwig 8

Yiddish, German language and 5
"Young Communists" 65

www.ingramcontent.com/pod-product-compliance
Ingram Content Group UK Ltd.
Pitfield, Milton Keynes, MK11 3LW, UK
UKHW050524150426
5217IPUK00026B/1788